# *Winds* of the *Spirit*

"*Winds of the Spirit* reminds us that Anabaptists in the South have much to teach us about how to reshape and revitalize Anabaptism in the North."
—*Juan Francisco Martínez, associate provost for diversity and international programs, Fuller Theological Seminary*

"A compact and informative thesaurus on emerging ecclesiastical and cultural meanings of 'Mennonite.' Christian faith today is not merely a *world* religion, but a substantially *non-Western* phenomenon."
—*Jonathan J. Bonk, executive director, Overseas Ministries Study Center*

"Provocative and thrilling, this book paints a picture of Anabaptism on the move around the world. Some will find the snapshot unsettling. Others will swell with gratitude and hope."
—*Mark R. Wenger, director of pastoral studies, Eastern Mennonite Seminary*

"*Winds of the Spirit* should prompt the Mennonite church in North America to reassess its place within the larger movement of God's Spirit in the world. I recommend it enthusiastically!"
—*John D. Roth, professor of history, Goshen College, and director of the Institute for the Study of Global Anabaptism*

# *Winds* of the *Spirit*

## A Profile of Anabaptist Churches in the Global South

Conrad L. Kanagy

Tilahun Beyene

Richard Showalter

**Herald Press**
Harrisonburg, Virginia
Waterloo, Ontario

**Library of Congress Cataloging-in-Publication Data**
Kanagy, Conrad L.
  Winds of the Spirit : a profile of Anabaptist churches in the global south / Conrad L. Kanagy, Tilahun Beyene, Richard Showalter; foreword by Philip Jenkins.
       p. cm.
  Includes bibliographical references.
  ISBN 978-0-8361-9636-8 (pbk.)
  1. Anabaptists. I. Telahun Beyene. II. Showalter, Richard. III. Title.
  BX4931.3.K36 2012
  284'.3—dc23

                                                              2012012202


All rights reserved. This publication may not be reproduced, stored in a retrieval system, or transmitted in whole or in part, in any form, by any means, electronic, mechanical, photocopying, recording or otherwise without prior permission of the copyright owners.

WINDS OF THE SPIRIT
Copyright © 2012 by Herald Press, Harrisonburg, Virginia 22802
   Released simultaneously in Canada by Herald Press,
   Waterloo, Ontario N2L 6H7. All rights reserved.
Library of Congress Control Number: 2012012202
International Standard Book Number: 978-0-8361-9636-8
Printed in United States of America
Cover design by Merrill R. Miller

16 15 14 13 12    10 9 8 7 6 5 4 3 2 1

To order or request information, please call 1-800-245-7894 in the U.S. or 1-800-631-6535 in Canada. Or visit www.heraldpress.com.

To the anchors of the Multi-Nation Anabaptist Profile whose partnership made the vision for this project a reality:
*Yemiru Tilahun and Tariku Gebre of
Meserete Kristos Church, Ethiopia;
Javier Xol and Galen Groff of Iglesia Nacional Evangélica
Menonita Guatemalteca, Guatemala;
Alfredo Cárcamo of Iglesia Evangélica Menonita
Hondureña, Honduras;
Carlos Marín Montoya of Organización Cristiana
Amor Viviente, Honduras;
Thomas Chacko and Blessan Abraham of Fellowship of
Christian Assemblies, India;
Kristina Setiawan and Andreas Wijaya of Persatuan
Gereja-Gereja Kristen Muria Indonesia, Indonesia;
Boniface Runji of Happy Church Ministries
International, Kenya;
Moses Otieno of Kenya Mennonite Church, Kenya;
Edgardo Docuyanan and Richard Rancap of
Integrated Mennonite Churches, Philippines;
Jumanne Magiri of Kanisa la Mennonite
Tanzania, Tanzania;
Karl Landis of Lancaster Mennonite
Conference, United States;
and
Trung Quang and Gerry Keener of Hoi Thanh Mennonite
Viet Nam, Vietnam.*

# Table of Contents

*Foreword by Philip Jenkins* . . . . . . . . . . . . . . . . . . . . . . 9
*Preface and Acknowledgments* . . . . . . . . . . . . . . . . . . 13

1. Introduction . . . . . . . . . . . . . . . . . . . . . . . . . . . . . . 17
2. A History of the Churches in the Profile . . . . . . . . . . 35
3. An Overview of the Profile . . . . . . . . . . . . . . . . . . . 53
4. Characteristics and Trajectories of
   Anabaptist Churches . . . . . . . . . . . . . . . . . . . . . . . 69
5. Anabaptist Beliefs and Practices . . . . . . . . . . . . . . 107
6. Congregational Life . . . . . . . . . . . . . . . . . . . . . . . 135
7. The Missionary Posture of Global Anabaptists . . . . . 153
8. Anabaptism from Sixteenth-Century Europe
   to the Twenty-First-Century Global South . . . . . . . . 175
9. The Holy Spirit's Movement among
   Global Anabaptists . . . . . . . . . . . . . . . . . . . . . . . 205

10. Emerging Visions of Anabaptism
   in the Global South . . . . . . . . . . . . . . . . . . . . . 233
*Bibliography* . . . . . . . . . . . . . . . . . . . . . . . . . . . . 253
*The Authors*. . . . . . . . . . . . . . . . . . . . . . . . . . . . 259

# Foreword

This is an exceptionally important book. Over the past quarter century, scholars and church leaders have recognized how fundamentally the atlas of world Christianity is changing through the upsurge of believers in the Global South and its impact on various denominations. From any number of examples we might point to the Assemblies of God, which was founded in the United States in 1914 but today finds a mere five percent of its adherents in North America.[1] While this may seem like an extreme case, similar shifts will transform all major denominations in coming decades.

I have suggested that, by 2050, fewer than twenty percent of all Christians worldwide will be non-Latino whites. To date, though, no study has tried to comprehensively assess the impact of such changes within a particular church tradition. None, certainly, has ever used the sophisticated quantitative evidence that we find in *Winds of the Spirit*, which is based on very large survey

---

1. *North America* in this book is a reference to Canada and the United States; Mexico is included within Latin America. While the data from the Multi-Nation Anabaptist Profile do not specifically address Canada, they do reference trends that are often true for both Canada and the United States.

samples from diverse corners of the world. In short, there really is nothing like this book, and it represents pioneering scholarship on an exceptionally important global issue.

*Winds of the Spirit* honestly and intelligently addresses questions that sooner or later will have to be confronted by each and every Christian denomination. Through the years churches have formed certain values and structures that work well for them and which, to a greater or lesser degree, reflect the needs of living within particular Euro-American cultures. But what happens when a majority of that church's members do not live in Euro-American cultural contexts and deal with radically different issues and dilemmas on a daily basis? Is it possible to maintain the sense of living in a global denomination when believers in Africa, say, have rather more in common with their Muslim or animist neighbors than with fellow Anglicans or Methodists or Mennonites in the United States?

We must ask at what point the values and standards of the newer non-European churches must be seen as the new normal and the true mainstream of the particular church in question. If we look at membership figures alone, Ethiopia's Meserete Kristos church already has a claim to stand at the heart of the Mennonite movement worldwide—and it is growing fast. Mere numbers are not everything, but they are certainly not nothing.

As an imaginative exercise, it is invaluable for Euro-American believers to think about the key theological issues that are so pressing for the newer churches and ask what relevance they might have for the Old Christendom. *Winds of the Spirit* identifies several, but foremost is the Pentecostal and charismatic impulse—the world of the Spirit—that so shapes attitudes about worship and belief. However that tradition may be derided in Western secular media, any exploration of worldwide Christianity tells us how centrally important it is to the present and future of the faith.[2] Growing from that charismatic theme,

---

2. In this book, *Western* and *North* are used rather synonymously, recognizing that both are problematic. But both continue to be used in scholarly literature—*Western* to point toward historic ideological

we have the critical issue of healing, without which the newer churches lose so much of their raison d'être.

Again, we think of the theological issues that necessarily arise from the social and cultural settings in which believers find themselves. For centuries, Western Christians have lived in societies composed mainly or exclusively of fellow believers, so they have had little need to consider the presence of competing faiths. Such attitudes are not possible for believers in societies that are equally divided between Christians and Muslims, like Ethiopia or Nigeria, or where they are small minorities, as in Vietnam or India. What do concepts such as mission or evangelism mean in worlds where trying to spread one's faith could provoke persecutions or pogroms? And how exactly should Christians regard those other faiths?

In many parts of the world, moreover, Christian life is shaped by the experience of prevailing poverty. Although this is not a theological issue in its own right, it profoundly affects matters as diverse as the understanding of the Bible and the obligations of social solidarity.

Charismatic faith, pervasive poverty, living as a religious minority, the daily encounter with other religions, the threat of persecution . . . however alien these experiences may be to Euro-American Christians, they are familiar and standard for hundreds of millions of believers worldwide. And in many ways, they recall the lives and practices of the oldest churches of apostolic times. Christianity is a faith that was born in Africa and Asia, which, in our own lifetimes, has decided to go home.

> —*Philip Jenkins, distinguished professor of history, Baylor University, and author of* Laying Down the Sword: Why We Can't Ignore the Bible's Violent Verses.

---

developments that have been relatively distinct from much of the rest of the world, and *North* as a hemispheric contrast to the Global South.

# Preface and Acknowledgments

This book is the culmination of four years of work by several teams of persons, without whose help and energy the project simply would not have been possible. My own vision for the Multi-Nation Anabaptist Profile (MNA Profile) came from a trip that I made with my son, Jacob, and several friends in 2003 to the Holy Spirit in Mission Conference in Addis Ababa, Ethiopia. I was greatly impressed by the energy and growth of the Mennonite church in Ethiopia, Meserete Kristos Church (MKC Ethiopia), and realized how little I had known of these brothers and sisters before our visit. I returned to the United States with a desire to tell the story of the growth of the global Anabaptist church from a sociological perspective.

In 2008, a commitment from Eastern Mennonite Missions (EMM) made it possible for us to study in depth twelve Anabaptist churches in ten countries. In addition to myself, the leadership team for the MNA Profile was composed of Richard Showalter (then president of EMM) and Tilahun Beyene (also of EMM). Mervin Charles also served on the team for several months until his resignation from EMM. The project required a substantial financial commitment from EMM, and Richard Showalter's enthusiastic support ensured its completion. Tilahun Beyene, originally from Ethiopia and one who experienced the decade-long persecution of MKC Ethiopia, brought valuable insight and an authentic perspective from the Global South.

Many others provided tremendous support:

- Cheryl Hock and Nita Landis, both executive administrative assistants at Eastern Mennonite Missions during the Profile study.

- Laura Livengood of Lancaster Mennonite Conference (LMC United States), who formatted all versions of the Profile questionnaires and assisted with a variety of other tasks.

- Leaders of the twelve participating churches, including Nguyen Quang Trung, Yesaya Abdi, P. C. Alexander, Kenna Dula, Keith Weaver, Philip Okeyo, John Nyagwegwe, Alfredo Siquuic, Luis Alonzo López, Javier Soler, Joseph Kamau, and Edgardo Docuyanan.

- Anchors who managed the Profile work in their churches, including Jumanne Magiri, Alfredo Cárcamo, Carlos Marín Montoya, Moses Otieno, Boniface Runji, Javier Xol, Galen Groff, Trung Quang, Gerry Keener, Karl Landis, Kristina Setiawan, Andreas Wijaya, Yemiru Tilahun, Tariku Gebre, Thomas Chacko, Blessan Abraham, and Richard Rancap.

- The more than 18,000 church members who completed questionnaires.

- Area representatives from Eastern Mennonite Missions, including Clair Good, Glenn Kauffman, Steve Shank, and Jewel Showalter.

- Antonio Ulloa, who designed our data entry system, communicated with Profile anchors, translated on many occasions, and was available at a moment's notice when I needed assistance.

*Preface and Acknowledgments* 15

- Students from my sociology of religion course at Elizabethtown College who read and commented on an early draft of this manuscript, including Kira Blome, Kristen Blome, Marshal Fettro, Natalie Hopkins, Allison Kinney, Julie Klaski, Sarah Knapp, Amanda McCaffrey, Amelia Moon, Tyler Norton, Barbara Prince, Ethan Shearer, Liesl Sieber, Nathan Smith, and Lauren Watt.

- The Elizabethtown Mennonite Church Sunday school class (Elvin Boll, Josh Gish, Mart Gish, Diane Herman, Hank Herman, Harold Keener, Ron Kratz, Joe Sherer, and Mary Ellen Shertzer) that read a late draft of the manuscript and energetically discussed it over a three-month period.

- Brinton Rutherford, Mike Schwartz, and Mark Wenger, who read and commented on drafts of the manuscript.

- Elizabethtown College, which graciously granted me a partial leave in the spring of 2010 to write this manuscript.

- Dr. Elizabeth Newell, chair of the Department of Sociology and Anthropology, for her ongoing support of my research among Anabaptists.

- The Schowalter Foundation, Eastern Mennonite Missions, and several generous individuals, for grants that permitted my research leave in the spring of 2010.

- The staff at Herald Press—including Amy Gingerich and Byron Rempel-Burkholder, among others—who carefully assisted in the various stages of publication of yet another Anabaptist profile.

Just as this project was getting underway in early 2008, my wife, Heidi, was diagnosed with cancer. Over the past four years, God has graciously cared for and protected her through surgery, chemotherapy, and recovery, and has once again shown himself to be Deliverer, Redeemer, Healer, and Savior (Psalm 103). Heidi has given me more support than anyone else for the various projects I have undertaken over the years, and I thank God for our partnership in ministry.

During this same season, our son, Jacob, attended and graduated from Eastern University with an interest in international politics and policy. I am amazed and blessed that our trip together more than eight years ago served as a catalyst for his own global interests.

This intensive, four-year project has been possible only because the Holy Spirit sustained and guided all of us who were part of the Profile. I have repeatedly stated that I cannot remember a project in which I so keenly sensed the winds of God's Spirit carrying the work. Every time we had a challenge or problem, someone was there to offer appropriate counsel or a helping hand. Every time we thought the mountain was too steep to climb, we received encouragement to continue. Whenever it seemed we would not make a deadline, somehow the work was accomplished. I pray that the same winds of the Spirit that we experienced—and about which we write in this book—will touch all who read it, bringing encouragement, understanding, renewal, and greater unity.

—*Conrad L. Kanagy*
*December 15, 2011*
*Elizabethtown, Pa.*

# 1

# *Introduction*

Conrad L. Kanagy[1]

The twentieth-century charismatic/Pentecostal renewal in the Holy Spirit has not entered the world scene on one single, sudden clear-cut occasion, nor even gradually over a hundred years. It has arrived in three distinct and separate surges or explosions sufficiently distinct and distinctive for us to label them the first wave (the Pentecostal renewal), the second wave (the charismatic renewal), and the third wave (the neo-charismatic renewal). All three waves share the same experience of the infilling power of the Holy Spirit, Third Person of the Triune God. The Spirit has entered and transformed the lives not simply of small numbers of heroic individuals and scattered communities . . . but of vast numbers of millions of Christians across the world today. . . . Charismatics are now found across the entire

---

1. Chapter 1 of this book is written by the lead author, Conrad L. Kanagy, as an introduction to the remainder of the book, which is coauthored with Tilahun Beyene and Richard Showalter.

spectrum of Christianity . . . in 9,000 ethnolinguistic cultures, speaking 8,000 languages covering 95 percent of the world's total population."[2] —*David Barrett, longtime analyst of world Christian trends*

During the mid-1980s, I lived for several months in a Quichua community in the rural highlands of Ecuador. While there, I questioned residents about the mass movement to evangelical Christianity that swept through their village in the 1960s. What I learned challenged the assertions of scholars who argue that such conversions are due primarily to the imposition of Western neocolonialist forces.[3] I observed peasants who, as former Catholics, had for decades felt abandoned by their church. They had found empowerment and autonomy in evangelical Christianity. As Catholics, the Quichua rarely interacted with their priests, who came to the community only to oversee major life course events such as baptism, marriage, and death. As evangelical Christians, these peasants were now responsible for their own religious life and for the rituals that gave life meaning.

By the 1980s, any evangelical missionary presence was long gone, and the church was overseen solely by Quichua pastors local to the community. The success of the evangelical movement among the Quichua was in its populist origins. Protestant evangelicalism fit more readily the relatively egalitarian structures of power in Quichua society than had Roman Catholicism. In many ways, evangelicalism enabled the church to reflect the Quichua sense of identity, leadership patterns, and cohesiveness. In sum, among the Quichua, evangelical expressions of the gospel were more readily contextualized than those of Roman Catholicism.

In addition to the cultural compatibility of the missionary message, other factors—religious, cultural, and economic—influenced the receptivity of Quichua peasants to the evangelical message. Such forces were also shaping the shifting religious

---

2. Barrett, 2001:381–83.
3. Kanagy, 1990.

Introduction 19

landscape in other parts of the Global South during the same period, providing a rich foundation for the growth of evangelical and charismatic expressions of Christianity in the decades that followed. Changes affecting the Roman Catholic Church globally, the national redistribution of landholdings from wealthy to impoverished, and national political turmoil contributed to a climate that made the Ecuadorian Quichua more likely to accept the teachings of evangelical missionaries. Conversion to evangelical Christianity connected these new converts with evangelical Christian non-governmental organizations (NGOs), which were more than willing to provide economic development assistance to the communities of the new converts. Sanitation programs, potable water projects, and agricultural development efforts became lifelines for communities that had been neglected by the Roman Catholic Church and government entities.[4]

Instead of being co-opted by Western neocolonial forces, the Quichua had made a rational religious choice—one that made sense to them—within the social, cultural, and political context in which they found themselves in the 1960s. Conversion for the Quichua was an act of empowerment: they stepped aside from a religious identity that felt distant and abstract and embraced a new identity that felt local and concrete. Far from being victims of neocolonialism, they were savvy religious entrepreneurs who, in coming to Christ, had found spiritual freedom, retained their cultural identity, and strengthened their community autonomy. Far from being Marx's "opiate of the masses," religious conversion became for the Quichua an "engine of hope."[5]

The debate about the nature of religious conversion and religious experience reflects a sociological tension that goes back to the nineteenth century. The assertions of Karl Marx—that

---

4. An analysis of conversion as I have described above for the Quichua does not discount the possibility of supernatural forces as contributing to such conversion. The empirical observation of such forces, however, is generally thought to be beyond the scope of sociological analysis.

5. Miller, 2009:284.

religion is nothing more than a drug—exist as a radical alternative to the more positive views of, for example, Emile Durkheim, who saw religion as a social glue, and Max Weber, who understood religion to be a factor in economic and social change.[6] At a personal level, the research described in this book connects back to my first sociological analysis in Ecuador in 1985. While the conversation about religion's impact on society has taken twists and turns in the quarter century since, the argument continues over whether religion is a drug or a catalyst for change.

### Emerging interest in global Christianity

The debate about religion's role and function has been informed over the last two decades by the rapid growth of Pentecostal forms of Christianity in Asia, Africa, and Latin America, which some refer to as the "Global South." While a number of scholars, including Andrew Walls, Lamin Saneh, and others, had been writing about the expansion of Christianity in the twentieth century, it was the publication of *The Next Christendom* by Philip Jenkins in 2002 that catalyzed scholars' and practitioners' interest in the important shift taking place in the global church.[7]

Jenkins argues that the growth of Christianity in the Global South over the past two decades is largely neglected by scholars in Europe and North America. This oversight, he says, is due in part to the lack of personal religiosity of many academicians, who still accept the early sociological notions that religion will eventually disappear with increased education and scientific awareness. But, he argues, the slowness to recognize Christianity's growth also reflects an academic skepticism about the Pentecostal type of Christianity that is rapidly expanding in the Global South.

In the 1960s, many assumed that if Christianity took root in the Global South at all, it would emerge from a liberation theology framework that emphasizes a need for a global

---

6. Marx, 1844; Durkheim, 1912; Weber, 1904.

7. Sanneh, 1993; Walls, 1996; Jenkins, 2002.

Introduction 21

redistribution of power and resources in order to bring about a more just and equitable society. Many expected this theologically-driven movement to be a vibrant catalyst for radical change that would usher in political revolution. Liberation theology did in fact mobilize the poor and create Christian communities in many places.[8] However, the Christianity that is expanding today in the Global South has relatively little to do with the neo-Marxist perspectives of liberation theologians.[9] Instead, it tends to be a conservative Pentecostalism that prefers capitalist modes of production and, where politically engaged, often embraces democratic means of voting, running for office, and legislation. As noted by Johnson and Ross in the *Atlas of Global Christianity*, the social and cultural forces leading such change are very similar to those that the Quichua experienced:

> Christianity as expressed in Pentecostalism has thrived in the Global South amongst peoples marginalized from power precisely because it both incorporates their cultural values . . . and responds to their deeply felt needs for healing and a voice in the midst of great poverty and socioeconomic and political marginalization.[10]

In 2003, I traveled with my two coauthors, Richard Showalter and Tilahun Beyene, to Ethiopia and Kenya to meet with Anabaptist leaders from Asia, Africa, and Latin America. What we found took me by surprise. While both a sociologist and a Mennonite

---

8. None of the churches in our study had their origins in the liberation theology movement, and most would likely see the movement as opposed to their understanding of Christian faith. In many places, liberation theology was aligned with Roman Catholicism, which itself discouraged the movement's development through the consistent appointment of conservative cardinals in the Global South.

9. Miroslav Volf argued in the late 1980s that though the impulses of liberation theology and Pentecostal theology were different in many respects, they shared a common commitment to a "material" salvation that distinguished them both from the "nonmaterial" nature of salvation in classic Protestantism.

10. Johnson and Ross, 2009:67.

pastor, I was largely unaware of the rapid growth of Mennonites (often referred to as Anabaptists) outside my own continent. In North America and Europe, church membership and attendance trends among many progressive denominations—including my own Mennonite denomination—have been downward for some time. Not only was I shocked at the upward trajectory of the churches in Africa; I was also impressed with the intentional way that this growth was nurtured and tracked by church leaders. Statistical measurements, monitoring of evangelism efforts, and intentional discipleship programs for every participating church revealed energy for recruitment and growth that was foreign to my experience as a North American Christian and pastor.

I returned to the United States with a vision for telling this story from a sociological perspective, tracking not just membership numbers (something on which much research about Christianity in the Global South is based) but also the beliefs, religious practices, values, and attitudes of ordinary members of these churches. Unable to locate funds for a global study of Anabaptists, several other colleagues and I succeeded in implementing a study of Anabaptist groups in the United States. As codirector of the 2006 Church Member Profile, I conducted a survey of members of Mennonite Church USA, the largest denomination of assimilated Mennonites in the United States.[11] The findings of the profile startled many members of Mennonite Church USA. To mention a few:

- The average age of members was fifty-four years, up from forty-nine years in 1989.

---

11. By "assimilated" I am referring to those Mennonites who over the last several decades have become increasingly like other Americans in residence patterns, educational levels, occupation, and who by and large have abandoned the distinctive dress and lifestyle that defined their ancestors and that continue to define Old Order Mennonites and Old Order Amish. Mennonite Church USA is a denomination representing two historic cultural streams of Mennonites—one from Switzerland and one from the Netherlands.

Introduction 23

- The percent of members within childbearing range (between eighteen and forty-five years of age) was 30%, a figure even lower than that among mainline Protestants and certainly among evangelicals.
- The "market share" of Mennonite Church USA of all Anabaptists globally had dropped to 7% from 15% in 1989.
- The church had declined in membership by 16.4% since the late 1980s.
- The percent of Mennonites with a four-year degree had doubled in just over thirty years to 38%, more than most other religious groups in the United States.
- Twenty-two percent of Mennonites expressed no interest in church planting—up from 8%.
- Only 2% of Mennonite members were new believers without previous church experience.
- One-third of Mennonites had never invited someone to church, up from 16% in 1972. Only 13% had invited others to church on a regular basis, monthly or more.
- Fifty-nine percent of Anglo Mennonites felt that the charismatic gifts of the Holy Spirit were genuine gifts of God's Spirit, and 44% had experienced the charismatic gifts at some point in their lives.[12]

While most Mennonites in the 2006 profile expressed agreement with questions related to Christian orthodoxy—such as Jesus was born of a virgin, Jesus physically rose from the dead, and the Bible is inspired—they exhibited little energy for evangelism and outreach, even while affirming the need to do so. Interestingly, however, members that were racial or ethnic

---

12. Kanagy, 2007.

24  Winds of the Spirit

minorities—many of them immigrants from the Global South—were much more likely than Anglo Mennonites to engage in evangelism and outreach and to embrace the charismatic gifts of the Spirit.

These findings among Mennonites in the United States reflect the vast changes that have taken place among U.S. Christians in general since World War II. Declining and aging memberships, minimal evangelical fervor, increased individualism, and changes in moral attitudes despite continued affirmation of orthodox beliefs characterize many denominations in the United States In other words, Mennonites in the 2006 profile largely mirror trends in North American mainline Protestantism in general.[13]

Not only had Mennonites in the United States changed dramatically since the first profile in 1972, but also they were quite different from the portrait of Global South Christians that Philip Jenkins sketched in *The Next Christendom*. Jenkins argues that the Christianity emerging in Africa, Asia, and Latin America is theologically conservative, charismatic in worship and experience, and evangelistic in its outreach. He adds that its adherents are young and that Christianity's growth is often in contexts of poverty and oppression.

### The Multi-Nation Anabaptist Profile

In early 2008, Eastern Mennonite Missions agreed to sponsor a study of Mennonite churches with origins in its mission-sending movement. In 1933, Eastern Mennonite Missions sent its first international missionaries to Tanganyika (now Tanzania) in Africa, and over the subsequent decades was actively engaged in evangelism and church planting in Asia, Africa, and Latin America, particularly in regions where an evangelical expression of the Christian church did not yet exist. Eastern Mennonite

---

13. For a useful analysis of recent trends among North American Christians, see *The Truth about Conservative Christians: What They Think and What They Believe* by Andrew Greeley and Michael Hout, 2006.

Missions' interest in a profile of global churches was to develop a "photograph" of the churches it had planted and to measure where these churches were on a host of religious and social variables.

This book is an effort to provide insight into the realities of these churches and to test a variety of sociological assertions that have been emerging over the past two decades as scholars of religion have increasingly turned their attention to the southern hemisphere. The empirical data supporting arguments in earlier studies of Christianity in the Global South have often been anecdotal, based on membership patterns, or gathered largely through ethnographic research. We do not know of anyone who has collected data on attitudes, values, and beliefs from ordinary church members as we have in the Multi-Nation Anabaptist Profile (MNA Profile). While our data are limited in that they do not represent all Anabaptists globally and are not representative of Christian groups outside the Anabaptist family, the Profile provides a new and useful window into the forces shaping Christianity in Asia, Africa, and Latin America today.

Some may criticize the Profile's research limitations and miss the more important story that the data reveal: a narrative consistent with what Jenkins and others have been reporting about Christianity's growth in the Global South. While important to strengthening future efforts, too much focus on the shortcomings of research methods can be a smokescreen to avoid realities that some of us in Europe and North America would like to deny about Christianity's demise in our own backyards. But frankly, it matters little what those of us in the West think about present or future trends of Christianity in the Global South. The precipitous declines in birth rates in Europe and North America and the lack of engagement in recruitment and evangelism have resulted in a Western church that is diminishing as quickly as the church in the Global South is expanding. Based on the data that are emerging, it is quite likely that the churches of Asia, Africa, and Latin America will have the last word in terms of what it means to be Christian in the twenty-first century.

At the same time, the MNA Profile data—as well as the history of Christianity—suggest that those in the Global South should not automatically assume that their current growth patterns will continue indefinitely. Demographic trends such as death rates, birth rates, life expectancy, and migration play a major role in the growth and decline of a church. Whether a church relies primarily on conversion and/or on reproduction helps to determine the future of that church. Historically, North American Anabaptist churches have relied on reproduction more than on recruitment for new members, but as members embraced family planning and birth control in the latter half of the twentieth century, the shortcomings of a "reproduction only" approach have become apparent. Barring the embrace of a conversion model, membership declines in Anabaptist churches in Europe and North America will continue unabated.

Sociologically, the growth and decline of churches as social organizations makes intuitive sense. New organizations recognize that their future depends on making new converts and recruiting new members. They are more evangelistic because they need to be. Older churches begin to take their existence for granted as multiple generations of believers meet Sunday after Sunday for worship. When their patterns of faith and practice become solidified, they become more mechanical and less passionate and lose the evangelistic fervor they once had. The loss of evangelistic activity is often accompanied by a decline in birth rates as the forces of modernity gain traction. It will take some time for churches in the Global South to recognize their vulnerability, since their birth rates are likely to remain high for a number of years. But over time, as in North American and European churches, reproduction without conversion will produce plateauing and eventual decline. As the history of the church has shown, early growth trajectories hold no promise of future growth or sustainability.

From the perspective of Christian believers, however, the growth in the South and the declines in the West are more than demographic phenomena. These trends seem to be connected to a stirring of the Holy Spirit that has made the Pentecostal movement the most rapidly growing expression of the Christian church over the past century. Regardless of one's own theological commitments and experience, it is difficult to deny the vitality of a movement sweeping so powerfully across the global church and encompassing so many diverse locations, ethnicities, cultures, and denominations. If the church in the Global South gets to define Christianity in the twenty-first century—and by all appearances this will be the case—it is fairly clear that the definition will include the words *Pentecostal* and *charismatic*.

## Our purpose

While Jenkins's purpose in *The Next Christendom* is to identify a new "Christendom" that appears to be emerging globally, our purpose is more modest—to describe the Anabaptist churches we studied and to address a number of emerging characteristics of churches in the Global South. It is important to carry out such empirical work before assertions about global Christian realities become too deeply embedded without sufficient analysis and reflection.

The data in the MNA Profile are a limited slice of global Anabaptism but will give scholars and church leaders one of the first systematic glimpses into the values, attitudes, beliefs, and practices of ordinary Christians in the Global South. Whether seen as a case study or as exploratory research, these findings may begin to correct a tendency of North American and European scholars to write about the church in the Global South without engaging that church itself. This study is important beyond the Anabaptist family of churches, since so little data have been collected at the grassroots level among ordinary members of any Christian faith tradition in Asia, Africa, and Latin America.

This profile reveals an interesting interplay between the historic Anabaptist movement and the Pentecostal movement of the Global South. A number of scholars have begun to point to the connections between these two movements and to argue that Pentecostalism is akin to the earlier Anabaptist movement that emerged in Reformation Europe.[14] In fact, recognizing the connections between these two faith traditions, Mennonite Church USA has been engaged in conversations with Pentecostal churches for several years. Contemporary Anabaptist churches in the Global South reflect many Pentecostal characteristics. If Pentecostalism owes something to early Anabaptism, as some contend and we concur, contemporary Anabaptism in the Global South is equally indebted to the Pentecostal movement.[15]

Philip Jenkins's work propelled global Christianity to the forefront of academic discussion in the fields of religion, sociology, and political science. But additional research, including the present study, is needed to further examine the realities of the global church and to explore and test Jenkins's and other hypotheses about it. To his credit, Jenkins recognizes the need for studies such as this one, noting, "The difficulty, of course, is deciding just what that vast and multifaceted entity described as the Third World actually does want or believe. As Southern churches grow and mature, they will increasingly define their own interests."[16] This profile of Anabaptists is an effort to do just that—to document what ordinary Christians in Asia, Africa, and Latin America believe and practice.

In sum, this book attempts to show the following among the churches in our sample:

---

14. Clark, 2004.

15. The extent to which the MNA Profile churches mirror Pentecostal characteristics varies across the churches. Amor Viviente Honduras, Happy Church Kenya, the Meserete Christos Church, and the Fellowship of Christian Assemblies may be most explicitly identifiable as within the Pentecostal stream. But as the data will show, all of the churches in the Global South lean in the direction of Pentecostal experience with the possible exception of the Indonesian church, which has a long history of resistance to speaking in tongues. In contrast to nearly all of the other churches stands the United States church, represented in our Profile by Lancaster Mennonite Conference, where experience with the charismatic gifts is much lower than for the Global Southern churches as a whole.

16. Jenkins, 2002:214.

1. The growth of Anabaptism in the Global South mirrors the numeric growth of other Christian groups in the southern hemisphere.

2. The nature and character of Anabaptism in the Global South parallels the broader, emerging Christianity of the Global South. It is orthodox in belief, conservative in moral commitments, and Pentecostal in orientation.

3. Anabaptism in the Global South has much in common with its sixteenth-century origins—perhaps more so than does contemporary Anabaptism in North America and Europe.

4. Both sixteenth-century Anabaptism and its contemporary expressions in the Global South reflect characteristics and qualities of the first three hundred years of pre-Christendom church history.

5. The decline of Christendom in North America and Europe may lead to greater convergence between the Global South and North in coming decades.

6. As one of many renewal movements that have occurred in the past two thousand years of church history, the growth of the Pentecostal movement may ensure the future sustainability of a vibrant Anabaptist witness, both in the Global North and the Global South.

## Definitions

Throughout this book we will refer to several concepts or words that we want to clarify at the outset. First, the term *Global South* has been used by many authors to refer to nation-states in Asia, Africa, and Latin America—particularly those that are low- to middle-income. While this phrase is useful for capturing a particular concept, it does not do so accurately, since some countries in these continents are located above the equator. We will use this term but also note more accurately the "countries of Asia, Africa, and Latin America." In addition, we sometimes refer to the West or to the Global North when discussing Europe and North America, as both continue to be used in the global literature.

Second, this book is specifically about a sample of Anabaptist churches in ten countries, all but one from Asia, Africa, and Latin America. The term *Anabaptist* refers to a group of sixteenth-century radical reformers who believed that the Protestant Reformation was falling short of New Testament Christianity. With origins in Switzerland and Germany as well as the Netherlands, these reformers insisted on believers baptism, rejected the protection of the state, refused to take up arms against those who disagreed with them, and, above all, chose to practice faithfulness to the teachings of Jesus in daily life. Many who embraced these commitments lost their lives at the hands of other reformers. By the early 1700s, many Anabaptists began to migrate to North America as they fled persecution in Europe.

The Anabaptist family is composed of numerous groups— too many to mention—including Mennonites (named after Anabaptist leader Menno Simons), Old Order Amish, Old Order Mennonites, Brethren in Christ, Church of the Brethren, and the English Baptists (the latter with historical connections to the Continental movement). All of the groups participating in the MNA Profile have historic connections to the Anabaptist or believers church family.

Third, our references to *Christendom* reflect the way that Western Christianity developed after Constantine's fourth-century conversion. Because of Constantine's conversion, Christianity became an official religion; the relationship between church and state virtually merged, blurring distinctions between Christian and non-Christian; and local mission efforts were abandoned (since all citizens were now Christians) in favor of foreign mission endeavors to reach the "true pagans" abroad.[17]

---

17. Kreider, 1999.

Our argument is that the kind of Christian context emerging in the Global South has more in common with pre-Christendom Christianity than it does with the Christendom faith of Europe and the United States. But, as many other scholars are suggesting, the historic forms of Christendom in the West are disintegrating and may well create a context in both North America and Europe that is more like pre-Christendom than has been the case for nearly seventeen hundred years. If this in fact occurs, we will likely see a convergence between a spiritually renewed Western church that has lost Christendom and a Spirit-filled Southern church that never experienced it.

Fourth, the story of Christianity in the Global South is replete with examples of the *contextualization* or *enculturation* of the gospel message, in which Christian teachings are adapted by the society to which they are introduced and take on the cultural forms of that society. Christianity, and particularly its Pentecostal form, has shown an uncanny ability to take root and prosper without sustained connections to a Western missionary presence. As Jenkins notes and as is true for some of the churches in our study, the greatest growth among some churches in the Global South occurs only after missionaries have gone home.[18] Included in the MNA Profile are fast growing churches that originated without any Western missionary witness and whose founders were from the Global South. At the same time, some leaders of churches in our study worry that syncretism, rather than contextualization or enculturation, sometimes occurs in their churches; indigenous religious expressions are mixed with Christian doctrine and practice, leading to outcomes, such as ancestor worship, that they feel do not meet the test of orthodox Christianity. But there is probably a continuum between syncretism and contextualization in all cultures. A Western eye is sometimes more likely to see syncretism where in fact appropriate contextualization has occurred.[19]

---

18. Jenkins, 2002.
19. Yong, 2005.

## Authors

While I have written the introduction and take the lead throughout this book, I am delighted to be writing with two others who have decades of experience in the churches that are part of the MNA Profile. Richard Showalter has lived and worked in numerous countries in the Global South and has been president of Eastern Mennonite Missions for seventeen years. Not only does he bring a wealth of experience and relationships, but he also knows well the missiological literature and context of the twentieth-century North American mission-sending movement. During his tenure as mission agency president, Richard observed firsthand the rapid growth of the churches in this study. Tilahun Beyene grew up in Ethiopia and was a leader in MKC Ethiopia for a number of years before migrating to the United States, where he formerly worked for Eastern Mennonite Missions. A member of one of our churches in the Profile, Tilahun both came to faith and became a Christian leader in the Global South. In addition, his responsibilities both in Ethiopia and in North America have involved a great deal of cross-cultural engagement, including with many of the churches in our Profile. While I bring to this book an understanding of the sociology of religion and social science methodologies, both Richard and Tilahun write from a perspective of intercultural mission engagement that is more concrete and "lived" than my own.

## Audience

Our intended audience in writing this book includes those with interest in the broader global evangelical movement, Anabaptists throughout the world, and members and leaders of participating churches in the MNA Profile. We believe that the findings of the Profile will contribute to a broader understanding of the Christian churches emerging in the Global South as well as speak to a global Anabaptist family that is tremendously diverse.

## Outline of chapters

The first three chapters of the book introduce the MNA Profile. Chapters 4, 5, and 6 describe its basic findings. Chapters 7 through 9 address topical areas on which the data shed important light, such as mission, Anabaptism, and the Holy Spirit. The tenth and final chapter offers several parameters that we believe will continue to shape the emergence of Anabaptism in the Global South.

More specifically, chapter 2 describes the historical origins and development of each of the churches in the Profile. Chapter 3 addresses prior research that has considered the global church, briefly introduces the participating MNA Profile churches, and reviews the methodology of the Profile. Chapter 4 looks at the demographic characteristics of Profile churches—including variables such as the age, gender, residence, education, occupation, and income of those who answered the Profile questionnaire. Chapter 5 considers the beliefs and practices of MNA Profile members and compares them across the churches. Chapter 6 describes the characteristics of Anabaptist congregations and the attitudes of members toward their congregations. The question of mission engagement among Profile churches is broached in chapter 7; faithfulness in mission has propelled these churches to their current positions and will undoubtedly continue to influence their trajectories. Chapter 8 evaluates the Anabaptist nature of the MNA Profile respondents, employing a brief summary of Anabaptist history. Chapter 9 considers the linkage between the growth and nature of churches in the Global South and the movement and work of the Holy Spirit as perceived by MNA Profile members. The chapter also discusses the character of the global Pentecostal movement. The concluding chapter, chapter 10, outlines parameters we believe will continue to shape global Anabaptism and Christianity more broadly into the twenty-first century.

2

# A History of the Churches in the Profile

> I appreciate your ongoing interest in what it means to be an Anabaptist. It is a much richer tradition than just not serving in the army and not swearing oaths. There was [in the sixteenth century Anabaptist reformation] a fresh encounter with the Bible, the Holy Spirit, evangelism, and the understanding that Jesus not only saves but transforms. The church is the new Body of Christ, called out of the world to be sent back into the world. I see elements of this in many of your groups. —*John Roth, Anabaptist historian, sharing his observations about the Profile data with participating churches*

When the Mennonites, or "Mennists," of continental Europe began migrating to North America in 1710, they came as religious and economic refugees along with many of their evangelical cousins. They first settled in eastern Pennsylvania not far from Philadelphia, along the colonial frontiers.[1]

---

1. Many streams of Anabaptists would come from other countries throughout the next three centuries. But the significance of including

Since the end of the Thirty Years War (1618–1648), Anabaptists in Europe had largely acquiesced to demands of their European magistrates and landlords that they not evangelize their neighbors. Nonetheless, embers of their ancestors' evangelistic fire in the previous century still glowed brightly and occasionally burst into flame. When it did, they were evicted, imprisoned, and even put to death for evangelizing. Hence, the shores of North America were a welcome sight for these Anabaptist faith communities with nearly two centuries of martyr memories.

Once in North America, Mennonites set immediately to clearing and farming their new landholdings, received in deeds from William Penn and his sons. They maintained the religious forms and many of the convictions inherited from their radical believers church origins. German was their language of choice, even though English was preferred by most immigrants in the newly emerging nation. In North America, they practiced their faith unhindered, reflecting the religious quietism that they had reluctantly accepted in the course of their stormy European trajectory. Their piety, however, seems to have had little spiritual fervor at times, with documents from the period reflecting more concern with material possessions and lifestyles than with the maintenance of a vibrant spirituality.[2] At least during some periods, faith as a living reality seems to have been quieted along with any outspoken witness.

### The origins of Mennonite mission

It was not until more than a century after their colonial arrival, about 1860, that Mennonites in the United States began to reconnect with the evangelistic core of the Anabaptist movement.

---

Lancaster Mennonite Conference churches in this study reflects not only the relationship of the conference to Eastern Mennonite Missions but also the fact that Lancaster Mennonite Conference—along with Franconia Conference—represents the earliest group of Mennonites going to North America from Europe.

2. Ruth, 2001.

This renewal occurred simultaneously with their adoption of the English language and a new ease of fellowship with other believers church movements. Missional influences that had once flowed from European Anabaptists to others on the continent now flowed back from Methodists, Baptists, and others to nineteenth century Pennsylvania Anabaptists.[3]

Between 1860 and 1910, a new evangelical movement took place among these Swiss-German Mennonites. Young evangelists, including J. S. Coffman and A. D. Wenger, preached for conversion. Sweeping away many of the quietist traditions of their elders, they reintroduced a missional fervor embedded in their Anabaptist beginnings. Although evangelical foreign mission movements were not new to North Americans—with Congregational and Baptist mission societies initiated in 1810 and 1813—Anabaptists had not yet participated in these mission-sending movements.

By the 1880s, a second wave of foreign missionary efforts occurred in the United States with the development of women's missionary societies and the Student Volunteer Movement. Mennonites by this time were ready to join, and within a few years several mission boards were established. One of these was Eastern Mennonite Missions, founded in 1894 in a farmhouse in Lancaster County, Pennsylvania.

At first, Eastern Mennonite Missions supported foreign missions through its national sister agency in Elkhart, Indiana (Mennonite Board of Missions). One of its founders led the first Mennonite foreign mission team to India in 1899. Later, beginning in 1933 with Tanganyika (now Tanzania), Eastern Mennonite Missions began forming and administering its own teams. In the next eighty years, Mennonite congregations were initiated beyond Tanzania in Kenya, Ethiopia, Vietnam, the Philippines, and other countries.

---

3. In our use of the word *missional*, we are referring to a commitment to "be sent" into the world with the gospel message. Early Anabaptists understood that they were both called to follow Jesus as well as then sent by Jesus into the world with the good news of salvation in Christ.

Before the twentieth century ended, new churches of the Global South planted by Lancaster Mennonite Conference (LMC United States) missionaries far outnumbered the sending congregations in eastern Pennsylvania. They functioned with ecclesiastical independence from LMC United States and other North American Mennonite church structures but maintained strong bonds of fellowship with them and with each other. These bonds were fostered through bilateral visits from United States bishops to mission churches and an annual global fellowship of mission leaders. In addition, most mission churches became members of the Mennonite World Conference, where leaders participated in triennial gatherings.

The experience of Mennonite missionaries as they came and went from Pennsylvania had an enormous impact on North American Mennonites, creating dialogue that was sometimes uncomfortable for all involved. Inevitably, mission activity created challenges for the church, since its religious and spiritual forms did not always function well within the culture receiving the gospel message. For example, missionaries to Tanganyika brought back a message of renewal from the East African Revival movement that created concern for some in LMC United States while revitalizing the faith of others. Questions of plain dress, so important to LMC United States bishops, were challenged by missionaries for whom such dress seemed irrelevant among their new converts. How should the gospel be appropriately contextualized? What should be the role of the sending church in eastern Pennsylvania? These and other questions would remain important for decades to come for both LMC United States and the missionaries it sent.

As Pentecostal movements spread in the United States and around the globe, missionaries were often among the first to become engaged. Some of the most rapidly growing Anabaptist churches planted by Eastern Mennonite Missions had experienced outpourings of the Holy Spirit that identified them in some way as "Pentecostal," even though neither Pentecostal theology nor Pentecostal experience had been part of the faith taught by their missionaries. Others churches, however, experienced significant growth apart from identification as Pentecostal. Nevertheless, in every case there appeared to be a connection between both numerical and spiritual growth and movements of spiritual renewal. The interplay of all these factors—intercultural mission engagement, renewal movements, and the missionaries who came and went—shaped the history of the global Mennonites who are part of this Profile.

## Churches in the MNA Profile

The participating church groups in the MNA Profile are all partners of Eastern Mennonite Missions (EMM), the mission agency of Lancaster Mennonite Conference (LMC United States). Each church in the Profile was selected according to their relationship to EMM. Eight of the churches were initiated by mission teams sent from EMM; three have worked with EMM in close partnership but were not initiated by EMM teams; and one (LMC United States) was EMM's primary constituent body. In this chapter we will give a brief historical introduction to each church.

### United States

**Lancaster Mennonite Conference (LMC United States).** Eastern Mennonite Missions has its origins in LMC United States, the largest regional conference of the Mennonite Church USA and one of the two oldest conferences in the denomination. As noted above, the beginnings of LMC United States can be traced to 1710, when Swiss-German Mennonites began settling on the frontier in Penn's Woods, east of the Susquehanna River, after disembarking in Philadelphia. LMC United States currently has a membership of about 15,500 persons in 167 congregations.[4]

---

4. The size of participating church bodies and the number of congregations presented here are figures reported publicly by the church bodies. The actual membership and congregational data that we received from participating churches and used to establish the population parameters of congregations and members in the Profile often

The beginnings of LMC United States include a bit of irony. Continental Europe was pleased to rid itself of the believers churches, troublesome as they were to the hegemony of the official state churches, both Protestant and Roman Catholic. Members of the believers churches flocked to the New World by the hundreds, escaping the suffering they had experienced in Europe. The Mennonites who formed LMC United States and other Mennonite groups throughout North America were descendants of the sixteenth-century Anabaptists. Victims of religious persecution on one continent, they became oppressors—if only latently—on another. In Pennsylvania, Mennonite farmers and families frequently benefited from broken treaties with Native Americans, contributing to the suffering and demise of those first nations. Although Mennonites themselves did not resort to physical violence against tribal groups, they reaped the benefits of the European invasion of North America.

The tendency toward isolationism while receiving economic benefits at the expense of others, including native peoples, was true not only for Eastern Pennsylvania Mennonites but for other Anabaptists as well, including the Dutch Mennonites from Russia. In writing the history of these Mennonites who settled in the midwestern United States in the late nineteenth century, historian Robert Epp criticizes their failure to recognize that they benefited from lands taken from native peoples by force and their ignorance of treaties with Indian tribes that whites broke at their own convenience:

> This concern for their own group . . . may also have been a weakness. At least, I should say it was not sufficiently counter-balanced by an awareness of what effect the total group might have on other groups. Their concern was always that they might have a place to worship God

---

differed from these public numbers. Such discrepancies may be due in part to (1) the rapid growth in some of these churches across the two years of the MNA Profile, (2) irregular record-keeping practices, or (3) membership criteria that differed from our relatively strict requirement of baptized members only.

as they saw fit, a place to teach their children the Faith. So long as they were assured of this they felt comfortable. This attitude, unfortunately, ignores the realities of life and does not measure up to the highest Christian insight. "And I have other sheep, that are not of this fold" (John 10:16).[5]

For seven generations, Mennonites in Pennsylvania spoke their native German in an otherwise English-speaking world, but by 1880 that wall of separation began to crumble. As already noted, they began to participate in revival movements taking place in North America. The cultural and spiritual changes taking place among Mennonites led to a loosening of traditional forms and normative behaviors, creating space for regeneration. The founding of Eastern Mennonite Missions in 1894 was a product of the Spirit's work in challenging and dismantling the traditional forms and structures that Lancaster Mennonites had come to take for granted since their arrival in North America. This awakening of evangelistic fervor led to the first foreign mission team to Tanganyika in 1933.

LMC United States was extraordinarily successful in engaging in foreign missions. Banding together, congregations created offering schedules for their church members that included eighteen annual mission offerings, all but two of these going directly to their mission agency. People gave generously, and foreign mission programs flourished. Since 1933, mission teams have worked on six continents and established more than twenty groups of churches in fifteen nations. Some of these churches are now much larger than LMC United States.

In their work, Mennonite missionaries often partnered with the Mennonite Central Committee (MCC), an inter-Mennonite relief and development agency in North America established in 1920. They found other partners as well.

In Indonesia, for example, they partnered with PIPKA, a Mennonite mission board founded in the 1960s by the GKMI Indonesia. In 1997, Eastern Mennonite Missions and three of

---

5. Epp, 1975:33.

its partner organizations initiated a global association of mission agencies, International Missions Association (IMA). It was attending an IMA gathering in Ethiopia (2003) that sparked lead author of this study Conrad Kanagy's vision for carrying out a church member profile among growing Anabaptist churches in Asia, Africa, and Latin America. In such a profile of churches, it seemed only right to include LMC United States, the sending church, along with the others selected for the Profile.

## Africa

**Kanisa la Mennonite Tanzania (KMT Tanzania).** KMT Tanzania is the oldest participating church planted by Eastern Mennonite Missions mission teams.[6] The missionaries who went to Tanganyika (now Tanzania) in 1933 settled on the eastern shores of Lake Victoria among unevangelized tribes. These foreign witnesses were generally Mennonite farmers, fervent in faith and eager to make disciples. The Tanzanians, on the other hand, were committed to traditional tribal religions but also open to the Western influences beginning to pervade their cultures. Congregations were slowly, persistently established among them.

In the 1940s, foreigners and Africans alike were touched by the flames of the East African Revival, a renewal movement sweeping the region. Unlike Pentecostal movements emphasizing supernatural signs and wonders, this renewal focused on the confession and repentance of sin and placed a strong emphasis on reconciling broken relationships. Breaking down cultural and spiritual barriers, the movement inspired missionaries to confess and ask forgiveness of African brothers and sisters. As a result, KMT Tanzania established a strong foundation that integrated

---

6. Although Eastern Mennonite Missions had been part of sending mission teams through its sister mission agency (Mennonite Board of Missions) in Elkhart, Indiana prior to 1933, the Tangyanika sending represented the first independent foreign involvement by Eastern Mennonite Missions.

strong Mennonite patterns imported from Pennsylvania with a dynamic African spirituality centered in Jesus.

The East African Revival did not emphasize planting or building new churches but rather focused on "walking in the light" with brothers and sisters. Transparency, quick confession of sin, keeping clear accounts, and reconciliation were major themes of the revival. The movement encouraged revived congregations and members to bloom where they were planted, with the assumption that the principles of the revival were equally valid for any church. Embraced by the first Tanzanian Mennonite bishop, the revival had powerful effects on the Mennonite church and resulted in an indigenous church that was distinctly different from its mother church and from the first missionaries who formed it.

The last foreign Mennonite bishop left Tanzania in the 1960s. As an intertribal church, KMT Tanzania has alternately experienced division, dependence, and a diversity of church forms and structures. For a time, LMC United States bishops mandated Swiss-German plain dress. The missionaries also created institutions that the church was ill-equipped to manage. Competing Tanzanian bishops struggled, divided, and reengaged. But in the end, KMT Tanzania remained a unified church body and continued growing. Today, it is a vigorous communion reaching into many parts of the nation and reporting more than 65,000 members and 400 congregations.

**Meserete Kristos Church (MKC Ethiopia).** Of the twelve churches in the MNA Profile, MKC Ethiopia has the most members. It is also the largest single Anabaptist communion in the world. The first Mennonite missionaries went to Ethiopia in 1948, and the church celebrated its fiftieth anniversary in 2002. In 2010, the church numbered 368,000 members and 580 local congregations.

The first American missionaries from LMC United States intended to evangelize among Ethiopia's Muslim peoples. But, due to a willing reception from traditional Orthodox Christians, the focus shifted rapidly to them. In the late 1960s, shortly after the church transitioned from foreign to local leadership, a spiritual revival broke out among Ethiopian youth who were taking English classes, studying the Gospel of John. This revival movement—like the East African Revival for the KMT Tanzania—transformed MKC Ethiopia. A more charismatic expression than the East African Revival, this movement's hallmarks were fervent prayer, healings, deliverance, and evangelism. Openness among Ethiopian leaders and missionaries allowed the movement to shape the direction of the church.

By 1981, the membership of MKC Ethiopia had reached 4,500 persons. Attendance at the largest congregation in Addis Ababa reached 2,500 in three services. The following year, the church was declared illegal by the Marxist government that had swept into power in Ethiopia. In response, MKC Ethiopia leaders established low-profile house fellowships. In 1991, when its public doors were again opened, the church's membership numbered as many as 50,000 members by some estimates—compared to 5,000 members at the time of its closure in 1982.

MKC Ethiopia is a discipling church as well as a church of prayer. Baptized members are a fraction of those who attend services. The church is well organized and effectively led, though leadership development is a constant challenge in such a rapidly growing church. MKC Ethiopia is also a sending church, with a vigorous mission department that sees to the planting of new churches beyond the reach of established congregations. MKC Ethiopia evangelists are beginning to enter surrounding nations, including Sudan, Somalia, and Djibouti, and are venturing much further afield among unreached peoples.

**Kenya Mennonite Church (KMC Kenya).** A fourth member of the MNA Profile, KMC Kenya is a close partner of KMT Tanzania. It was planted by both Tanzanian and North American missionaries but is best understood as a natural outgrowth of the Tanzanian church on the Kenyan side of the border. It resulted in part from the return to southwest Kenya of KMT Tanzania members in 1962. Thus, as the Tanzanian church began to expand into Luo tribal territory in Kenya, the first witnesses to Kenya were African.

KMC Kenya's numerical strength is along Lake Victoria among the Luo population that extends across the border from Tanzania. The Luos are strong in KMT Tanzania but not as dominant as in KMC Kenya. KMC Kenya remained under the bishopric of the KMT Tanzania until 1988, when the first Kenyan bishops were appointed. There are currently seven dioceses, with more than 6,000 members in 110 congregations. In 2008, KMC Kenya ordained its first female pastor, joining LMC United States as the only churches in the Profile to formally ordain women.

**Happy Church Ministries International (Happy Church Kenya).** Another Kenyan participant in the MNA Profile, Happy Church Kenya has different origins than KMC Kenya. Its founder, Bishop Joseph Kamau, traveled to the United States in the late 1970s to study at Rosedale Bible College, where he connected with Mennonites. While originally intending to become a medical doctor, he returned to Kenya with a vision for church planting. Working in the intertribal Rift Valley, he and his team experienced great church growth. They held nightly evangelistic meetings, where many people came to Christ and experienced miraculous healings. The impact of these conversions created resistance, causing the church to move its activities to a rented high school hall, where many young people were exposed to the gospel.

With most of its churches in the Rift Valley, Happy Church Kenya is multiethnic and mostly urban. For this reason, the post-election violence that rocked Kenya in 2007 was particularly devastating to Happy Church Kenya congregations, accounting for the loss of many of its members. United with KMC Kenya in 1989, a decade later it was registered as a stand-alone entity. Still reeling from the effects of intertribal violence, Happy Church Kenya is now rebuilding and estimates a size of 7,000 members in more than 60 congregations.

## Asia

**Hoi Thanh Mennonite Viet Nam (HTM Vietnam).** There are four Asian churches in the MNA Profile. Of these, the one planted most directly by Mennonite mission teams from LMC United States is HTM Vietnam. American missionaries first went to Vietnam in 1957 following relief work begun there by MCC five years earlier. By 1975, the end of the American-Vietnamese War, a Mennonite fellowship existed in the southern part of the country. Officially disbanded at the end of the war, it continued a quiet, unofficial existence for many years, patiently shepherded by Pastor Nguyen Quang Trung, who had worked with the churches since 1965.

In the past fifteen years, a group of churches known as "Mennonite" gradually emerged under Pastor Trung's tutelage. In the late 1990s, Mennonite missionaries from North America once again began to walk with the churches, and in 2008, the Vietnamese government officially recognized the church. The church now has more than 8,000 members in 90 congregations and is actively engaged in developing new leaders and starting new churches, as well as educational classes for women and children. Many churches have affiliated with HTM Vietnam because of their affinity for the 1995 *Confession of Faith in a Mennonite Perspective*, in which they found a unity of faith and practice that they could embrace.

**Persatuan Gereja-Gereja Kristen Muria Indonesia (GKM Indonesia).** GKM Indonesia dates its origin to 1920, when a missionary sent by the Dutch Mennonite mission board, Nicolai Thiessen, baptized a small group of Chinese Indonesians. GKM Indonesia grew first among Indonesians of Chinese origin, planting nine churches between 1920 and 1951 around Muria Mountain, a region designated for Mennonite missions by the Dutch colonists of Indonesia. Although it struggled to move beyond this region, when its mission board (PIPKA) was established in 1965, the church began to reach out to Javanese and Indonesians of other cultural groups on different islands, including Sumatra and Kalimantan. In 1974, Eastern Mennonite Missions created a partnership with PIPKA, and the two have been working together for more than thirty years. GKM Indonesia currently reports 18,880 members in 102 congregations.

**Fellowship of Christian Assemblies (FCA India).** FCA India has its headquarters in Delhi. Seeking Anabaptist connections, FCA India began to partner with Eastern Mennonite Missions in 2002. Its founder, P. C. Alexander, is a South Indian missionary who leads the Pocket Testament League of India. In 1990, P. C. Alexander began leading his team to plant churches, recognizing that Scripture distribution and leading people to faith in Christ were not sufficient to develop faithful disciples and form new fellowships. He met some resistance in doing so, but his persistence has led to rapidly growing and thriving congregations.

The first FCA India church planter ministered for three years before baptizing the first Christian convert. Today, FCA has a total of 270 missionaries, 250 of them trained in their own mission training institute. FCA India is entering some of the most challenging mission areas of India but has grown to 100 fellowships and nearly 20,000 members in these fellowships. Education has been an important part of FCA India's work, and it has established four schools to aid in the spread of the gospel. FCA India is the most rapidly growing church group in the MNA Profile, with nearly all of its growth occurring in the past two decades. The majority of new converts are young people.

**Integrated Mennonite Church of the Philippines (IMC Philippines).** A Mennonite witness existed in the Philippines since the late 1940s with MCC's presence in the country, but IMC Philippines did not form until 1991, after a small group of churches that had walked with Eastern Mennonite Missions mission teams since 1972 decided to create their own fellowship. The church has faced a variety of challenges, including leadership divisions, constitutional struggles, and the untimely death of a key mission leader. Simultaneously, however, it has demonstrated great resilience and produced outstanding global Anabaptist leaders. Today, IMC Philippines has 20 congregations and just over 700 members.

## Latin America

**Iglesia Evangélica Menonita Hondureña (IEM Honduras).** The three Latin American participant groups in the MNA Profile represent two Central American nations, Honduras and Guatemala. The first of these to be planted was IEM Honduras. Eastern Mennonite Missions' work in Honduras started in 1950 in and around La Ceiba, Trujillo, and San Pedro Sula. For the first twenty-five years of its existence, the church was largely rural, farming, and relatively poor. As it grew, it expanded into the mountains and along the coast.

Poverty, the Cuban War, and the early transfer of mission property to the Honduran church to mitigate the risk of losing it to a communist insurgency have left their imprint on the church. IEM Honduras has also been shaped by the confluence of Central American Pentecostal streams of renewal and Anabaptist streams from North and Central America. These varied influences have given rise to some struggles with identity, but the church has generally managed these tensions effectively and is currently flourishing. While migration of members because of poverty and unemployment affects the membership of local congregations, in 2010 the church reported 136 congregations with 5,450 baptized members.

**Organización Cristiana Amor Viviente (Amor Viviente Honduras).** In contrast to most other churches planted by North American Mennonites, Amor Viviente Honduras traces its beginning to a single missionary couple, Ed and Gloria King, who began their formal missionary work in Honduras in 1973. Shaped by the second wave charismatic movement in the United States, the Kings began a Bible study or coffee house in their home with young people who came in off the streets. The Kings also organized annual music festivals that attracted many young people.

Church growth was rapid and led to the formation of local congregations and a national movement. In 2008, the church reported 32 congregations with 8,642 members. Amor Viviente Honduras has a strong emphasis on discipleship, with a unique three-year curriculum for every member. Evangelism

A History of the Churches in the Profile    49

and mission are at the core of its identity, and Amor Viviente Honduras churches are being planted globally, not only in Hispanic communities but also in other unreached groups, including in the United States, Spain, and China.

**Iglesia Nacional Evangélica Menonita Guatemalteca (INEM Guatemala).** The third participating group from Latin America is INEM Guatemala, sometimes referred to as the Kekchi Evangelical Mennonite Church of Guatemala. The first congregation was started in 1971 following the arrival of Eastern Mennonite Missions missionaries in 1969. The church grew rapidly during thirty years of civil war in Guatemala, with fifty congregations in place by 1985.

From 1969 to the present, approximately twenty Eastern Mennonite Missions missionaries have served among the Kekchi of INEM Guatemala, but today the church has complete autonomy. Membership estimates vary with 115 congregations and at least 15,000 baptized members. The Kekchi are an indigenous group (one of the earliest people groups in the Americas) whose people are regarded as second-class citizens in their native land. Among all the participating groups, their poverty and relative lack of education set them apart from others.

### Age of churches

Figure 2.1 provides a timeline for the approximate origins of the churches in the MNA Profile. Throughout the book, we will discuss the impact of maturation on the Profile churches, arguing that as churches age, they begin to take on characteristics common to older churches. One of the key changes we see in the Profile is a tendency for maturing churches to rely on reproduction (the birth and conversion of their own children) rather than on the recruitment of new members for growth. Doing so inevitably leads to a plateauing of membership and eventual decline, particularly if the church embraces family planning and birth control. Keeping in mind the chronological age of each church is useful in understanding these churches.

Table 2.1 Approximate dates of origin for Profile

| | |
|---|---|
| United States | 1710 |
| Indonesia | 1920 |
| Tanzania | 1933 |
| Ethiopia | 1951 |
| Honduras (Mennonite) | 1950 |
| Vietnam | 1957 |
| Kenya (Mennonite) | 1962 |
| Guatemala | 1969 |
| Honduras (Amor Viviente) | 1973 |
| Kenya (Happy) | 1983 |
| India | 1990 |
| Philippines | 1991 |

## Conclusion

The twelve church groups in the MNA Profile vary substantially in culture, ethnicity, language, socioeconomic status, geography, national identity, literacy, size, year of the church's origins, and more. Studying these characteristics helps explain other differences among the churches in the Profile. But, as distinct as the churches are, the following chapters will show that they share much. All of the churches reflect deep Christian devotion, commitment to the fundamental beliefs of Christianity, and a concern for the ongoing mission of God. While they are shaped by the cultural, social, and political forces in their different contexts, each has retained a clear witness of Christian faith and practice.

It is important to recognize that the present realities of the churches in the Profile reflect in part the identities of the missionaries they received. The first missionaries to Tanganyika had a conservative cultural and religious perspective that shaped how they presented the Christian gospel. Just over a decade later, when missionaries went to Ethiopia, they communicated a more progressive strain of Mennonite faith, with less emphasis on particular forms of dress, more egalitarian leadership, and a deep commitment to the cultural contextualization of the gospel. In all of the churches initiated by missionaries from North America, the impact of that early missionary activity remains, reflected, for example, in KMT Tanzania's liturgy and order of service, MKC Ethiopia's leadership development patterns, Amor Viviente Honduras's discipleship programs, and IEM Honduras's holistic witness.[7] While early mission activity has shaped these churches, the gospel has been contextualized in all of these locations after missionaries exited and released control of the church and its institutions to local Christians. Missionary origins matter, but Christianity throughout the world has been contextualized and indigenized in places where missionaries do not have a sustained presence.

---

7. In Ethiopia the resistance of new MKC members to the hierarchy of the Orthodox Church—from which they had converted—also prevented the development of a bishop structure like that among Mennonites in Lancaster.

# 3

# *An Overview of the Profile*

There were various positive findings. We want to congratulate our congregations and at the same time call attention to changes that need to happen. The question about Allah and God requires more teaching. We found a very high awareness of missions in our church—we want to move this forward in concrete ways; people clearly have a vision for missions. The high number of young people was a great surprise and we want to take advantage of this resource. How do we transition to give opportunities to these young people? We are concerned that, even though evangelism is very high, our churches should be fuller.
—*Carlos Marin, Amor Viviente Honduras, commenting on the results of the MNA Profile*

Even though our results were not ideal, the snapshot nonetheless was very useful. Hearing the results was great. Please bear with us as we continue to ask questions. If Mennonites in Lancaster are so rich in literature and score so low in Bible reading, what is the point of writing so much literature? —*Jumanne Magiri, Tanzania Mennonite Church, commenting on the results of the MNA Profile*

From 2005 to 2007, Conrad Kanagy helped direct a sociological profile of three Anabaptist groups in the United States and subsequently wrote *Road Signs for the Journey: A Profile of Mennonite Church USA*. That book documents the challenges facing Mennonite Church USA, the largest Mennonite denomination in the United States. In 2008, Eastern Mennonite Missions committed funds to carry out a two-year study of Anabaptist churches on four continents whose historic origins were related to the activity of its mission teams and that had at least five thousand members.[1] Several other churches were invited to participate because of their contemporary relationship with EMM, even though their origins were not in its missionary activity.

Richard Showalter, then president of Eastern Mennonite Missions, appreciated the continuity of this project with previous efforts to learn from EMM's partner churches in the Global South. He was particularly interested in a profile of churches that would connect churches outside of North America, believing that such a study would create a foundation for greater missional synergy and a baseline against which to measure future changes in these churches. He also hoped that doing such a profile would allow participating churches to connect with and understand one another more fully.[2] The MNA Profile was envisioned in order to offer church leaders and their respective churches a snapshot of the values, practices, and beliefs of their

---

1. When using the language of *church* or *churches* in this book we typically are referring to the church bodies or denominations that participated in the MNA Profile, not to local congregations.

2. The objectives of the original MNA Profile proposal included strengthening God's mission globally; utilizing information gathered for the missional, spiritual, and ecclesiological health of Anabaptist churches globally; giving voice to southern hemisphere churches; providing feedback for the global church and a baseline against which to measure future growth and change among these churches; and increasing the potential for North to South Anabaptist church conversations.

members.[3] The findings would enable them to better understand their members, track changes in their churches over time, and develop more effective ministries in response.

## Previous studies

There are no previous global sociological studies of Anabaptists comparable to the Multi-Nation Anabaptist Profile. Few, if any, other Christian bodies have attempted to carry out profiles of this magnitude. Exceptions include the Seventh Day Adventists, the Church of Jesus Christ of Latter Day Saints, and the Church of the Nazarene—who each require some form of reporting from their global churches.[4]

Relatively few sociologists anywhere have conducted social science surveys in low- and middle-income countries, with the notable exception of Ronald Inglehart and the World Values Survey (WVS) affiliated with the University of Michigan. Since 1981, WVS has conducted national surveys in 97 societies representing 90 percent of the world's population. The survey has focused on changing values within these societies and the impact of these changes on social and political life. WVS relies on interviews of representative member samples from each participating nation and has asked questions about religion, gender roles, work motivations, democracy, governance, political participation, tolerance of other groups, environmental protection, and subjective well-being.[5]

Another example of the use of survey research in an international context is the 2010 Pew Research Center's study of more than

---

3. Originally called the Multi-Nation Anabaptist Profile I, with the hope that other profiles including additional churches might follow, we have dropped the "I" from the title of the project for purposes of convenience in writing, but still anticipate that future profiles might be conducted that expand our understanding of Anabaptists in churches and regions not represented in the current study.

4. The First Adventist World Survey was carried out in 1994 and included samples from more than one hundred countries.

5. For more information about the WVS see www.worldvaluessurvey.org.

2,000 evangelical leaders from 166 countries who participated in the Third Lausanne Conference of World Evangelization in Cape Town, South Africa. In that study, global leaders were asked about a variety of religious and social issues, some quite similar to the kinds of questions asked in the MNA Profile.[6]

Prior to beginning the MNA Profile, Conrad Kanagy consulted with researchers from the Seventh Day Adventist Church, the Church of the Nazarene, and the World Values Survey. In particular, Peter Ester, a Dutch sociologist who has contributed to the World Values Survey in Europe, encouraged the development and implementation of a global study of Anabaptists. He suggested that, while it would be complicated and less precise than such studies in the West, such a study would provide a new window into Anabaptist Christianity in the Global South.

With this encouragement, we proceeded with the Profile, recognizing that many of the challenges of social science survey methods in North American and European contexts would be exacerbated in contexts in the Global South with lower educational levels and greater illiteracy. Until now, much of what we know about Christianity's growth in the Global South is largely based on membership data. While such data are important in painting broad strokes in terms of religious trends, our own experience with this study verifies the difficulties of relying on membership data, which are often reported irregularly and sometimes more for political purposes than to track actual trends. In addition, membership data—upon which much global church research is built—do not reveal the underlying social forces shaping Christianity's growth in the Global South. While some may criticize our efforts to gather survey data in places where such endeavors are rare, we believe that the information we have gathered gives a legitimate window into the underlying forces shaping the membership numbers that many researchers are presenting as their primary source of data.

While the MNA Profile is the first sociological analysis of global Anabaptists, it is preceded by the Global Mennonite

---

6. The Pew Forum on Religion and Public Life, 2011.

History Project (GMHP) sponsored by Mennonite World Conference and edited by John A. Lapp and C. Arnold Snyder. The project is a series of books representing five continental regions and authored by writers from those regions. The purpose of the project is to relate the origins, development, and mission of Anabaptist churches in each region, with the hope that doing so will bring about a "renewal and extension of Anabaptist Christianity worldwide." It is also expected that the project will reveal more about "the shift in church energy, leadership, and numbers from North to South, from developed to developing nations."[7]

Beyond the fairly limited efforts of particular denominations to study the Christianity of the Global South, scholars of religion, history, and sociology by and large ignored the rapid growth of Christianity in the southern hemisphere until the publication of *The Next Christendom* by Philip Jenkins in 2002. In his groundbreaking book, Jenkins argues that Christianity in the Global South represents a new Christendom, distinctly unlike the Christendom that originated with Constantine's conversion in the fourth century AD and experienced the effects of Enlightenment rationality.

The Christendom of the Global South, says Jenkins, is characterized by charismatic expressions of Christian faith, a focus on social justice, and a more conservative theology than its cousin in the northern hemisphere. At the same time, Jenkins reminds readers that the southern hemisphere is not without its own very early expressions of Christianity, which are often ignored by scholars and the church in Europe and North America. He asserts that the rapid growth of Christianity in the Global South has been ignored because it has not met Enlightenment expectations about the declining future of religion. As secularization brought stagnation and decline in Europe and North America,

---

7. For more information see the Mennonite World Conference website at http://www.mwc-cmm.org/en15/index.php?option=com_content&view=article&id=24&Itemid=37. Three volumes have been released to date: *Anabaptist Songs in African Hearts* (2006), *Testing Faith and Tradition* (2006), and *Mission and Migration* (2010).

sociologists more than a century ago projected that religion would disappear within one hundred years. Clearly this has not been the case, and the growth of churches in the Global South exemplifies the absurdity of such projections.

Although Jenkins's work is not without its critics, it has resulted in a burst of scholarly work examining mission, globalization's effect on religion, and religious trends of the Global South. Two recent works in both sociology and history include Robert Wuthnow's *Boundless Faith: The Global Outreach of American Churches* (2009) and Mark Noll's *The New Shape of World Christianity: How American Experience Reflects Global Faith* (2009). Jenkins himself has written additional books on the nature of Christianity in the Global South, including *The New Faces of Christianity* (2006).

While the findings of the MNA Profile will contribute to a greater understanding of Anabaptist churches around the world, the relative lack of such data from Christian churches in the Global South in general will make it a rich resource for hypotheses and generalizations extending beyond Anabaptists.

### Anabaptist Christians in the global context

The twelve churches in our study total 1,441 congregations with 261,102 members.[8] Working with Mennonite World Conference membership data from 2009, which reports 1,616,126 Anabaptists globally, we estimate that the Profile churches represent between 15% and 20% of all Anabaptists globally, including Old Order Mennonites, Amish, and Brethren in Christ.[9]

---

8. Again, our sample size of members is lower than figures often reported for these churches. This is true for a variety of reasons including that we specified baptized adult members. In other contexts, some churches publicly report children and unbaptized members.

9. Find Mennonite World Conference membership statistics at http://www.mwc-cmm.org/en15/files/MWC%20Map%202009%20Oct%20FINAL.pdf. Two churches in the Profile—Fellowship of Christian Assemblies and Happy Church Ministries International—are not members of Mennonite World Conference.

An Overview of the Profile    59

However, there has been substantial change from 1978 to 2009 in Anabaptist membership by continent (see Table 3.1). While 51% of Anabaptists were in North America in 1978, in 2009 North Americans represent only 32% of the Anabaptist family, despite a threefold increase among the Brethren in Christ since 1972 and the continued growth of Old Order Amish and Old Order Mennonite groups. European Anabaptists have declined from 16% of all Anabaptists in 1978 to just 4% today. Africa, Asia, and Latin America have all experienced growth, with Africa's increase being the greatest—from 14% of all Anabaptists in 1978 to 37% today. Africa now represents the continent with the highest number of Anabaptists.

Table 3.1 Growth and decline of Anabaptists—1978 to 2009

|  | 1978 | 2009 |
|---|---|---|
| Latin America | 44,211 | 169,864 |
| Asia | 74,257 | 265,447 |
| Africa | 85,771 | 592,106 |
| Europe | 96,011 | 64,740 |
| North America | 313,000 | 523,969 |

*The number of Anabaptists globally increased from 613,250 in 1978 to 1,616,126 in 2009.
**Data from Mennonite World Conference

Table 3.2 Changes in percentage of Anabaptists by continent—1978 to 2009

|  | 1978 | 2009 |
|---|---|---|
| Latin America | 7% | 10% |
| Asia | 12% | 16% |
| Africa | 14% | 37% |
| Europe | 16% | 4% |
| North America | 51% | 32% |

*Data from Mennonite World Conference

60　*Winds of the Spirit*

Today, there are fewer Anabaptists in North America and Europe combined (588,709) than in the continent of Africa (592,106), even though in 1978 there were nearly five times as many Mennonites in Europe and North America as in Africa. These data indicate the dramatic shift from North to South in terms of membership size and growth.

### Churches in the Profile

Table 3.3 provides information about each participating church in the MNA Profile, including the number of congregations in each church and in the selected sample of each church, total membership in each church and in each church sample, and the final number of members and congregations that participated.[10]

Response rates of congregations in the Profile—that is, the percent of local congregations in each church body's sample that agreed to participate—were relatively high. The lowest congregational response was in GKM Indonesia, where fourteen of thirty selected congregations participated (47%). In four church bodies, all of the congregations chosen for the Profile agreed to be included. Ultimately, 281 congregations participated, and the average response rate for congregations was 80%.

Responses of members within congregations also varied from church to church, ranging from GKM Indonesia, where 5% of the total members in the sample agreed to participate, to IMC Philippines, where 87% of the members participated.[11] In GKM Indonesia, we ended up with 462 useable questionnaires from an original sample size of 8,565 members, as compared to IMC Philippines, where we received 609 useable questionnaires from an original sample of 701 members. For all twelve church

---

10. Some congregations reported zero members. These congregations were included in the sampling frames from which congregations were randomly drawn.

11. Because of the small size of the Philippine church, we invited all members to participate, resulting in what we typically call a saturated sample.

An Overview of the Profile 61

bodies, the average response rate for members was 38%, and the final sample was composed of 18,201 respondents.

Table 3.3 Response rates of participating churches

|  | Respondents |  | Response Rates |  |
|---|---|---|---|---|
| Church | Congregations | Members | Congregations | Members |
| Fellowship of Christian Assemblies | 25 | 1,159 | 100% | 74% |
| Persatuan Gereja-Gereja Kristen Muria Indonesia | 14 | 462 | 47% | 5% |
| Hoi Thanh Mennonite Viet Nam | 27 | 802 | 90% | 61% |
| Meserete Kristos Church | 24 | 5,507 | 90% | 58% |
| Kenya Mennonite Church | 19 | 817 | 76% | 33% |
| Happy Church Ministries International | 27 | 1,902 | 100% | 63% |
| Kanisa la Mennonite Tanzania | 22 | 1,002 | 63% | 17% |
| Organizacion Cristiana Amor Viviente | 15 | 2,700 | 100% | 49% |
| Iglesia Evangelica Menonita Hondurena | 31 | 1,385 | 78% | 69% |
| Iglesia Nacional Evangelica Menonita Guatemalteca | 33 | 1,096 | 94% | 28% |
| Integrated Mennonite Church of the Philippines | 20 | 609 | 100% | 87% |
| Lancaster Mennonite Conference | 24 | 760 | 62% | 19% |
| Total | 281 | 18,201 | 80% | 38% |

## Research methods

The MNA Profile formally began with a consultation in Delhi, India, in September 2008. The consultation was held in conjunction with the annual International Missions Association (IMA) meeting. Participants at the consultation included research associates, or anchors, appointed by each participating church to lead the Profile in its respective church. The research methods

62  Winds of the Spirit

and questionnaire for the MNA Profile were designed with the anchors' input and participation.[12] Anchors decided on a paper and pencil questionnaire to be completed by members of participating local congregations in the context of a worship service or other congregational gathering. The questionnaire was distributed in twelve languages: Amharic, Dholuo, English, Hindi, Indonesian, Kekchi, Oromo, Spanish, Swahili, Tagalog, Tamil, and Vietnamese. Before their distribution, all translations were back-translated into English to allow comparison with the original English version.

The survey was to be distributed to congregational members eighteen years of age and older, though some churches involved younger members. Anchors were responsible for implementing the Profile, which included training others to administer the questionnaire when they could not do so themselves. Once anchors received data back from congregations, they were responsible for entering them into spreadsheets and sending them to Conrad Kanagy for analysis.

## Sample

In order to select congregations and members to participate in the Profile, the authors requested that anchors submit a list of congregations in their churches that included each congregation's region or diocese and membership size. The churches

---

12. The anchors were Jumanne Magiri of Kanisa la Mennonite Tanzania, Alfredo Carcamo of Iglesia Evangélica Menonita Hondureña, Carlos Marin Montoya of the Organización Cristiana Amor Viviente, Moses Otieno of the Kenya Mennonite Church, Boniface Runji of the Happy Church Ministries International, Javier Xol and Galen Groff of the Iglesia Nacional Evangélica Menonita Guatemalteca, Trung Quang and Gerry Keener of the Hoi Thanh Mennonite Viet Nam, Karl Landis of Lancaster Mennonite Conference, Kristina Setiawan and Andreas Wijaya of the Persatuan Gereja-Gereja Kristen Muria Indonesia, Yemiru Tilahun and Tariku Gebre of the Meserete Kristos Church, Thomas Chacko and Blessan Abraham of the Fellowship of Christian Assemblies, and Edgardo Docuyanan and Richard Rancap of the Integrated Mennonite Church of the Philippines.

An Overview of the Profile 63

were treated as separate strata within which each congregation, or cluster, had an equal probability of selection. All members in each congregation also had an equal probability of selection. This type of sampling is called "one stage cluster sampling."

From the list of congregations submitted by each church, congregations were randomly selected for participation in the Profile. In the process, attention was paid to the overall regional distribution of the prospective sample as well as its number of congregations and members. The overall sample size of each church depended on the size of local congregations and the total number of congregations selected.

Anchors were then asked to review and authorize the list of congregations. In some cases, they suggested deleting or adding a few congregations due to their viability, geographic location, or strategic importance. With the exception of KMT Tanzania, there was relatively little deviation from the original sample in terms of additions and deletions. However, not all congregations elected to participate in the Profile, meaning that congregational response rates varied from church to church. In a few cases, congregations that chose not to participate in the Profile were replaced with others.

All members of selected congregations were invited to complete the questionnaire. In some instances, anchors distributed the questionnaires. In other cases, regional leaders or local pastors were responsible for the distribution. In congregations with low levels of literacy, anchors met with small groups to guide them through the process of completing the questionnaire by reading questions and response categories aloud for respondents. The number of members who completed a questionnaire was often lower than the number of members originally listed for a given congregation. In a few instances, however, the number of members who completed a questionnaire was higher than the number of members originally reported by the church.[13]

---

13. It is possible that church leaders underestimated a congregation's membership at the outset, or that the congregation grew between the

## Challenges

Implementation of the MNA Profile presented a number of challenges for Profile anchors and congregations.

- In India, FCA pastors understood the term *Anabaptist* as meaning *Baptist* and resisted implementation until the leader of FCA India explained it to them. It became an educational opportunity for a rapidly growing church in which many are not familiar with the terms *Anabaptist* or *Mennonite*. Indian anchors demonstrated great commitment to their Profile work; one anchor logged nearly ten thousand kilometers by train, walked extensively, rode the bus, and traveled by motorcycle to accomplish the task.

- In Guatemala, questionnaires were distributed by boat to the Kekchi of INEM Guatemala. Church members' low levels of education and literacy required several unique adjustments to the questionnaire, primarily creating fewer response categories for some questions.

- In the case of MKC Ethiopia, the geography of the country required the use of donkeys to deliver and return questionnaires for some congregations.

- In the Philippines, illiteracy, loss of electricity, and concerns about the national revenue service created challenges for IMC Philippines. But in the end, the

---

time of the original membership estimate and the Profile's implementation. Unlike the United States, where the membership of Mennonite Church USA declined during the time we were conducting the Profile from 2005–2007, in some of the participating churches in the MNA Profile memberships grew during the Profile's implementation. A third possibility for discrepancies in some congregations has to do with how membership is defined and measured in that particular church (something that also varies in the United States). For example, a leader of one church stated that an individual is considered a member whenever that person indicates such, as long as they are attending and giving regularly.

engagement of young people—including a Muslim youth who expressed interest in helping—allowed this church to accomplish its task.

## Questionnaire

The MNA Profile questionnaire was originally intended to be composed of approximately 75% core questions shared by all churches and 25% unique questions customized for each church. However, as anchors worked together in Delhi, they agreed to share as many questions as possible. In the end, we developed two questionnaires, one with thirty-seven questions and one with five additional questions that some churches chose to include. Churches that departed slightly from the core include HTM Vietnam, GKM Indonesia, MKC Ethiopia, and INEM Guatemala. As mentioned earlier, substantial changes were made in INEM Guatemala to accommodate the local culture and literacy levels.

The MNA Profile included demographic information (e.g., age, income, education, occupation, residence), questions regarding church participation (e.g., attendance, financial contributions, volunteer service), religious identity, spiritual biography and history, commitment to church planting, beliefs about Jesus, experience with charismatic gifts of the Holy Spirit, attitudes about social and moral issues, personal devotional life, witnessing and evangelism, social outreach, commitment to one's congregation, Anabaptist values, and worship preferences.

## Reporting the results

In August 2010, anchors and church leaders from the twelve participating churches met for a four-day consultation in Thika, Kenya, to present and review the findings of the MNA Profile. During the Thika consultation, anchors presented their church's data to all participants. Churches then spent substantial time reflecting together on what had been learned from one another and discussing how the MNA Profile data might be used to implement changes in their church bodies. These were exciting days, as leaders prayed together, listened to one another, and challenged each other to greater Christian faithfulness. Particular points of discussion that emerged included the following:

- *How should Christians engage with Muslims?* Islam is growing rapidly alongside some of the churches in the Profile. Indeed, the Islamic call to prayer each morning in Thika reminded consultation participants of the proximity of a rapidly growing Islam to many of the churches in the Profile. Churches differ in their understanding of how Christians should understand Islam and how to best respond to Islamic activity. Some emphasize evangelism and are inspired by the possibilities of Christian insider movements in Islamic communities. Others express anxiety about the growth of other religions and are encouraging their Christian young people to engage in political activities and become politicians so they can support an endangered church.

- *Should women be ordained?* The Profile revealed that a majority of members in all of the churches support the ordination of women—raising questions for leaders at the Thika consultation, given that most of the Profile churches do not ordain women. The discrepancy between members' views and the reality of most churches suggests a challenge and opportunity for Anabaptist churches around the world. Interestingly, in one of the few churches that does ordain women (LMC United States), support for doing so is the lowest.

- *Do Christians experience health and wealth?* Respondents were asked whether they believed that Christians experience good health and financial blessings because of their faith. Seventy-five percent of members in all churches except LMC United States affirm this belief; only 27% of LMC United States members affirm it. When pressed, leaders at the Thika consultation talked openly about the economic improvement that their members experience when they become Christians and abandon lifestyles that are socially, emotionally, and economically destructive. For these leaders, coming to Jesus means new economic hope and the motivation to better care for one's self and one's family. But what does it mean that so few in the wealthiest church in the Profile affirm this statement? Is this a rejection of a prosperity gospel? Is it a failure to recognize the Giver of all good gifts? Is it a belief that such gifts are the result primarily of hard work and individual effort? Or does it reflect some embarrassment about the inequities between so many in North America and those in the rest of the world? While no clear answers were suggested, Global South leaders seemed particularly intrigued and puzzled by the response of LMC United States members to this question.

- *What does it mean to be Anabaptist?* And how committed are leaders and members in the MNA Profile churches to being Anabaptist? There were various understandings of Anabaptism among participants at the consultation in Thika, but by and large most seemed keenly interested in faithfully following Jesus in an Anabaptist way. Many focused on nonviolence as the primary Anabaptist distinctive, while others encouraged a broader understanding of Anabaptism and reflected on the evidence of Anabaptist distinctives apparent in the churches represented at the consultation.

After listening to our partners at the final consultation for this project, it became clear that the Profile is extremely useful for their churches in planning and providing direction for the future. Many leaders expressed surprise at the low average age of members per congregation in the Profile and talked about how younger members should shape the direction of the church. Other leaders expressed concern about what they saw as moral lapses among some members and expressed the need for discipleship programs to support new believers. Others were encouraged to see the faithfulness of their members in mission and evangelism. Overall, the MNA Profile provided a snapshot for leaders to see their church in a systematic way for the first time.

As noted previously, we believe the results of this study about Anabaptist Christians provide a window into the religious identity and expressions of Christianity in the Global South in general. The paucity of public opinion data from ordinary Christians in Asia, Africa, and Latin America makes these findings particularly useful in pointing to religious and ecclesiastical dynamics not revealed in prior research.

4

# Characteristics and Trajectories of Anabaptist Churches

The genius of Pentecostalism is that it was a populist religion which affirmed the "priesthood of all believers," and so the missionaries could easily be replaced by indigenous leaders. Furthermore, anyone who was called by the Holy Spirit could be a minister of the gospel, which resulted in many bi-vocational clergy— even to this day. These men and women were powered by the Spirit rather than by titles, salaries, and pension plans. Many Pentecostal clergy have little formal theological training. Instead, they are schooled in the biblical narratives of personal transformation and find empirical verification for their beliefs in self-transcending experiences where God intervenes in their life.[1] —*Donald E. Miller*

---

1. Miller, 2009:284.

## The Enlightenment and belief

After conducting a major ethnographic study of Pentecostal groups in the Global South, Donald Miller suggests that the churches of Asia, Africa, and Latin America have "leapfrogged" the Enlightenment, that period of early modernity in eighteenth century Europe when science and positivistic approaches to knowledge took precedence over divine or supernatural ways of knowing.[2] In eighteenth-century Europe, the microscope and the telescope overtook the Bible and mysticism in their power to shape the way people understood the universe's origins and human purposes within it. The material or empirical world separated from the spiritual world, with the latter increasingly considered irrelevant. Following this trajectory, it made sense that early sociologists would predict the eventual disappearance of religion.

The effects of the Enlightenment were compounded by the rise of the Industrial Revolution. The Enlightenment's focus on science and rationality supported the efficient mass production of material goods in the Industrial Revolution; the materialism and consumption fostered by the Industrial Revolution fed the empirical and material emphasis of the Enlightenment. Both the Enlightenment and Industrial Revolution had cultural ramifications, shaping popular values and beliefs. They also had structural implications, determining how societies organized themselves and how power was distributed.

Because the Global South bypassed the Enlightenment, or was only indirectly affected by it, its people there remain more open to beliefs in the supernatural and the divine and miraculous manifestations characteristic of the Pentecostal movement. Societies in the South are less likely to be caught in the divide between matter and spirit that so characterized Enlightenment thinkers and those who followed in their steps in Europe and North America. In Western societies, the focus on empirical ways of knowing—using the senses to gather data and

---

2. Miller, 2009.

information—limited the development of other ways of knowing. Many in North America and Europe see dreams, visions, and other supernatural interventions as merely part of the superstitious backwaters of the Middle Ages. In addition, the privatization of religion—allocating spirituality to the personal or individual realm—stole the tongues of many Christian believers in the West, who became uncomfortable with expressing their faith in public beyond a few close acquaintances. Personal testimonies and faith stories are often hard to find even within communities of believers in North America and Europe. In the Global South, personal stories of experiences with God and miraculous events flow freely in everyday conversations. Where the Enlightenment's shadow is lighter, God's activity is better understood to be present and relevant to one's life and experiences. Where the material and the spiritual are less divided, religious faith and commitment are not relegated to the private corners of one's existence. Religiosity in the Global South is more about a personal relationship with God than about intellectual or cognitive belief—though it should not be assumed that Christians in the Global South see the two as mutually exclusive. This personal relationship with God readily expresses itself in testimonies and stories of how Jesus Christ changed the direction of one's life.

## The Enlightenment and social order

The Enlightenment's effects are not limited to shaping worldviews, attitudes, and beliefs. The move toward modernity has also affected the organization of society, leading not only to "rational" ways of knowing but also to "rational" ways of doing and organizing.[3] Writing in the early twentieth century,

---

3. While much has been written about the onset of post-modernity and the post-Enlightenment, no one is clear if and when such a period will be upon us. The reality is that globalization continues, by and large, to diffuse the values and structures of modernity through the world—values and structures deeply embedded in the Enlightenment and Industrial Revolution. The arrival of post-modernity will not occur (or has not

sociologist Max Weber worried that ways of organizing society that flow from the Enlightenment lead to a bureaucratic society that inevitably traps its members in "an iron cage of rationality."[4] Who can resist the dehumanizing forces of a bureaucratic world? George Ritzer notes,

> In Weber's view, bureaucracies are cages in the sense that people are trapped in them, their basic humanity denied.... He anticipated a society of people locked into a series of rational structures, who could move only from one rational system to another—rationalized educational institutions . . . rationalized workplaces . . . rationalized recreational settings . . . rationalized homes.[5]

Such rationalized structures, including denominations and local congregations, are organized with efficiency and productivity as their most important values, often losing in the process the vision for mission and ministry that birthed them. In the end, vitality is replaced by the barrenness of doing things because they have "always been done that way." As Weber predicted, inertia and ritualism in the modern world eventually replaced meaningful relationships with others and with God. Without intervention, such rationalized societies and structures produce what Weber predicted as "mechanized petrification embellished with a sort of convulsive self-importance" managed by "specialists without spirit, sensualists without heart."[6]

But Weber was not without hope that something might intervene to free humans from the bonds of Enlightenment rationality, and though not religious himself, he speaks of such intervention with near-religious zeal. He hoped that in the last

---

occurred) without deep connection to that which preceded it—in many ways a post-modern period will simply be an extension or maturation of modernity and will reflect much of its qualities and characteristics.

4. Weber, 1904.
5. Ritzer, 2008:27.
6. Weber, 1904:182.

phases of modernity, there might rise "entirely new prophets" or the "great rebirth of old ideas and ideals."[7] Weber staked his hope for society's future on an old fashioned revival that breaks the chains of Enlightenment tyranny. In uncanny language—given the rapidly growing Pentecostal movement that emerged at the time he was writing—Weber argues that only charisma and charismatic leaders can bring such a revival.[8] By virtue of their unusual character and personalities, such leaders could redefine society and reveal the entrapment and dehumanization of modern persons.

Within the framework of Weber's analysis, the Pentecostal movement in North America at the beginning of the twentieth century can easily be understood as a reaction to lifeless religious forms that needed the Spirit's inbreaking. The flourishing of the same movement in the Global South is due to the absence of the Enlightenment worldviews and social structures that affected the decline of religious vitality in the North. If the constraints of modernity gave birth to contemporary Pentecostalism, the freedom from such constraints in the Global South brought the movement to maturity. The absence of "iron cages" in Asia, Africa, and Latin America created a space for the movement and flow of ideas and beliefs about the supernatural that continue to face barriers in Western societies that are just now emerging from the clutches of modernity into postmodern realities. The Pentecostal movement found fertile ground in societies that missed the Enlightenment and where indigenous religions emphasize supernatural intervention in everyday life.[9]

---

7. Weber, 1904:182.

8. Weber, 1904.

9. It is true that North American and European missionaries inserted bureaucratic, rationalized structures into their mission activity, often building educational institutions, medical facilities, and development agencies. It is arguable, however, that the use of such structures had less effect in a context where a rationalized worldview was less pervasive. In fact, social and economic development literature contains many stories of failures by Westerners who assumed that modern techniques

## Church characteristics

If it is indeed true that the churches of the Global South have missed the direct effects of the Enlightenment and Industrial Revolution, we should expect to find a variety of differences between them and churches in North America and Europe. Beginning with this chapter, we will look at the characteristics of churches revealed in the MNA Profile. This chapter is largely descriptive and will outline similarities and differences among churches in terms of demographic variables such as gender, residence, and educational level. In this chapter, we will also consider the growth and decline of churches in the MNA Profile.

**Table 4.1 Membership size of congregations by church body**

| Church | Membership Size |
| --- | --- |
| Fellowship of Christian Assemblies | 58 |
| Persatuan Gereja-Gereja Kristen Muria Indonesia | 185 |
| Hoi Thanh Mennonite Viet Nam | 34 |
| Meserete Kristos Church | 342 |
| Kenya Mennonite Church | 90 |
| Happy Church Ministries International | 83 |
| Kanisa la Mennonite Tanzania | 152 |
| Organizacion Christiana Amor Viviente | 270 |
| Iglesia Evangelica Menonita Hondurena | 35 |
| Iglesia Nacional Evangelica Menonita Guatemalteca | 114 |
| Integrated Mennonite Church of the Philippines | 35 |
| Lancaster Mennonite Conference | 96 |
| Total | 124 |

---

and approaches would work seamlessly in non-Western contexts just as they had in the United States or Europe. Such failures resulted in the recognition of the need for social impact assessment by development agencies.

### Characteristics and Trajectories of Anabaptist Churches 75

**Average size of congregations.** The average size of congregations in the MNA Profile range from 34 members in HTM Vietnam to 342 in MKC Ethiopia. The church with the second largest average congregational size is Amor Viviente Honduras (270 members), followed by GKM Indonesia (185 members) and KMT Tanzania (152 members). FCA India, KMC Kenya, Happy Church Kenya, and LMC United States average fewer than 100 members per congregation. Churches with the smallest congregational sizes are IMC Philippines and IEM Honduras, each with an average of 35 members per congregation.

The size of a congregation can be affected by multiple sociological factors, including the reception of or resistance to Christianity in the local community surrounding a congregation, the rate of population growth or decline within a country or region, the overall growth trajectory of the church nationally, the birth and death rates of members of a congregation, and immigration into and out of a local community. Other factors include the history of normative congregational size (typically small congregations tend to remain that way), competition among different churches in a community or region, and geographic factors that may affect population distribution. The size of congregations also depends on their evangelistic activity and the extent to which members are engaged in recruitment efforts to win new members to the church.

**Gender, residence, and marriage.** Members of the MNA Profile churches are more likely to be female than male; only two churches (HTM Vietnam and MKC Ethiopia) have higher proportions of men than women. FCA India congregations are evenly split by gender. IMC Philippines, Amor Viviente Honduras, and Happy Church Kenya are nearly two-thirds women.

The greater proportion of women to men is typical for churches in the Global South and comes as no surprise based on what others are learning about the churches of Asia, Africa, and Latin America. The appeal of Christianity for women in the Global South should not be overlooked. As Jenkins notes, "No account of the Southern movements can fail to recognize the pervasive role of women in these structures, if not as leaders then as the devoted core members . . . the new churches play a vital role in reshaping women's lives, in allowing them to find their voices."[10] Coming to the newly emerging churches, women are finding a new reality and identity as well as new possibilities for marriage partners who have come to understand their role as responsible fathers and husbands (which has been suggested as the "reformation of machismo" among Christian men).[11] For some, the church represents a more egalitarian community than is true of the societies in which these churches are emerging.

Members in the Profile sample are more likely to live in rural communities than in urban ones. A question on the MNA Profile provides respondents with two categories, rural and urban, and their definition of where they live is a subjective one. The three churches with more urban than rural residents are Happy Church Kenya, IEM Honduras, and Amor Viviente Honduras. Both Happy Church and Amor Viviente are known as urban churches, so this finding came as no surprise. The Profile churches with the most rural populations are INEM Guatemala, FCA India, KMC Kenya, IMC Philippines, KMT Tanzania, and HTM Vietnam.[12]

The Profile reveals that where one lives correlates with other demographic variables such as occupation and education. Rural churches also tend to have lower levels of education and to be more engaged in agriculture. As urbanization encroaches on rural communities, and as rural residents migrate to urban areas, the churches in the Profile are likely to experience changes not dissimilar to those of North American churches—rural churches declining in size, the loss of rural church members to urban congregations, and an increase in educational levels among members.

---

10. Jenkins, 2002:75.

11. Brusco, 1995; in Jenkins, 2002.

12. The Honduran Mennonite church is thought by many to be largely rural, meaning that either the sample failed to reflect what is known for the population as a whole, or respondents subjectively answered "urban" for what leaders of that church believe to be a largely rural church.

Characteristics and Trajectories of Anabaptist Churches 77

Table 4.2 Percent who are urban and rural

| Church | Rural | Urban |
|---|---|---|
| Fellowship of Christian Assemblies | 81% | 19% |
| Persatuan Gereja-Gereja Muria Indonesia | 71% | 29% |
| Hoi Thanh Mennonite Viet Nam | 79% | 21% |
| Meserete Kristos Church | 65% | 35% |
| Kenya Mennonite Church | 87% | 13% |
| Happy Church Ministries International | 45% | 55% |
| Kanisa la Mennonite Tanzania | 80% | 20% |
| Organizacion Christiana Amor Viviente | 6% | 94% |
| Iglesia Evangelica Menonita Hondurena | 27% | 73% |
| Iglesia Nacional Evangelica Menonita Guatemalteca | 91% | 9% |
| Integrated Mennonite Church of the Philippines | 77% | 23% |
| Lancaster Mennonite Conference | 60% | 40% |
| Total | 56% | 44% |

**Marital status.** MNA Profile respondents are more likely to be married than single. Only three churches (MKC Ethiopia, KMT Tanzania, and Amor Viviente Honduras) have more single members than married members. Divorce rates are low in all churches. In the Global South, the highest percentage of divorced members is 2.6% (Amor Viviente Honduras), compared to LMC United States, with an average of 4.8% divorced members. All of the African churches have a small percentage of members in polygamous marriages: Happy Church Kenya (1.6%), KMC Kenya (3.2%), KMT Tanzania (2.6%), and MKC Ethiopia (2.6%).[13]

**Education.** Fewer than 80% of members have completed high school in the following churches: INEM Guatemala, HTM Vietnam, and KMT Tanzania. In Tanzania, only 8% of Profile church

---

13. Typically, Anabaptist churches in Africa have permitted first generation converts who were in polygamous relationships to be members of churches without asking them to disrupt their marital relationships or families. However, such converts are usually restricted from positions of leadership and are asked to teach their children that polygamy is not an acceptable Christian arrangement.

members have a high school education. The highest levels of education are found in LMC United States, Amor Viviente Honduras, and GKM Indonesia—where 85%, 70%, and 64% are high school graduates, respectively. IMC Philippines and Happy Church Kenya also have relatively high educational levels. Churches with the most college graduates are LMC United States, GKM Indonesia, IMC Philippines, and Amor Viviente Honduras.

Table 4.3 Percent who are high school graduates

| Church | High School Graduates |
|---|---|
| Fellowship of Christian Assemblies | 31% |
| Persatuan Gereja-Gereja Muria Indonesia | 64% |
| Hoi Thanh Mennonite Viet Nam | 18% |
| Meserete Kristos Church | 34% |
| Kenya Mennonite Church | 18% |
| Happy Church Ministries International | 48% |
| Kanisa la Mennonite Tanzania | 9% |
| Organizacion Christiana Amor Viviente | 70% |
| Iglesia Evangelica Menonita Hondurena | 38% |
| Iglesia Nacional Evangelica Menonita Guatemalteca | 8% |
| Integrated Mennonite Church of the Philippines | 53% |
| Lancaster Mennonite Conference | 85% |
| Total | 42% |

**Occupation.** Occupations vary among churches in the Profile. The churches' locations in rural or urban communities affect members' occupational choices, as well as their level of education. Agricultural occupations are most present among the members of rural churches INEM Guatemala, HTM Vietnam, KMC Kenya, and KMT Tanzania—where at least one-third of members are engaged in agriculture. Churches with the highest percentage of professional and white-collar occupations are GKM Indonesia, Amor Viviente Honduras, Happy Church Kenya, and LMC United States. Churches reporting the most homemakers are INEM Guatemala, Amor Viviente Honduras, IEM Honduras, and IMC Philippines.

## Table 4.4 Occupations of members

| Church | Professional | Farmer | Homemaker |
|---|---|---|---|
| Fellowship of Christian Assemblies | 36% | 17% | 19% |
| Persatuan Gereja-Gereja Muria Indonesia | 45% | 17% | 0% |
| Hoi Thanh Mennonite Viet Nam | 8% | 50% | 10% |
| Meserete Kristos Church | 21% | 25% | 11% |
| Kenya Mennonite Church | 23% | 42% | 11% |
| Happy Church Ministries International | 45% | 11% | 16% |
| Kanisa la Mennonite Tanzania | 19% | 46% | N/A |
| Organizacion Christiana Amor Viviente | 59% | 1% | 28% |
| Iglesia Evangelica Menonita Hondurena | 31% | 6% | 41% |
| Iglesia Nacional Evangelica Menonita Guatemalteca | 12% | 35% | 40% |
| Integrated Mennonite Church of the Philippines | 28% | 28% | 30% |
| Lancaster Mennonite Conference | 55% | 8% | 14% |
| **Total** | 32% | 21% | 19% |

**Income.** Income levels are generally low for MNA Profile churches, with the exception of LMC United States and Amor Viviente Honduras. Income categories were created by the anchors to fit the economic context of their countries. Still, it became evident that most members in these churches are making very low incomes. In Ethiopia, a sizeable proportion of members earn higher incomes than those in other churches, reflecting—according to our Ethiopian anchor—government subsidies that some farmers receive from the current government.

When asking demographic questions on the Profile, we intentionally chose not to inquire about political affiliation or racial and ethnic identities. It was too complicated to create a question about political identity that could be asked across all of the churches, given the variation in political parties in each country. And church leaders were hesitant to ask about racial and ethnic

80  Winds of the Spirit

identity, because they can be sources of tension. In India, differences of caste and ethnicity create challenges for developing a church that represents a cross-section of Indian society. Among KMC Kenya congregations, one tribal group (Luo) dominates, and the church has not been successful starting churches among other groups. Multiethnic Happy Church Kenya congregations experienced extreme tension in the post-election violence of 2007 and 2008, and a number of Happy Church congregations have been decimated by ethnic conflicts fanned by the tribal violence experienced in their society. Because of these complications, with the exception of HTM Vietnam, all Profile churches chose not to ask about racial or ethnic identity.

### Global trends in Christianity

The *Atlas of Global Christianity*, the most comprehensive analysis of global religious changes, reports that the statistical center of gravity of Christianity (a measure based on the global population of Christians) has shifted from Spain in 1910 into the heart of Africa today. Its projection is that this center will move further and further south over the next century.[14] Mark Noll describes the growth of the Global South this way:

> In a word, the Christian church has experienced a larger geographical redistribution in the last fifty years than in any comparable period in its history, with the exception of the very earliest years of church history. Some of this change comes from the general growth of world population, but much also arises from remarkable rates of evangelization in parts of Asia, Africa, Latin America and the islands of the South Pacific—but also from a nearly unprecedented relative decline of Christian adherence in Europe. The result of population changes—in general for the world, specifically for the churches—is a series of mind-blowing realities: More than all of the Christian adherents in the whole history of the church have been

---

14. Johnson and Ross, 2009.

alive in the last one hundred years.... The magnitude of recent change means that all believers, including those in the former Christian heartlands of Europe and North America, are faced with the prospect of reorientation.[15]

Specifically, the *Atlas of Global Christianity* outlines the following global Christian trends over the century:

- *Fewer Christians in the West.* In 1910, 80% of the world's Christians were from Europe or North America. One hundred years later only 45% are from these two continents.[16]

- *The proportion of Christians globally has declined slightly.* In 1910, Christians represented 35% of all religious adherents globally (approximately six hundred million persons). In 2010, Christians represent 33% (nearly two and one-quarter billon persons).

- *Europe's share of Christians has declined remarkably.* In 1910, Europe contained two-thirds of the world's Christians. One hundred years later, just over one-quarter live in Europe.

- *The proportion of Christians in the United States has dropped slightly.* In 1910, 15% of global Christians were from the United States, as compared to 12% in 2010.

---

15. Noll, 2009:21–22.

16. Johnson and Ross, 2009. The statistics for the *Atlas of Global Christianity* refer to total Christian numbers (including Roman Catholic, Orthodox, etc.) and not only to evangelical or Pentecostal membership data. There has been, in fact, striking growth in the twentieth century in evangelical and Pentecostal numbers. This is particularly important to note, given that there has been essentially no overall Christian growth in Latin America in the past century despite huge gains among evangelical and Pentecostal churches on that continent. These global figures also include most of the population of Europe, which is overwhelmingly nominal and has suffered serious declines in religious commitment.

- *The greatest Christian gains proportionately have been in Asia, Africa, and Latin America.* These three continents today represent 61% of all Christians: 15% are Asian, 22% are African, and 24% are Latin American.

- *The strongest growth proportionately for any continent over the past one hundred years is in Africa.* While 9% of all Africans were Christian in 1910, 48% are Christian today. Asia increased from 2.4% to 8.5%.

- *Both Europe and North America experienced substantial declines in Christian adherents as a proportion of their total populations.* Nearly 95% of Europeans were Christian one hundred years ago, as compared to 80% today. In North America, 97% were Christian in 1910, as compared to 81% today.

- *The proportion of Christians to population growth globally has been nearly flat over the last century.* Christian growth (3.8% annually) has exceeded population growth in Africa (2.1% annually) and Asia (between 2.7% and 1.4%), while the inverse is true for North America and Europe. In Latin America, Christian growth as compared to population growth was essentially flat in the last century.

- *The fastest growing Christian populations are in the Global South.* Of the ten countries with fastest growing Christian populations since 1910, six are in Africa and four are in Asia.

- *Since 1910, the Pentecostal movement represents the fastest-growing sector of Christianity.* The Pentecostal population has grown at five times the rate of global Christianity. Today, 51% of Pentecostal churches are independent, 23% are Catholic, 22% are Protestant, and 3% are Anglican. In eighteen different countries—fifteen of them in Asia or Africa—more than one-half of Christians are Pentecostal.

Important projections for the future of Christianity include the following:

- *Christian growth will be exceeded by the growth of Islam.* The percentage of Christians is expected to rise from 33% today (2010) to 35% by 2050, but Muslim growth is projected to be greater, from 22% in 2010 to 27% in 2050.

- *Globally, fewer will be nonreligious.* The growth of nonreligious individuals in the United States has exceeded that of any other religious grouping in recent years.[17] But globally, the percent of religious *nones* (no religious affiliation) has been declining, accounting for 20% of the world's population in 1970 but only 11% today. This decline is expected to continue and the global percentage of religious *nones* is projected to be only 7.5% in 2050.[18]

MNA Profile data reveal that trends among Christians globally are mirrored among Anabaptists—growth in the Global South and decline in the North. While Christianity's worldwide presence has been relatively flat for the last century in terms of the total proportion of the global population that is Christian, that presence has been geographically redistributed over the same time period. This redistribution will have important implications for the articulation of Christian theology and practice over the next century; North America and Europe will become increasingly marginal to such conversations. One of the major sources of discussion will involve Islam's rapid growth, which Christians in the Global South will have a greater stake in addressing than have North Americans and Europeans, who to date have responded more often with confrontation than with dialogue. Such a reaction makes little sense and is less common among Christians in the Global South, whose neighbors, family

---

17. U.S. Religious Landscape Survey, 2008.
18. Johnson and Ross, 2009.

members, and coworkers are Muslim. Finally, the Pentecostal strain of Christianity that has swept the globe over the past century shows no sign of ebbing and will likely continue to define global Christianity for some time to come.

## Trends among North American Mennonites

In Kanagy's analysis of Mennonite Church USA in 2006, the most stunning finding for many church members and leaders is the rapid numerical decline and aging of church membership. The reasons for this decline are fairly straightforward: low birth rates, low levels of evangelism, loss of young people, and the aging of members. Several of these declines exceed what other denominations in the United States and the nation's population as a whole have been experiencing.[19] Specifically, the number of members in Mennonite Church USA declined from more than 130,000 in 1989 to 109,000 in 2006. Of all Anabaptists in the United States, the proportion claiming membership in Mennonite Church USA decreased from 49% in 1989 to 22% in 2006. Likewise, the membership of Mennonite Church USA as a percentage of the total global Anabaptist fellowship declined from 15% in 1989 to 7% in 2006.[20]

Although many have sensed these changes through personal experiences—smaller crowds in worship services, fewer children in Sunday school, and shrinking congregational and denominational budgets—the actual numbers reinforce this new reality. There is no longer any denying that North American Anabaptists face the same difficult challenges that are faced by other denominations in the United States, particularly the liberal and mainline ones.[21] The decline among historically large and influential denominations has been well documented, with "little doubt as to the vulnerability of Liberal Christianity,

---

19. Kanagy, 2007.

20. Kanagy, 2007.

21. More conservative and evangelical Anabaptist groups have been growing, including the Brethren in Christ and the Old Order Amish.

however big its battalions."[22] In the United States, the only denominations that are growing in the early twenty-first century are Pentecostal, Roman Catholic, and Seventh Day Adventist. Even those with historic growth, such as Southern Baptist, have been declining in recent years.[23]

Mennonites in North America have become increasingly assimilated into the broader culture and now have among the highest levels of education of any religious group in the United States. Sociological sources of this enculturation include migration away from farms and rural areas, more emphasis on higher education, and more professional employment. In two generations, Mennonites in North America have found their way solidly into the middle class. Doing so has reduced family size, dampened commitment to evangelization and outreach, and resulted in rapid membership declines in the denomination.[24] For a denomination like Mennonite Church USA—with an aging membership and a declining percentage of young people—long-term sustainability is impossible without a renewal of evangelistic activity.

The only segment of Mennonite Church USA experiencing growth is among Asian-American, African-American, and Hispanic-American congregations. Not only are these churches growing in numbers, but also the average age of their members is much younger. These churches include many immigrants from Asia, Africa, and Latin America, where Anabaptist churches are growing rapidly. The future of Anabaptist churches in the United States may depend in large part on the continued influx of members from the Global South for whom growth is already normative and whose presence brings a renewed commitment to evangelism and outreach.

---

22. Martin, 2002:3.
23. Linder, 2011.
24. Kanagy, 2007, has shown a relationship between one's educational level and commitment to evangelism—as education goes up evangelistic activity goes down among members of Mennonite Church USA.

Just as the 2006 study of Mennonite Church USA brought a new image of reality to denominational leaders, the Multi-Nation Anabaptist Profile generates for leaders of the Global South a similarly reorienting effect—but for different reasons. For example, as we met Profile anchors in Thika, Kenya, we repeatedly heard them exclaim, "We had no idea that we had so many children and young people!" The MNA Profile has provided them with an affirming self-awareness of their churches' youth.

### Secularization debunked?

While scholars now generally agree on the direction of global Christianity, debate about the implications of this shift continues. For decades, sociologists of religion have argued over the evidence for secularization or the decline of religion. The "secularization thesis" is rather simple. It is assumed that the modern world has a debilitating effect on religion and that the forces of modernization—including science, education, urban living, increased consumption and materialism, and individualism—reduce the role and importance of religion in individual lives and society as a whole. As discussed earlier, sociologists at the turn of the twentieth century expected religion to disappear from society as people became more educated and the effects of the Enlightenment more widespread. Indeed, the trajectory of Europe seemed to support this argument. With Europe leading the way, it was relatively easy for scholars to assume that the United States was next in line. And in fact, the declines described above for Mennonite Church USA as well as for many mainline denominations seem to mirror Europe's experience.

At the same time, while individuals in the United States are less likely to go to church or synagogue today than in the past, they are still very likely to say that they believe in God, believe in life after death, and pray.[25] This reflects the fact that the nature of religion has changed in the United States from a corporate

---

25. Christiano et al., 2008.

practice to an individualistic form of spirituality.[26] Observing this shift, scholars have challenged the secularization thesis and suggested that religion in the United States is not declining as in Europe, but rather is developing a new face—one that is more private than public, more individual than corporate, and more "spiritual" than "religious."[27]

Scholars' emerging interest in Christianity's growth in the Global South raises further questions about the veracity of the secularization thesis. While the European experience seems to support conclusions about secularization, the rapid growth of religious commitments in Asia, Africa, and Latin America—even in places that are modernizing rapidly—has challenged assumptions about the weakness and unsustainability of religion, and particularly of Christianity. In the Global South, urbanization, modernization, and professionalization do not seem, at least at the moment, to be leading to the kinds of decline in religiosity predicted by sociologists a century ago. If upward mobility and religious vitality continue to coexist in the Global South, this phenomenon will be one more challenge to the secularization thesis that many once took for granted.

## Trends among churches in the Multi-Nation Anabaptist Profile

Not surprisingly, as we consider the churches in the Multi-Nation Anabaptist Profile, North Americans are strikingly different from the rest of the churches in many of the variables we examine here. The average age of LMC United States is fifty-three years. The next closest average age—forty-one years—is in IMC Philippines and IEM Honduras. Four churches—KMT Tanzania, Amor Viviente Honduras, HTM Vietnam, and GKM Indonesia—share an average age of thirty-eight years. KMC Kenya and INEM Guatemala average thirty-seven years, FCA

---
26. Bellah et al., 1985.
27. Berger, 1999.

India averages thirty-four years, and Happy Church Kenya's average age is thirty-three years. The youngest average age is thirty-two years, in MKC Ethiopia.

Table 4.5 Mean age of members

| Church | Mean Age of All Members 18+ | Mean Age of All Members in Sample |
|---|---|---|
| Fellowship of Christian Assemblies | 34 | 32 |
| Persatuan Gereja-Gereja Muria Indonesia | 38 | 36 |
| Hoi Thanh Mennonite Viet Nam | 38 | 36 |
| Meserete Kristos Church | 32 | 28 |
| Kenya Mennonite Church | 37 | 35 |
| Happy Church Ministries International | 33 | 32 |
| Kanisa la Mennonite Tanzania | 38 | 32 |
| Organizacion Christiana Amor Viviente | 38 | 36 |
| Iglesia Evangelica Menonita Hondurena | 41 | 37 |
| Iglesia Nacional Evangelica Menonita Guatemalteca | 37 | 35 |
| Integrated Mennonite Church of the Philippines | 41 | 37 |
| Lancaster Mennonite Conference | 53 | 53 |
| Total | 37 | 34 |

The years of age between eighteen and forty-five are what demographers often refer to as childbearing age, when most women give birth. For churches that depend on reproduction for growth, the higher the percentage of members between the ages of eighteen and forty-five years, the longer the sustainability of the church. The lower the percentage, the more likely the church will struggle to remain viable into the future. Of Profile churches, LMC United States has the fewest persons in this age category—only 33%. Happy Church Kenya has the highest proportion (88%), followed by MKC Ethiopia (86%) and FCA India (83%).

In the other eight churches, between 63% and 74% of members are between the ages of eighteen and forty-five. At the opposite end of the age spectrum, 26% of LMC United States members are older than sixty-five years of age, while all of the other Profile churches range between 1% and 10% for this age group. Among Anabaptist churches in the Global South, the percentage of members between the ages of eighteen and forty-five is much higher than any denomination in the United States. For Mennonite Church USA, 30% of members are between eighteen and forty-five years of age. Among mainline denominations, 45% of members are within this age range. And for conservative Protestants, 52% are within childbearing age.[28] For churches in Asia, Africa, and Latin America, the combination of high birth rates and the large proportion of members still having children indicates strong growth into the future. But for the United States, opposite patterns of low birth rates and fewer people having children portend continued declines.

Table 4.6 Percent of members within childbearing age (18–45 years)

| Church | 18–45 |
| --- | --- |
| Fellowship of Christian Assemblies | 83% |
| Persatuan Gereja-Gereja Muria Indonesia | 72% |
| Hoi Thanh Mennonite Viet Nam | 66% |
| Meserete Kristos Church | 86% |
| Kenya Mennonite Church | 74% |
| Happy Church Ministries International | 88% |
| Kanisa la Mennonite Tanzania | 70% |
| Organizacion Christiana Amor Viviente | 70% |
| Iglesia Evangelica Menonita Hondurena | 63% |
| Iglesia Nacional Evangelica Menonita Guatemalteca | 73% |
| Integrated Mennonite Church of the Philippines | 66% |
| Lancaster Mennonite Conference | 33% |
| Total | 74% |

---

28. Greeley and Hout, 2006.

**Childbirth.** The birth rate among women ages eighteen to forty-five differs substantially from church to church and is an important variable in the growth of these churches. LMC United States and GKM Indonesia are barely replacing themselves, with an average of 2.0 children per woman. Birth rates are much higher in the other churches: 4.6 in KMT Tanzania and MKC Ethiopia, 4.3 in INEM Guatemala, and 4.2 in KMC Kenya. The two most urban churches, Happy Church Kenya and Amor Viviente Honduras, have lower rates of 2.8 and 2.4, respectively.

Table 4.7 Average number of births among women 18–45 years of age

| Church | Number of Children |
|---|---|
| Fellowship of Christian Assemblies | 2.59 |
| Persatuan Gereja-Gereja Muria Indonesia | 1.99 |
| Hoi Thanh Mennonite Viet Nam | 2.18 |
| Meserete Kristos Church | 4.63 |
| Kenya Mennonite Church | 4.2 |
| Happy Church Ministries International | 2.78 |
| Kanisa la Mennonite Tanzania | 4.63 |
| Organizacion Christiana Amor Viviente | 2.35 |
| Iglesia Evangelica Menonita Hondurena | 2.89 |
| Iglesia Nacional Evangelica Menonita Guatemalteca | 4.25 |
| Integrated Mennonite Church of the Philippines | 2.91 |
| Lancaster Mennonite Conference | 2.00 |
| Total | 3.15 |

The low average age, high percent of members in the age of childbearing, and high fertility rates make it clear that the current growth of the churches in Africa, Asia, and Latin America will continue for decades to come, even if these churches were to depend solely on natural reproduction rather than on gaining new converts. This reproductive strength in the Global South will be reinforced by continued growth through conversions, as enthusiasm for evangelism is much greater there than in North America and Europe. Therefore, we can expect rapid growth to continue. Alongside the upward trajectory in the Global South, however, Mennonites in the United States will continue to decline, since natural reproduction, rather than conversion, has always been their primary engine of membership growth. As the number of children per family has declined among Mennonites in North America, congregations have declined in size over time. In sum, this means that the current differences in membership between churches in the Global South and churches in North America and Europe will grow greater, barring some unforeseen change.

Table 4.8 Average year of conversion

| Church | Year |
|---|---|
| Fellowship of Christian Assemblies | 2003 |
| Persatuan Gereja-Gereja Muria Indonesia | 1988 |
| Hoi Thanh Mennonite Viet Nam | 1994 |
| Meserete Kristos Church | 1997 |
| Kenya Mennonite Church | 1986 |
| Happy Church Ministries International | 1997 |
| Kanisa la Mennonite Tanzania | 1992 |
| Organizacion Christiana Amor Viviente | 1997 |
| Iglesia Evangelica Menonita Hondurena | 1997 |
| Iglesia Nacional Evangelica Menonita Guatemalteca | 1995 |
| Integrated Mennonite Church of the Philippines | 1993 |
| Lancaster Mennonite Conference | 1970 |
| Total | 1995 |

**Conversion trends.** In the Profile, we asked members the year they were converted to Christianity. Again, the United States is the exception to the rule. It is the oldest church in the Profile in terms of date of origin, has the highest proportion of elderly, and has the lowest rate of recent growth. The average member of LMC United States came to Christ in 1970, sixteen years before the average year of conversion in KMC Kenya and eighteen years before the average conversion of GKM Indonesia members. In eight other churches, the average year of conversion ranges from 1992 to 1997. In FCA India, the average year of conversion is 2003.

**Previous church involvements.** The MNA Profile asked members if they had been baptized in another church before becoming part of a Mennonite church. This question provides a means of distinguishing between new converts (with no Christian commitment prior to their membership in their present church) and Christians who had switched congregations, as is now so often the case in North America. Happy Church Kenya, GKM Indonesia, LMC United States, and HTM Vietnam have the highest proportion of members previously baptized in other churches. MKC Ethiopia, KMT Tanzania, and FCA India have the lowest proportion of such members.

Table 4.9 Percent who were baptized in another church

| Church | Baptized |
| --- | --- |
| Fellowship of Christian Assemblies | 14% |
| Persatuan Gereja-Gereja Muria Indonesia | 40% |
| Hoi Thanh Mennonite Viet Nam | 35% |
| Meserete Kristos Church | 11% |
| Kenya Mennonite Church | 17% |
| Happy Church Ministries International | 49% |
| Kanisa la Mennonite Tanzania | 11% |
| Organizacion Christiana Amor Viviente | 23% |
| Iglesia Evangelica Menonita Hondurena | 24% |
| Iglesia Nacional Evangelica Menonita Guatemalteca | 19% |
| Integrated Mennonite Church of the Philippines | 19% |
| Lancaster Mennonite Conference | 35% |
| Total | 21% |

We also asked respondents about former church memberships. In general, a higher proportion of members in most churches acknowledge former membership than acknowledge baptism in other churches. In INEM Guatemala, whose members were largely Roman Catholic before conversion, few state that they were previously baptized (19%)—though it is likely that most were baptized as infants—but 73% indicate having been part of another church before joining the Mennonite Church. This suggests that members of INEM Guatemala recognize their former membership in the Roman Catholic Church but do not legitimize their baptism as infants. A similar though less pronounced dynamic exists in Honduras and the Philippines (also countries where Roman Catholicism is dominant); members of Amor Viviente Honduras, IEM Honduras, and IMC Philippines are nearly two times more likely to recognize their membership in another church than baptism in another church (again likely as an infant). This pattern—recognizing former church membership but not baptism—may reflect the importance of believers baptism among these Anabaptist groups.

Table 4.10 Percent who were former members of another church

| Church | From Another Church |
|---|---|
| Fellowship of Christian Assemblies | 26% |
| Persatuan Gereja-Gereja Muria Indonesia | 37% |
| Hoi Thanh Mennonite Viet Nam | 61% |
| Meserete Kristos Church | 25% |
| Kenya Mennonite Church | 52% |
| Happy Church Ministries International | 24% |
| Kanisa la Mennonite Tanzania | 21% |
| Organizacion Christiana Amor Viviente | 52% |
| Iglesia Evangelica Menonita Hondurena | 54% |
| Iglesia Nacional Evangelica Menonita Guatemalteca | 73% |
| Integrated Mennonite Church of the Philippines | 56% |
| Lancaster Mennonite Conference | 55% |
| Total | 43% |

Interestingly, however, in MKC Ethiopia, many members who most likely were Orthodox before joining the Mennonite Church are unwilling to recognize either previous membership or baptism, with only 25% saying they were ever members of another church and even fewer saying that they were baptized in another church (11%).

## 94  Winds of the Spirit

### Table 4.11 Mean years of membership

| Church | Mean Years of Membership |
|---|---|
| Fellowship of Christian Assemblies | 5 |
| Persatuan Gereja-Gereja Muria Indonesia | 15 |
| Hoi Thanh Mennonite Viet Nam | 5 |
| Meserete Kristos Church | 11 |
| Kenya Mennonite Church | 17 |
| Happy Church Ministries International | 7 |
| Kanisa la Mennonite Tanzania | 17 |
| Organizacion Christiana Amor Viviente | 10 |
| Iglesia Evangelica Menonita Hondurena | 9 |
| Iglesia Nacional Evangelica Menonita Guatemalteca | 12 |
| Integrated Mennonite Church of the Philippines | 15 |
| Lancaster Mennonite Conference | 30 |
| Total | 11 |

**Average years of membership.** In the MNA Profile, the average time that individuals have been members of their congregations is often closely correlated to the year of their conversion, though many found Christ in other churches before transferring to the one they currently attend. Average years of membership also correlates with the date of origin of the church, particularly in the churches that have leaned most heavily on childbearing for membership growth: LMC United States, GKM Indonesia, and KMT Tanzania.[29] These three churches also lean away from a Pentecostal expression of faith, unlike the most rapidly growing churches in our sample. While, given its early origins in the 1950s, one might expect the average years of membership in MKC Ethiopia to be higher than it is (11 years), the average years of membership are lower, because the church has depended heavily on conversion and recruitment rather than solely on reproduction. Profile data reveal that the more a

---

29. These three churches would also be among the least Pentecostal in our sample.

congregation relies on reproduction, the higher its average years of membership.

The average length of time that a person has been a member of a church differs substantially across churches. The United States has members with by far the longest tenure, reflecting the fact that it is the oldest church in the Profile and that, more than others, it has ceased growing. Were LMC United States recruiting new members, the average years of membership would be lower. Churches where members on average have the fewest years of membership reflect their newness in terms of dates of origin and also the success of their recruitment efforts.

Profile data suggest that new churches recruit new converts and older churches do not. Churches with the longest average memberships are also among the oldest churches in the Profile: LMC United States, GKM Indonesia, KMC Kenya, and KMT Tanzania. Again, while this reflects the length of time these churches have been in existence, other Profile data suggest that these churches have also slowed their recruitment efforts and are depending more on reproduction for growth than are newer churches in the Profile. Although MKC Ethiopia was planted in the 1950s, its greatest growth did not occur until later. The low average years of membership in that church is influenced by its large number of young converts.

**Parents as members.** In an effort to determine the proportion of members who are first generation Mennonites, the MNA Profile also asked whether the parents of members were in a Mennonite church when the member was a child. KMT Tanzania and GKM Indonesia have by far the greatest proportion of members who had at least one Mennonite parent when they were children. INEM Guatemala, IMC Philippines, KMC Kenya, and LMC United States are next, with 50% or more of their members identifying themselves as second-generation Mennonites. The two Honduran churches and Happy Church Kenya have the lowest percentages of second-generation Anabaptists—approximately 25% of their members.

## 96  Winds of the Spirit

Table 4.12 Percent whose parents (one or more) were members of the same church as respondent

| Church | Parents Were Members |
|---|---|
| Fellowship of Christian Assemblies | 34% |
| Persatuan Gereja-Gereja Muria Indonesia | 71% |
| Hoi Thanh Mennonite Viet Nam | 37% |
| Meserete Kristos Church | 46% |
| Kenya Mennonite Church | 55% |
| Happy Church Ministries International | 23% |
| Kanisa la Mennonite Tanzania | 81% |
| Organizacion Christiana Amor Viviente | 23% |
| Iglesia Evangelica Menonita Hondurena | 27% |
| Iglesia Nacional Evangelica Menonita Guatemalteca | 58% |
| Integrated Mennonite Church of the Philippines | 52% |
| Lancaster Mennonite Conference | 54% |
| Total | 42% |

**Conversion by decade.** The decades of greatest growth are starkly different by hemisphere. In North America, 20% of current members came to Christ between 1990 and the present. In FCA India, 95% received Christ during the last two decades, followed by churches in descending order: HTM Vietnam (85%), Happy Church Kenya (80%), MKC Ethiopia (80%), Amor Viviente Honduras (77%), IEM Honduras (76%), INEM Guatemala (71%), IMC Philippines (64%), KMT Tanzania (62%), KMC Kenya (48%), and GKM Indonesia (47%).

Table 4.13 Conversion by decade

| Church | Before 1980 | 1981-1990 | 1991-2000 | 2001-2009 |
|---|---|---|---|---|
| Fellowship of Christian Assemblies | 2% | 4% | 18% | 77% |
| Persatuan Gereja-Gereja Muria Indonesia | 31% | 22% | 26% | 21% |
| Hoi Thanh Mennonite Viet Nam | 4% | 12% | 64% | 21% |
| Meserete Kristos Church | 5% | 14% | 43% | 37% |

## Characteristics and Trajectories of Anabaptist Churches 97

| Church | Before 1980 | 1981-1990 | 1991-2000 | 2001-2009 |
|---|---|---|---|---|
| Kenya Mennonite Church | 33% | 20% | 32% | 16% |
| Happy Church Ministries International | 6% | 14% | 41% | 39% |
| Kanisa la Mennonite Tanzania | 22% | 16% | 25% | 37% |
| Organizacion Christiana Amor Viviente | 6% | 17% | 40% | 37% |
| Iglesia Evangelica Menonita Hondurena | 10% | 15% | 32% | 44% |
| Iglesia Nacional Evangelica Menonita Guatemalteca | 14% | 15% | 29% | 42% |
| Integrated Mennonite Church of the Philippines | 16% | 21% | 34% | 30% |
| Lancaster Mennonite Conference | 66% | 14% | 14% | 6% |
| **Total** | 12% | 15% | 36% | 37% |

**Age of conversion.** We also looked at the average age a member became a Christian. Given that one often tends to think of the Global South movement as driven by young people, what we found surprised us. The churches with the greatest growth in the last two decades have relatively high average ages of conversion. And in general, churches that are growing most slowly have the lowest ages of conversion. These data show that rapidly growing churches in the Global South are reaching into the adult population of their societies—persons who are currently Roman Catholic, Orthodox, Muslim, Hindu, Buddhist, agnostic, or practicing indigenous religions. On the other hand, churches that are growing most slowly are depending largely on their own reproduction for growth, resulting in younger converts on average. Interestingly, one would expect that a true believers church will have higher ages of conversion, while a church that depends on natural reproduction will have lower ages of conversion.[30]

---

30. To further investigate the relationship between year of conversion and year of birth, we calculated an "R-squared" as a measure to help us

98　Winds of the Spirit

**Table 4.14 Mean age of conversion**

| Church | Mean Age of Conversion |
|---|---|
| Fellowship of Christian Assemblies | 28 |
| Persatuan Gereja-Gereja Muria Indonesia | 21 |
| Hoi Thanh Mennonite Viet Nam | 24 |
| Meserete Kristos Church | 20 |
| Kenya Mennonite Church | 17 |
| Happy Church Ministries International | 21 |
| Kanisa la Mennonite Tanzania | 19 |
| Organizacion Christiana Amor Viviente | 25 |
| Iglesia Evangelica Menonita Hondurena | 27 |
| Iglesia Nacional Evangelica Menonita Guatemalteca | 23 |
| Integrated Mennonite Church of the Philippines | 25 |
| Lancaster Mennonite Conference | 14 |
| Total | 23 |

The four slowest growing churches—LMC United States, KMC Kenya, KMT Tanzania, and GKM Indonesia—are also among the four oldest churches in the MNA Profile in terms of their dates of origin. These findings begin to suggest that, over time, all churches regardless of culture face the possibility of a life course trajectory that begins with growth, leads to plateauing, and then shifts into decline—unless turned around by some

identify which churches were relying most on their own members for growth as opposed to the conversion of adults. In doing so, we found that in North America, more than one-half of the variation in year of conversion is explained by year of birth. This is extraordinarily high for an R-squared value that can range between zero and one. This means that for Lancaster Conference, year of birth—more than any other factor—explains when one is converted. On the other hand, within the North Indian church—which is the most rapidly growing church in the MNA Profile—the R-square is zero. In India, year of birth does not at all explain the year that one becomes a Christian. As with previous findings, the earliest churches in the MNA Profile have higher R-square values. The longer ago a church's origins, the more likely those churches are today to depend on their children for current membership growth.

intervention such as renewal, increased birth rates, or more intentional evangelism.

## Discovering youthfulness

As mentioned earlier, the issue of age and its significance was not missed by the MNA Profile anchors who gathered in Thika, Kenya, in 2010 to review the findings of the Profile. Surprisingly, a number of leaders had not recognized just how young their churches were until they saw the data. Some recognized both an opportunity and a challenge in this dynamic. Others, including Amor Viviente Honduras, expressed surprise, even while mentioning their efforts to mentor and train young people for ministry. One leader said, "Without youth we are nothing. If you are old enough to be baptized, then you are old enough to be discipled. Young people come first, and then they bring their parents. The main people doing the real work are not the leaders, it's the young people."

Kekchi leaders from INEM Guatemala saw certain challenges in the changing age dynamic in their church, which is now made up of more members from first generation converts than second generation members. Needing employment, some of their Mennonite youth find jobs in military, security, and police sectors—creating questions about how to disciple these young people with Anabaptist understandings of peacemaking and the separation of church and state. Similarly, leaders of IEM Honduras expressed concern that they have a large number of young people who do not come from Mennonite homes and need to discipled in Anabaptist principles and doctrines.

The leaders of MKC Ethiopia are very intentional about retaining their young people, even as they leave for educational opportunities and urban settings. According to their leaders, they are doing

> everything we can so that our children will finish their life within the church. When they go to college and university they need a ministry that follows them and supports them. When they go to assignments in different

parts of the country with government work we keep track of them. When they get four or five people to gather for worship around them, we send an evangelist and help plant a church.

It was apparent during the Thika convention that the leaders of churches in the Global South are focused on the youthfulness of their churches and consider it both a challenge and an opportunity. American Mennonites, on the other hand, like American churches in general, are faced with the challenge of how to rejuvenate a church in which more than one-fourth of its members are of retirement age and members are not birthing enough children to replace themselves.

## Causes of decline in Profile churches

So what do we make of these findings? North American Anabaptists appear to be in a free-fall in terms of their growth trajectory. Older members, fewer young people, and low birth rates mean an inevitable decline—barring a new reliance on conversion. Several of the chronologically older churches in the Global South also seem to be plateauing or on the doorstep of decline. This should serve as a caution to churches, regardless of denomination or geography, that they face the same challenges that many organizations face over time—a shift from development and growth to a focus on survival and maintenance. In the process, churches tend to abandon evangelism efforts and growth strategies in order to devote their resources to program development, new institutions, construction of physical facilities, and the overall maintenance of these.

The findings of the MNA Profile call into question once again the assumptions of the secularization debate. Perhaps secularization of entire societies or nations is less the question than the possibility that churches—both congregations and denominations—have a proclivity to transition over time from growth to maintenance to decline. For example, while mainline churches are declining rapidly in the United States, Roman Catholicism and evangelical denominations are experiencing less decline, and charismatic churches are still experiencing some growth. The movement of Christianity's center of gravity from Jerusalem in AD 33, around the Mediterranean, and into central Africa over the course of two millennia may say less about secularization trends and more about the fickleness of human beings as well as the life course of Christian churches, which tend to spike in one century and decline in another. This shift may also point to the eternal motivation of God's Spirit to move wherever it finds receptivity and welcome, regardless of geography, ethnicity, or other factors.

Perhaps churches since the Protestant Reformation—and certainly since their modern reinvention within North American Christianity—are burdened with a rationalizing tendency that necessarily drives them toward bureaucratization, institutionalization, and maintenance and away from the visions that birthed them. When the needs of Hellenist widows arose in the early church, the office of deacon was created (Acts 6)—a clear movement toward structure with the potential to pull energy away from mission and outreach. The question, then, is to what extent the movement toward institutionalization might become part of the history of global Christianity in the South.

## A Pentecostal ethic

These risks for decline suggest that some caution is appropriate when talking about the rapid growth of the church in the Global South. It is possible that the churches there, as in North America, may face a time when tendencies toward maintenance overwhelm their current evangelistic bent. While growth may be in the air today, decline may be just as present tomorrow.

Some researchers have suggested that the rapid growth of charismatic churches in the Global South may be as subject to a Pentecostal ethic as mainline and evangelical churches in North America have been to a Protestant ethic.[31] Max Weber is responsible for the Protestant Ethic argument, maintaining

---

31. Miller and Yamamori, 2007.

that as people live a Christian lifestyle that demands a strong work ethic, saving money, and living simply (he was referencing Puritan immigrants to the northeastern United States), they or their offspring will necessarily move into higher socioeconomic statuses. In doing so, Weber argues, they will be less likely to retain their religious commitments and more likely to embrace the material world that their parents and grandparents worked so hard to resist.[32]

Donald Miller and Tetsunao Yamamori, following their ethnographic study of Pentecostal churches in the Global South, have suggested that churches in the Global South may yet experience a Pentecostal ethic as a result of the economic improvement that the Pentecostal movement is creating in societies in the Global South. It is well documented that the rapidly growing charismatic movement is moving people out of poverty and into the middle class, while also remaining widely attractive to those already in the middle class.[33] This upward mobility may create a secularizing effect for churches in the Global South. In the MNA Profile, many anchors talked about the greater economic well-being that their members experience when they become Christians. Arguing somewhat along the lines of Miller and Yamamori, David Martin contends that, as a late phase of modernity, Pentecostalism may potentially enter decline: "Put crudely, Pentecostalism in the developing world is likely to follow a trajectory of incline and decline, until its devotees all too successfully better themselves, relax their rigor, and 'go to school.'"[34]

## Challenges to church growth

The MNA Profile data suggest that those in the Global South should not assume that their current growth patterns will continue indefinitely. Demographic trends, conversion trends, the

---

32. Weber, 1904.
33. Miller and Yamamori, 2007.
34. Martin, 2002:2.

nature of potential converts, the social status of church members, and the need for socialization of new converts all play major roles in the growth and decline of a church. Following is a more detailed discussion of these challenges.

**Reliance on reproduction or conversion or growth.** The extent to which a church relies on conversion and/or reproduction invariably determines its future trajectory. North American Anabaptist churches have historically relied on reproduction, but as assimilated members embrace family planning and birth control, the shortcomings of a reproduction-only approach have become apparent. Barring the transition to a conversion model, declines for the North American church will surely continue. And given that so many North American Anabaptists have literally "gone to school"—having among the highest educational levels in North America—a renewal of evangelistic activity may be unlikely.

In the Global South, much of the current growth among Anabaptists is through the conversion of adult nonbelievers, alongside reproduction. But there is evidence in the MNA Profile that all churches regardless of hemisphere may follow a kind of life course that causes them to begin to rely on reproduction instead of conversion. As noted above, in older churches (in terms of date of origin) in the MNA Profile, the mean age of conversion is lower than in churches with more recent origins. Sociologically this makes sense—older churches rely on their children to become new members while churches that are new recognize that their growth and vitality depends on the making of new adult converts from outside the church. Newer churches are necessarily more evangelistic because they need to be. Older churches begin to take their existence and the multiple generations of converts in their midst for granted and, as a result, lose the evangelistic fervor they once had. Among the Global South churches, there seems to be some connection between a church's enthusiasm and commitment to evangelism and its level of recent growth. In fact, the four churches with the slowest growth in the last two decades are also the four churches for whom the highest proportion of members indicate they are not interested in church planting: LMC United States, KMC Kenya, KMT Tanzania, and GKM Indonesia.

While Enlightenment values and structures are less present in Asia, Africa, and Latin America, demographic forces that come with social and economic development may well shape the churches in ways that limit growth and eventually lead to decline. Western forms of family planning, higher education, and employment of women are trends likely to continue in developing countries. These are precisely the social forces that demographers have shown to lower birth rates and reproductive capacity; in a consumer culture where both parents work, children become an economic liability rather than an asset. As birth rates continue to drop in the Global South, churches that depend on reproduction without the conversion of adult believers will find themselves on a trajectory similar to that of North American and European churches.

**Increasing resistance among potential converts.** Another factor that may lower conversion rates in Asia, Africa, and Latin America is the possibility that rapidly growing churches in the Profile have initially been winning over the least resistant individuals in their communities and, over time, may run into greater challenges in their soul-winning efforts. In FCA India, conversions are currently highest among lower caste members, with upper caste members resisting conversion to Christianity. Those in the lower castes consider conversion a means of upward mobility, autonomy, and empowerment and an avenue for participation in the democratic processes of their country. As lower caste members disproportionately convert, the church will begin to look like a "lower caste" church, and those in upper castes will have little desire to join a movement that appears to threaten their upward mobility and status.

**Higher social status of members.** While not the case in FCA India, a question that many churches will need to deal with is how they are preparing for the challenges they will face as they become older and more mature and as their members gain greater social status. For example, in some places in Latin America, upwardly mobile individuals are rejecting the evangelical church for the same reasons they have rejected the Roman Catholic Church, their rejection owing to a loss of faith as well as disillusionment with religious requirements in an ever secular context.

**The need for socialization of converts.** This points to another challenge facing churches in the Global South: new believers must be socialized, or discipled, in the beliefs and practices of their church.[35] Rapid growth can mitigate the leaders' ability to ensure the socialization of new believers through meaningful discipleship programs and the development of new, effective leaders who are deeply converted. We heard this concern expressed at the Thika consultation by leaders of rapidly growing churches, including MKC Ethiopia. Failure to socialize new believers can lead to nominal Christian converts and weak reproduction of faith in their children. There is much evidence that the leadership of the MNA Profile churches is deeply concerned about the socialization of their members and the reproduction of the faith, but this concern will need to be accompanied by intentional plans for discipleship that stems nominalism.

**Conclusion.** Despite the rapid growth of many of global southern churches, a question that all will need to deal with is this: How are these churches preparing for the challenges they will face as they become older and more mature, and as their members gain greater status in their societies? The trajectory of North American churches should not be considered an anomaly by leaders of churches in the Global South. Rather, it may be a prophetic word about the challenges and direction churches of Asia, Africa, and Latin America will face as they increase in numbers and get further from their dates of origin and the visions that birthed them.

---

35. Theologically, we often refer to such religious socialization as discipleship, whereby new believers learn the norms, values, and beliefs of their new religious identity. In this book we use these two terms synonymously.

On the other hand, while we should recognize the possibilities of decline in Global South, it may be just as reasonable to argue that it is less likely than in North America and Europe. Earlier, we suggested that openness to the Spirit's movement in the Global South came from the weakness of the Enlightenment's influence in Asia, Africa, and Latin America. If this is the case, we should not so readily assume that the same kinds of routinization will occur there. Enlightenment forces that limit belief in the supernatural and create organizational structures that hinder the Spirit's movement in the West are less prevalent in the Global South. It may be that the freedom that led to the Spirit's dramatic movement in the Global South will also create an enduring space to sustain that movement.

5

# Anabaptist Beliefs and Practices

> The early Christians were alert to the dominant cultural patterns of their civilization. They faced the task of inculturating their message in societies whose narratives and folkways they needed to evaluate; some they used, some they adopted, some they rejected. . . . Thinking missiologically, they asked in case after case whether a given practice was life-giving or whether it led to bondage. Regarding bondage and addiction, early Christian thinkers and catechists were particularly sensitive to the way that conventional folkways—doing what everybody did—trapped people in deathly, demon-beset cages. . . . These were missiological insights, for they pointed to areas in which the good news of Jesus could set people free.[1] —*Mennonite historian Alan Kreider*

## Belief and behavior in the early church

In the early church, right belief and right behavior were strongly connected when it came to discipling converts. New Christians

---

1. Kreider, 1999:10.

were expected to believe and to behave differently, since "Christian *belief* led to a discerning of areas of demonic power in society that enslaved people; but the freedom Christ brought liberated people from addiction and compulsion and led to distinctive forms of *behavior*."[2] For early Christians, belief and behavior went hand in hand, for Jesus transformed both. The ritual act of adult baptism was at the center of this transformation.

As the church matured following Constantine's conversion in the fourth century, it was increasingly co-opted by the larger society, the connection between belief and behavior became more tenuous. It became enough to just believe; in fact, it was assumed that everyone believed. In this process, the distinction between pagan and Christian disappeared within Christendom. The new social distinction that emerged was between clergy and monastics and the laity rather than between pagan and Christian. Only clergy and monastics were expected to hold to the highest behavioral standards of early church converts, while laity simply had to believe the right things and belong to the church. Behavior in the Constantinian church was largely irrelevant, overridden by belief and conformity to an institution now embraced by the broader society. As time evolved, membership in the church became a status symbol that required little change of behavior; it was merely an embrace of the dominant values of the dominant society.[3] Christianity had become its own worst enemy, lowering the standards of a people who suddenly had every reason to believe that they were all Christians.[4]

## Belief and behavior in the global church

In this chapter, we will examine the beliefs and practices of members in the twelve MNA Profile churches. In doing so, we will

---

2. Kreider, 1999:5.

3. Kreider, 1999.

4. For an excellent statement of the effects of Constantine's conversion on Christianity, see Lee C. Camp, *Mere Discipleship*, Brazos Press, 2003.

observe substantial differences in patterns between LMC United States responses and those of church members in the Global South. As we met in Thika, Kenya, with anchors and leaders of the participating Profile churches, we were surprised by the concern that many leaders in the Global South showed as they viewed the results of their profiles. Looking with dismay at the relatively small percentage of members who deviated from the expected normative behaviors in their churches (relative to the larger number in LMC United States), they were heard asking, "Who are these people?" In turn, they had questions for North American leaders about the laxness and apathy that they saw in LMC United States responses and about which North American leaders expressed little consternation.

It became clear that one of the major differences between the churches in the Global South and the church in North America is the concern for consistency of belief and behavior. Perhaps this difference has to do with the effects of Christendom in North America—where the residual presence of belonging is more important—and the lack of such in the Global South. Or perhaps it has more to do with the similarities in contexts between the Global South and the early church. Like early church leaders, leaders in the Global South are aware that the very sustainability of their churches depends on socializing faithful converts to differentiate themselves from their non-Christian surroundings. Leaders recognize that they are constructing a new reality for their converts, calling them out from a society and culture seen as pagan. Like the early church, many Profile churches understand that they are missionaries in their local context: members expect to be witnesses to their communities and extended families. In fact, living in pagan and non-Christian contexts, new Christians are witnesses even without saying anything to their neighbors, friends, or family. They have made a choice, often a costly one, to step out of their traditional religious communities in order to join the church.

One sometimes hears North American Christians complaining that they are not effective evangelists because they do not know how or because they have not been trained in evangelism. When Christians have to be trained to be evangelists, might there be too little difference between their lifestyle and that of the world around them? Or it is that North Americans simply do not have much to share about the difference Jesus has made in their lives? It is possible that, where testimonies fail to erupt, there simply is not testimony to give. As children of Christendom, North Americans live with a sense that we are not that much different from the world around us and that right behavior is less important than right belief. In writing about how Christendom separated belief from behavior, Lee Camp notes,

> With the rise of Christendom, the content of the "Christian ethic" was transformed: the empire began to call upon the church to guide and approve the deeds of the emperor, deeds that the early church rejected. But since Christianity was now legally mandatory, one's inner nature, one's "heart," now served as the central focal point of discipleship. An outwardly disciplined life became reserved for a special class of "religious," but was certainly not expected of the Christian masses.... To use different language, the Christendom project separated "doctrine" and "ethics" into two separable categories.[5]

This failure of North American churches may be related to its Christendom context. Or it may be the influence of North American evangelicalism, which some suggest has placed more emphasis on salvation and belief in Jesus and less on obedience to Jesus in everyday life.[6] Or perhaps it is the nature of American civil religion, which has minimized Christian commitment in exchange for patriotic commitment to the nation-state and worship of a generic god who oversees America's manifest destiny and assists her domination of the rest of the world. Whatever the case, it became clear at the 2010 consultation in Thika that the

---

5. Camp, 2003:35–36.
6. Camp, 2003.

concerns about the connection of belief and behavior expressed by church leaders in the Global South were close to the concerns of early Christian leaders in the first several centuries.

## Beliefs and the MNA Profile

Differentiating between orthodoxy (right belief) and orthopraxy (right practice), we see immediately that MNA Profile churches share much regarding right belief but diverge on issues relating to behavior.

**Beliefs about Jesus.** MNA churches are orthodox in belief, whether located in Asia, Africa, or the Americas. As members of Anabaptist churches, they vary little from one another on the central tenets of faith—such as who Jesus is, the truth of the Bible, and Jesus' return to earth. The beliefs of all the churches fall squarely into that great tradition of what "all Christians in all places have believed all of the time." The elements of the Apostles' Creed, the authority of the Bible, the importance of salvation, and the centrality of the church are all important aspects of the faith of these widely scattered groups.

Table 5.1 Percent who believe Jesus was born of a virgin

| Church | Believe |
| --- | --- |
| Fellowship of Christian Assemblies | 100% |
| Persatuan Gereja-Gereja Muria Indonesia | 98% |
| Hoi Thanh Mennonite Viet Nam | 99% |
| Meserete Kristos Church | 97% |
| Kenya Mennonite Church | 97% |
| Happy Church Ministries International | 97% |
| Kanisa la Mennonite Tanzania | 97% |
| Organizacion Christiana Amor Viviente | 96% |
| Iglesia Evangelica Menonita Hondurena | 97% |
| Iglesia Nacional Evangelica Menonita Guatemalteca | 99% |
| Integrated Mennonite Church of the Philippines | 95% |
| Lancaster Mennonite Conference | 96% |
| Total | 97% |

112  *Winds of the Spirit*

Ninety-seven percent of respondents across all churches confess that Jesus was born of a virgin. Overwhelmingly, they believe that Jesus physically rose from the dead, with 96% affirming this statement. And 99% assert that God created the heavens and the earth. As evident, there is little variation among churches about these beliefs.

Table 5.2 Percent who believe Jesus rose from the dead

| Church | Believe |
| --- | --- |
| Fellowship of Christian Assemblies | 100% |
| Persatuan Gereja-Gereja Muria Indonesia | 98% |
| Hoi Thanh Mennonite Viet Nam | 97% |
| Meserete Kristos Church | 96% |
| Kenya Mennonite Church | 97% |
| Happy Church Ministries International | 96% |
| Kanisa la Mennonite Tanzania | 96% |
| Organizacion Christiana Amor Viviente | 95% |
| Iglesia Evangelica Menonita Hondurena | 92% |
| Iglesia Nacional Evangelica Menonita Guatemalteca | 100% |
| Integrated Mennonite Church of the Philippines | 88% |
| Lancaster Mennonite Conference | 97% |
| Total | 96% |

With one exception (IMC Philippines), more than 80% believe that Jesus will physically return to the earth. All of the churches confess strongly that the Bible is the inspired Word of God. Furthermore, with only one significant exception (LMC United States), 90% or more believe that God performs the same kind of miracles today as are reported in Scripture.

Anabaptist Beliefs and Practices 113

Table 5.3 Percent who believe the Bible is inspired

| Church | Believe |
|---|---|
| Fellowship of Christian Assemblies | 100% |
| Persatuan Gereja-Gereja Muria Indonesia | 100% |
| Hoi Thanh Mennonite Viet Nam | 99% |
| Meserete Kristos Church | 96% |
| Kenya Mennonite Church | 94% |
| Happy Church Ministries International | 98% |
| Kanisa la Mennonite Tanzania | 89% |
| Organizacion Christiana Amor Viviente | 98% |
| Iglesia Evangelica Menonita Hondurena | 98% |
| Iglesia Nacional Evangelica Menonita Guatemalteca | 99% |
| Integrated Mennonite Church of the Philippines | 97% |
| Lancaster Mennonite Conference | 96% |
| Total | 97% |

Table 5.4 Percent who believe that miracles today are same as in the Bible

| Church | Believe |
|---|---|
| Fellowship of Christian Assemblies | 100% |
| Persatuan Gereja-Gereja Muria Indonesia | 99% |
| Hoi Thanh Mennonite Viet Nam | 98% |
| Meserete Kristos Church | 97% |
| Kenya Mennonite Church | 95% |
| Happy Church Ministries International | 95% |
| Kanisa la Mennonite Tanzania | 92% |
| Organizacion Christiana Amor Viviente | 95% |
| Iglesia Evangelica Menonita Hondurena | 96% |
| Iglesia Nacional Evangelica Menonita Guatemalteca | 100% |
| Integrated Mennonite Church of the Philippines | 88% |
| Lancaster Mennonite Conference | 77% |
| Total | 95% |

**Beliefs about the devil.** There is somewhat more variation in belief about whether the devil, as a personal being, is active in the world today. Members of KMT Tanzania (68%) and KMC Kenya (62%) are unsure that the devil is active. In neighboring MKC Ethiopia, 20% do not profess certainty that the devil is active. All others churches claim a greater degree of certainty.

Table 5.5 Percent who believe the devil is active today

| Church | Believe |
| --- | --- |
| Fellowship of Christian Assemblies | 97% |
| Persatuan Gereja-Gereja Muria Indonesia | 96% |
| Hoi Thanh Mennonite Viet Nam | 91% |
| Meserete Kristos Church | 80% |
| Kenya Mennonite Church | 62% |
| Happy Church Ministries International | 89% |
| Kanisa la Mennonite Tanzania | 68% |
| Organizacion Christiana Amor Viviente | 95% |
| Iglesia Evangelica Menonita Hondurena | 94% |
| Iglesia Nacional Evangelica Menonita Guatemalteca | 89% |
| Integrated Mennonite Church of the Philippines | 86% |
| Lancaster Mennonite Conference | 91% |
| Total | 86% |

Why the lower scores for Satan in East Africa, a region where there is historically greater awareness of demonic power? Perhaps the lower emphases on the devil in Africa simply reveal a greater confidence that Christ has defeated Satan. The recognition of spiritual forces in African religions may lead to greater certainty among African Christians of the enemy's defeat through the work of Jesus Christ and the devil's decreased power and activity as a result.

The churches overwhelmingly believe that there is a real heaven and a real hell where people are rewarded or punished. Tanzanian believers, however, are less certain about both than the others, particularly about heaven.

Anabaptist Beliefs and Practices 115

Table 5.6 Percent who believe heaven is real

| Church | Believe |
|---|---|
| Fellowship of Christian Assemblies | 100% |
| Persatuan Gereja-Gereja Muria Indonesia | 97% |
| Hoi Thanh Mennonite Viet Nam | 99% |
| Meserete Kristos Church | 86% |
| Kenya Mennonite Church | 93% |
| Happy Church Ministries International | 94% |
| Kanisa la Mennonite Tanzania | 59% |
| Organizacion Christiana Amor Viviente | 96% |
| Iglesia Evangelica Menonita Hondurena | 97% |
| Iglesia Nacional Evangelica Menonita Guatemalteca | 99% |
| Integrated Mennonite Church of the Philippines | 96% |
| Lancaster Mennonite Conference | 94% |
| Total | 91% |

Table 5.7 Percent who believe that followers of Christ experience good health and finances

| Church | Believe |
|---|---|
| Fellowship of Christian Assemblies | 91% |
| Persatuan Gereja-Gereja Muria Indonesia | 84% |
| Hoi Thanh Mennonite Viet Nam | 82% |
| Meserete Kristos Church | 89% |
| Kenya Mennonite Church | 76% |
| Happy Church Ministries International | 85% |
| Kanisa la Mennonite Tanzania | 79% |
| Organizacion Christiana Amor Viviente | 78% |
| Iglesia Evangelica Menonita Hondurena | 85% |
| Iglesia Nacional Evangelica Menonita Guatemalteca | 91% |
| Integrated Mennonite Church of the Philippines | 79% |
| Lancaster Mennonite Conference | 27% |
| Total | 83% |

**Beliefs about prosperity.** Except for LMC United States, churches in the MNA Profile believe that Christians experience good health and financial blessings as a result of their faith. In LMC United States, only 27% believe this. It seems ironic that, in one of the nations with the highest standards of living in the world, Christians seem less inclined to attribute good health and financial blessings to God. Perhaps it is the very ubiquity of material wealth in the United States that makes it harder to see God in it. Christians in the United States may believe that good health and financial blessings come primarily from good medical care and hard work. Or perhaps they have less frequently experienced the personal and community transformation that occurs when people stop drinking, start loving their spouses and children, and become productive citizens. Many Christians in the United States minimize the idea that God is the source of good health and financial success and consider such attribution evidence of a prosperity gospel: the belief that God wants all his people to be wealthy and that loads of "cargo" will come to those who claim it by faith, whether that cargo is new cars, fine homes, or an independent lifestyle.[7] The prosperity gospel is an issue in many places, the United States included. But in conversations with Profile leaders, there was little if any evidence of such prosperity teaching. Rather, they communicated the simple testimony that, when people become Christians, their lives are transformed and God blesses them. Many Profile members live in relative poverty; nevertheless, they thank God for the good health and financial blessings that are theirs.

Regarding the question of God's provision of health and financial blessings, some of our anchors noted the following:

- Boniface Runji of Happy Church Kenya said, "Being a developing country with challenges of food, people

---

7. "Cargo" refers to the cargo cults of Melanesia, which were the result of World War II GIs and American missionaries. Melanesians developed apocalyptic and messianic religious beliefs around material goods that these Americans brought to them, mixing Christian beliefs with a desire for Western items.

run to the church because it gives them hope. Not the prosperity gospel. But we give them hope. It's out of that kind of hope that people trust that followers of Jesus will have good health."

- Carlos Marin of Amor Viviente Honduras stated, "It's interesting that the churches of India and Guatemala, which have the lowest incomes, also believe that God is blessing them as they follow him. They're not only talking about health and wealth. They are comparing their present state to their previous one."

- Observing Profile results from LMC United States churches, Yemiru Tilahun of MKC Ethiopia said, "LMC does not have financial needs. They have good health insurance. In Ethiopia we have to pray every day and expect from the Lord. We are looking to God for material things. The poorer churches are constantly looking to God for health and financial needs."

**Islam and Christianity.** Many Anabaptist churches in the Global South are on the boundaries of the great world religions, including Islam. We found substantial variation among members when we asked, "Do Christians and Muslims worship the same God?" While not a question that appears in the creeds, it is useful for defining the boundaries of theological persuasion among world religions.

Only one group (FCA India) answers with a resounding "no" of 97%. Some, including HTM Vietnam, KMC Kenya, Happy Church Kenya, and KMT Tanzania are split quite evenly. The rest give a majority answer of "no" but with a strong minority responding "yes."

The same diversity seen among church members in the Profile was evidenced among church leaders at the 2010 consultation in Thika. This question evoked some of the most disparate answers of any question on the survey. Leaders asked how they can learn about Islam, respond to its political push, and witness effectively without resorting to political solutions based on a push-back of Christian power.

## Table 5.8 Percent who believe Muslims and Christians worship the same God

| Church | Believe |
| --- | --- |
| Fellowship of Christian Assemblies | 3% |
| Persatuan Gereja-Gereja Muria Indonesia | 26% |
| Hoi Thanh Mennonite Viet Nam | 57% |
| Meserete Kristos Church | 26% |
| Kenya Mennonite Church | 58% |
| Happy Church Ministries International | 32% |
| Kanisa la Mennonite Tanzania | 63% |
| Organizacion Christiana Amor Viviente | 24% |
| Iglesia Evangelica Menonita Hondurena | 33% |
| Iglesia Nacional Evangelica Menonita Guatemalteca | N/A |
| Integrated Mennonite Church of the Philippines | 34% |
| Lancaster Mennonite Conference | 29% |
| Total | 30% |

Clearly, the sociopolitical context of each region affects relationships between Christians and Muslims. In some contexts, church leaders consider Islam and other religions a threat. Church leaders in FCA India are socializing their young people to consider political careers as a response to radical Hinduism. One Indian leader said, "many Hindu fundamentalists are getting involved in politics. . . . perhaps Christians should get more involved to vote against the anti-conversion laws that are being implemented."

In Indonesia, Muslims have burned six Mennonite churches, and Christians are concerned about living peacefully with Islamic believers. One Indonesian leader responded that his country's constitution states, "We believe in one God." He continued, "We worship Allah through Jesus Christ. We try not to offend Muslims. We are trying to build good relations with them."

The churches from Kenya reveal differences in their approach and response to Islam. Fifty-eight percent of Happy Church members say that Christians and Muslims worship the same God, compared to 26% of KMC members. Some young

KMC members have attended a Christian-Muslim dialogue in Nairobi. Happy Church leaders, on the other hand, have approached the question of Islam by developing specific teachings about the differences between Muslims and Christians. One leader notes:

> In Kenya, many Christians don't understand the Muslims. We need to educate our people about what Muslims believe. We need to teach people about evangelizing Muslims. We need to understand that Allah is not the God of the Bible. . . . members don't really understand differences between Christianity and Islam.

Language also affects how people interpret this question about God. In India, Christians and Hindus use different words for God. In Indonesia, a country with more than 204 million Muslims, there is one word for God.

Perhaps the variation in answers to this question is due to the ambiguity of the question rather than to actual differences of perspective among the respondents. Yet the differences in responses cannot be completely dismissed by critiquing the question, for such questions arise repeatedly at the boundaries of the great world religions. Who is this God, and how has God revealed himself both through Jesus Christ and in other ways? To what extent has God revealed himself in the fabric of Islam? Is the sincere Muslim believer indeed worshiping the same God as is the Christian believer, but doing so amiss or incompletely because of lack of knowledge? Or is that believer in fact worshiping a different god? The answers churches give will do much to shape the way they share the good news with adherents of other faiths.

## Behaviors

In the first part of this chapter, we examined the nature of Anabaptist beliefs and found that MNA Profile churches have much in common in their views of Jesus, the Bible, and the afterlife. The next part of the chapter considers the religious practices and behaviors of members, reporting their level and intensity in the areas of moral practices, devotional life, corporate worship, and service.

**Moral behaviors.** Profile respondents were asked a set of questions related to their attitudes about certain behaviors and practices. The general question stated, "People have different views of the behaviors listed below. Please indicate how wrong you consider each behavior to be." The categories that respondents could choose from were "Always wrong," "Usually wrong," "Sometimes wrong," "Rarely wrong," and "Never wrong." Some of the items on the list generate general agreement that the behaviors are always wrong. These include drug use, abortion, receiving or offering a bribe, viewing pornographic material, profanity, immodest clothing, gambling, premarital sex, extramarital sex, homosexuality, smoking, and watching pornographic movies.

Table 5.9 Percent who believe a bribe is always wrong

| Church | Believe It Is Always Wrong |
|---|---|
| Fellowship of Christian Assemblies | 98% |
| Persatuan Gereja-Gereja Muria Indonesia | 89% |
| Hoi Thanh Mennonite Viet Nam | 92% |
| Meserete Kristos Church | 78% |
| Kenya Mennonite Church | 72% |
| Happy Church Ministries International | 85% |
| Kanisa la Mennonite Tanzania | 78% |
| Organizacion Christiana Amor Viviente | 94% |
| Iglesia Evangelica Menonita Hondurena | 92% |
| Iglesia Nacional Evangelica Menonita Guatemalteca | 96% |
| Integrated Mennonite Church of the Philippines | 91% |
| Lancaster Mennonite Conference | 82% |
| Total | 86% |

Anabaptist Beliefs and Practices 121

Table 5.10 Percent who believe premarital sex is always wrong

| Church | Believe It Is Always Wrong |
|---|---|
| Fellowship of Christian Assemblies | 99% |
| Persatuan Gereja-Gereja Muria Indonesia | 95% |
| Hoi Thanh Mennonite Viet Nam | 89% |
| Meserete Kristos Church | 85% |
| Kenya Mennonite Church | 70% |
| Happy Church Ministries International | 90% |
| Kanisa la Mennonite Tanzania | 78% |
| Organizacion Christiana Amor Viviente | 90% |
| Iglesia Evangelica Menonita Hondurena | 93% |
| Iglesia Nacional Evangelica Menonita Guatemalteca | 95% |
| Integrated Mennonite Church of the Philippines | 84% |
| Lancaster Mennonite Conference | 88% |
| Total | 88% |

Table 5.11 Percent who believe homosexual relations are always wrong

| Church | Believe It Is Always Wrong |
|---|---|
| Fellowship of Christian Assemblies | 97% |
| Persatuan Gereja-Gereja Muria Indonesia | 95% |
| Hoi Thanh Mennonite Viet Nam | 95% |
| Meserete Kristos Church | 91% |
| Kenya Mennonite Church | 69% |
| Happy Church Ministries International | 89% |
| Kanisa la Mennonite Tanzania | 80% |
| Organizacion Christiana Amor Viviente | 96% |
| Iglesia Evangelica Menonita Hondurena | 96% |
| Iglesia Nacional Evangelica Menonita Guatemalteca | 92% |
| Integrated Mennonite Church of the Philippines | 92% |
| Lancaster Mennonite Conference | 86% |
| Total | 91% |

122  Winds of the Spirit

Table 5.12 Percent who believe voting is always wrong

| Church | Believe It Is Always Wrong |
|---|---|
| Fellowship of Christian Assemblies | 6% |
| Persatuan Gereja-Gereja Muria Indonesia | 5% |
| Hoi Thanh Mennonite Viet Nam | 29% |
| Meserete Kristos Church | 36% |
| Kenya Mennonite Church | 16% |
| Happy Church Ministries International | 25% |
| Kanisa la Mennonite Tanzania | 23% |
| Organizacion Christiana Amor Viviente | 12% |
| Iglesia Evangelica Menonita Hondurena | 30% |
| Iglesia Nacional Evangelica Menonita Guatemalteca | 34% |
| Integrated Mennonite Church of the Philippines | 12% |
| Lancaster Mennonite Conference | 4% |
| Total | 24% |

Only one behavior, voting, is generally considered completely acceptable in all churches. Just one-third or fewer of members in all churches believe that it is wrong.

Responses to other behaviors demonstrate much diversity of opinion. For example, only 13% of LMC United States participants say that divorce is always wrong. The church with views closest to LMC United States is Amor Viviente Honduras, with 56% saying that divorce is always wrong. In all other churches, at least 64% state that divorce is always wrong. In four churches, more than 80% of members respond this way. Clearly, LMC United States is the outlier on this particular question.

Drinking alcohol is another behavior where LMC United States opinions differ from the Global South churches: only 33% of LMC members say that drinking alcohol is always wrong. But more than 70% of all other churches indicate that this behavior is always wrong, with 80% or more of members in seven churches calling drinking always wrong.

When asked whether marriage between a Christian and a non-Christian is wrong, churches vary widely in their responses.

Anabaptist Beliefs and Practices 123

In seven churches, 60% or fewer members say that this behavior is always wrong: LMC United States, IMC Philippines, both Honduran churches, both Kenyan churches, and KMT Tanzania. But for all churches, affirmation that this practice is always wrong is lower than for some of the other practices in the survey.

Table 5.13 Percent who believe divorce is always wrong

| Church | Believe It Is Always Wrong |
|---|---|
| Fellowship of Christian Assemblies | 90% |
| Persatuan Gereja-Gereja Muria Indonesia | 90% |
| Hoi Thanh Mennonite Viet Nam | 84% |
| Meserete Kristos Church | 68% |
| Kenya Mennonite Church | 64% |
| Happy Church Ministries International | 65% |
| Kanisa la Mennonite Tanzania | 66% |
| Organizacion Christiana Amor Viviente | 56% |
| Iglesia Evangelica Menonita Hondurena | 71% |
| Iglesia Nacional Evangelica Menonita Guatemalteca | 95% |
| Integrated Mennonite Church of the Philippines | 71% |
| Lancaster Mennonite Conference | 13% |
| Total | 68% |

When asked about polygamy, the African churches are less likely than other churches to say that this practice is always wrong, ranging between 58% and 82% across the four African Profile churches. This finding makes sense, given that these are the churches that most often face this question. In most other churches, nearly 90% state that this practice is always wrong.

Belief in good luck had many diverse responses, with churches varying between 37% and 91% in their affirmation that it is wrong.

Responses also vary regarding the performance of non-Christian religious ceremonies, with between 63% and 95% of church memberships saying it is always wrong. Eating food offered to idols is considered least wrong in LMC United States—57% of LMC members say it is always wrong—while 70% or more in all other churches state that this behavior is wrong.

When asked about being present at ancestral worship, all churches but KMT Tanzania strongly affirm that this practice is always wrong; in KMT Tanzania, only 43% of respondents say that it is always wrong. On the other end of the spectrum, FCA India, INEM Guatemala, and GKM Indonesia affirm most strongly that this is wrong (97%, 95%, and 93%, respectively).

There is substantial disagreement about participating in the armed forces. Only 4% of FCA India members say that participation is always wrong, compared to 76% of INEM Guatemala and 50% or more of respondents in HTM Vietnam, KMC Kenya, MKC Ethiopia, IEM Honduras, and IMC Philippines. Just 29% of LMC United States members say that entering the armed forces is always wrong. Individuals' attitudes about serving as a police officer parallel attitudes about the armed forces, with a range of 3% (FCA India) to 65% (INEM Guatemala).

Table 5.14 Percent who believe entering the armed forces is always wrong

| Church | Believe It Is Always Wrong |
| --- | --- |
| Fellowship of Christian Assemblies | 4% |
| Persatuan Gereja-Gereja Muria Indonesia | 11% |
| Hoi Thanh Mennonite Viet Nam | 55% |
| Meserete Kristos Church | 47% |
| Kenya Mennonite Church | 53% |
| Happy Church Ministries International | 12% |
| Kanisa la Mennonite Tanzania | 38% |
| Organizacion Christiana Amor Viviente | 17% |
| Iglesia Evangelica Menonita Hondurena | 51% |
| Iglesia Nacional Evangelica Menonita Guatemalteca | 76% |
| Integrated Mennonite Church of the Philippines | 47% |
| Lancaster Mennonite Conference | 29% |
| Total | 37% |

**Fellowship and giving.** The extent to which members of the MNA Profile churches regularly meet together varies from church to church. Small group participation is strongest in FCA India, INEM Guatemala, and HTM Vietnam, and lowest in the churches in Honduras, Kenya, and the Philippines. The remaining churches range from 66% to 73% of members meeting in small groups two to three times a month or more.

With the exception of IMC Philippines, at least 82% of members in all churches report attending public worship on a weekly basis or more; IMC Philippines' weekly attendance is just over two-thirds (68%). Whether or not members attend more than once a week varies from church to church and depends in part on how services are organized in their regular worship schedule. Weekly church attendance is highest in INEM Guatemala and HTM Vietnam, followed closely by IEM Honduras and LMC United States.

**Table 5.15 Percent who attend worship services at least weekly**

| Church | Attend Weekly or More |
|---|---|
| Fellowship of Christian Assemblies | 83% |
| Persatuan Gereja-Gereja Muria Indonesia | 83% |
| Hoi Thanh Mennonite Viet Nam | 95% |
| Meserete Kristos Church | 87% |
| Kenya Mennonite Church | 88% |
| Happy Church Ministries International | 87% |
| Kanisa la Mennonite Tanzania | 82% |
| Organizacion Christiana Amor Viviente | 83% |
| Iglesia Evangelica Menonita Hondurena | 93% |
| Iglesia Nacional Evangelica Menonita Guatemalteca | 98% |
| Integrated Mennonite Church of the Philippines | 68% |
| Lancaster Mennonite Conference | 92% |
| Total | 87% |

Rates of giving are highest in the poorest church, INEM Guatemala, where 87% report giving 10% or more of their income to the church or to charitable causes. Among the Kekchi of INEM Guatemala, who are largely subsistence farmers and earn very little monetary income, giving to the church is sometimes in the form of first fruits from their land, such as bags of corn and live chickens. In the rural churches of FCA India, farmers tithe from the crops they harvest up to three times per year. Levels of giving are lowest in MKC Ethiopia and KMT Tanzania.

Table 5.16 Percent who give 10% or more of income

| Church | Give 10% or More |
|---|---|
| Fellowship of Christian Assemblies | 73% |
| Persatuan Gereja-Gereja Muria Indonesia | 59% |
| Hoi Thanh Mennonite Viet Nam | 63% |
| Meserete Kristos Church | 48% |
| Kenya Mennonite Church | 66% |
| Happy Church Ministries International | 67% |
| Kanisa la Mennonite Tanzania | 43% |
| Organizacion Christiana Amor Viviente | 54% |
| Iglesia Evangelica Menonita Hondurena | 58% |
| Iglesia Nacional Evangelica Menonita Guatemalteca | 87% |
| Integrated Mennonite Church of the Philippines | 65% |
| Lancaster Mennonite Conference | 75% |
| Total | 60% |

**Worship preferences.** Members in the MNA Profile were given the opportunity to express their worship preferences from a list of possibilities that included singing locally composed songs, using flags in worship, praying spontaneously, and more. Relative to many other worship practices, singing without instruments receives relatively little support from most churches. By far, GKM Indonesia members are least likely to opt for singing without instruments, while members of HTM Vietnam feel the most positive about the practice.[8]

---

8. Among the Kekchi, the MNA Profile was modified to address issues of literacy and educational levels. This particular question about worship practices had three categories rather than five—Negative,

Anabaptist Beliefs and Practices

**Table 5.17 Percent who feel very positive about singing without instruments**

| Church | Feel Very Positive |
|---|---|
| Fellowship of Christian Assemblies | 24% |
| Persatuan Gereja-Gereja Muria Indonesia | 8% |
| Hoi Thanh Mennonite Viet Nam | 48% |
| Meserete Kristos Church | 19% |
| Kenya Mennonite Church | 22% |
| Happy Church Ministries International | 23% |
| Kanisa la Mennonite Tanzania | 28% |
| Organizacion Christiana Amor Viviente | 23% |
| Iglesia Evangelica Menonita Hondurena | 25% |
| Iglesia Nacional Evangelica Menonita Guatemalteca | 86% |
| Integrated Mennonite Church of the Philippines | 26% |
| Lancaster Mennonite Conference | 29% |
| Total | 22% |

Singing in four-part harmony is most preferred by KMT Tanzania and least preferred in FCA India, GKM Indonesia, and Amor Viviente Honduras. In all other churches, one-third or more members feel very positive about this practice. Support is strongest in LMC United States and in the churches planted early by Eastern Mennonite missionaries: KMT Tanzania, MKC Ethiopia, and KMC Kenya.

In general, instruments in worship are least preferred in GKM Indonesia and LMC United States. Contemporary praise songs receive little support in GKM Indonesia and relatively low levels of support in FCA India and LMC United States. Among all other churches, more than 50% of members feel very strongly about the value of these songs in worship, and 60% or more of members in eight churches support singing these songs.

---

Neutral, and Positive—making it impossible to compare directly with the eleven other churches in the Profile. As a result, we do not include the Kekchi responses in this discussion when comparing churches (their responses are available in the tables that we include here).

A similar but somewhat different question addresses member preferences for locally composed songs. In LMC United States, IMC Philippines, and GKM Indonesia, fewer than one-fourth of members endorse such songs. But in all other churches, 40% or more do so, with support being highest in Latin American churches.

Several questions inquired about the use of physical movement in worship. LMC United States, GKM Indonesia, and IMC Philippines members are least likely to prefer kneeling for prayer during services. In all other churches, 50% or more of members feel strongly that kneeling is important in worship. A question about altar calls reveals a similar pattern of response, with the same three churches feeling less positive about the practice. Although more positive about altar calls than these three, FCA India and KMT Tanzania are less positive about alter calls than they are about kneeling. In the remaining churches, 50% or more believe that altar calls are important.

Table 5.18 Percent who feel very positive about dancing in worship

| Church | Feel Very Positive |
| --- | --- |
| Fellowship of Christian Assemblies | 26% |
| Persatuan Gereja-Gereja Muria Indonesia | 4% |
| Hoi Thanh Mennonite Viet Nam | 46% |
| Meserete Kristos Church | 37% |
| Kenya Mennonite Church | 56% |
| Happy Church Ministries International | 52% |
| Kanisa la Mennonite Tanzania | 32% |
| Organizacion Christiana Amor Viviente | 67% |
| Iglesia Evangelica Menonita Hondurena | 60% |
| Iglesia Nacional Evangelica Menonita Guatemalteca | 90% |
| Integrated Mennonite Church of the Philippines | 24% |
| Lancaster Mennonite Conference | 12% |
| Total | 41% |

When asked about dancing in worship, churches express greater ambivalence about the practice than they do regarding some of the other practices. LMC United States and GKM Indonesia are least likely to appreciate dancing, followed by IMC Philippines and FCA India. The churches from Honduras (Amor Viviente and IEM) and Kenya (Happy Church and KMC) most readily embrace dancing in worship. The two other African churches, KMT Tanzania and MKC Ethiopia, are less exuberant about dancing than their Kenyan brothers and sisters.

Clapping with music is more strongly supported than a number of other practices. While lowest in LMC United States and GKM Indonesia (in keeping with their evident dislike of a number of other expressive worship activities), more members in these churches feel positive about clapping than anticipated. The Kenyan (Happy Church and KMC), Honduran (Amor Viviente and IEM), and Vietnamese (HTM) churches are most favorable about clapping, followed by KMT Tanzania and FCA India.

With the exception of singing without instruments, using flags in worship receives less endorsement than any of the worship activities discussed to this point. LMC United States, GKM Indonesia, and IMC Philippines show little support for flags in worship. The greatest support is in the Honduran churches (Amor Viviente and IEM). Among other churches, the preference for flags varies substantially; it is low in KMC Kenya, KMT Tanzania, and MCK Ethiopia churches but higher in Happy Church Kenya and HTM Vietnam.

LMC United States, FCA India, IMC Philippines, and GKM Indonesia are the least likely to appreciate spontaneous prayer. Support is highest in Happy Church Kenya and HTM Vietnam. Litanies and responsive readings are by far most affirmed by HTM Vietnam. Those least likely to affirm litanies and responsive readings are LMC United States, Amor Viviente Honduras, IMC Philippines, GKM Indonesia, and FCA India.

Of all the worship preferences we have described, respondents in all of the churches feel most positive about sharing testimonies in their worship services. Forty-five percent or more of respondents in each church feel strongly that testimonies are an important part of the worship experience. Clearly, there is something about shared experience, the struggle of human souls, and the faithfulness of a loving God that echoes in the hearts of Anabaptist Christians.

Table 5.19 Percent who feel very positive about testimonies in worship

| Church | Feel Very Positive |
| --- | --- |
| Fellowship of Christian Assemblies | 49% |
| Persatuan Gereja-Gereja Muria Indonesia | 45% |
| Hoi Thanh Mennonite Viet Nam | 67% |
| Meserete Kristos Church | 57% |
| Kenya Mennonite Church | 66% |
| Happy Church Ministries International | 70% |
| Kanisa la Mennonite Tanzania | 66% |
| Organizacion Christiana Amor Viviente | 77% |
| Iglesia Evangelica Menonita Hondurena | 76% |
| Iglesia Nacional Evangelica Menonita Guatemalteca | 95% |
| Integrated Mennonite Church of the Philippines | 54% |
| Lancaster Mennonite Conference | 45% |
| Total | 59% |

Previous research suggests that Pentecostal churches are the most likely to have expressive forms of worship, and we found this to be true among the MNA Profile churches. As Miller notes, "the music that flows out of Pentecostal churches is populist in tone, resonating with the cultural taste of the common person."[9]

In general, Profile churches in the Global South prefer expressive worship relative to the North Americans in the study (LMC United States). Honduran (Amor Viviente and IEM) and Kenyan (Happy Church and KMC) churches are most

---

9. Miller, 2009:285.

affirming of expressive forms of worship; LMC United States, IMC Philippines, and GKM Indonesia are consistently the lowest.

The influence of early Mennonite missionaries may affect current worship forms in some of the churches, with KMT Tanzania being an obvious example. As the earliest target of the LMC United States mission movement, KMT Tanzania developed worship expressions and other norms that reflect those of LMC United States in the early twentieth century more strongly than other churches in the Profile, which received their mission presence a decade or two later. Each of the churches in the Profile has integrated the missionary message (both theology and practice) with local customs, stories, and history—but the timing of the missionary message and the forms in which it arrived continue to have an effect on them. The extent to which local context and culture shape the message compared to how the message shapes the context and culture seems to vary.

**Service.** Respondents were asked whether their congregation allows them to express and put into practice their spiritual gifts. Between 84% and 95% of members in all churches believe that their churches do so. Levels of agreement are highest in FCA India and lowest in MKC Ethiopia. All other churches cluster between 89% and 95% of their members reporting the opportunity to use their spiritual gifts.

In many regions where MNA Profile churches are located, HIV/AIDS has been a critical health issue, and churches have struggled to know how to respond. Knowing that some churches are actively engaging this issue and the health crisis it has created, the Profile asked about the extent to which congregations are working at alleviating the crisis and reaching out to persons who have the disease and their families. Compared to the churches in the Global South, relatively few LMC United States members indicate that their congregations are addressing HIV/AIDS (17%), but among other churches affirmation is strong. The only exceptions to this other than LMC United States are the Honduran churches (Amor Viviente and IEM) and IMC

Philippines. In all other churches, 64% or more of members affirm that their church life includes such ministries.

How HIV/AIDS ministries are defined, however, is not clear. In some churches where we know that there are no specific HIV/AIDS ministries, some respondents respond that they have such ministries, perhaps indicating that their churches are open to ministering to individuals with HIV/AIDS. Other Profile churches, including MKC Ethiopia, have active ministries to those with HIV/AIDS and its victims—often children—left in the wake of the disease. MKC has organized worship choirs for people with AIDS, programs to alleviate AIDS suffering, and counseling to assist affected families and congregations.

The desire to serve is strong among the Anabaptist churches in the MNA Profile. At least 84% of members in all churches agree "Christians should do all they can to promote social justice," with as many as 99% of members in several churches affirming this value. At the individual level, members dedicate on average between 3.5 and 6.7 hours per week in volunteer work for their churches.

Table 5.20 Percent who agree that Christians should promote social justice

| Church | Agree |
| --- | --- |
| Fellowship of Christian Assemblies | 99% |
| Persatuan Gereja-Gereja Muria Indonesia | 98% |
| Hoi Thanh Mennonite Viet Nam | 84% |
| Meserete Kristos Church | 88% |
| Kenya Mennonite Church | 95% |
| Happy Church Ministries International | 92% |
| Kanisa la Mennonite Tanzania | 88% |
| Organizacion Christiana Amor Viviente | 91% |
| Iglesia Evangelica Menonita Hondurena | 88% |
| Iglesia Nacional Evangelica Menonita Guatemalteca | 98% |
| Integrated Mennonite Church of the Philippines | 89% |
| Lancaster Mennonite Conference | 92% |
| Total | 91% |

## Conclusion

As we have seen in this chapter, there are few differences between profiled Christians in the Global South and those in LMC United States regarding the orthodox Christian beliefs about Jesus, the Bible, and heaven. There are major differences, however, in attitudes about some moral behaviors that remain very important to Christians in the Global South. The differences in responses between LMC United States members and the others in the MNA Profile suggest that North Americans are much less interested in a commitment to certain moral practices than are their brothers and sisters in the Global South.

It is also interesting to note that, regarding several important indicators of Anabaptist commitments such as entering the armed forces and voting, LMC United States members are less likely to consider them "always wrong" than are other churches in the MNA Profile. North Americans have been known to question whether or not Mennonites in the Global South are truly Anabaptist in their theology and commitments. Justification for that critique is not consistently supported by data in the MNA Profile. Beliefs regarding joining the armed forces and serving in the police force are two examples of Christians in the Global South remaining faithful to traditional Anabaptist perspectives.

The concern for right behavior among churches in the Global South is particularly evident in several countries. In India, for example, baptism occurs only after the convert's pastor is convinced that he or she has found victory over the temptations and vices that were part of their preconversion lifestyle. In some cases, this requires up to three years of intentional discipleship training. MKC Ethiopia offers a discipleship program that all new converts are expected to traverse, regardless of which congregation they join—reflecting the fact that the church maintains a standard set of discipleship expectations for new believers.

Early Anabaptists argued that it was the practice of faith in daily life that gave evidence of one's beliefs. For these followers of Jesus, faithfulness was only as deep as one's lived out commitments to serve others, engage in the Scriptures, and assemble together in worship. All of the churches in the MNA Profile agree that service is a key to the Christian faith, and most members feel positively about the use of their spiritual gifts to serve in their local congregations. The churches of the Global South also consistently link social action and service with a commitment to evangelism and outreach. Word and deed are one in these churches.

This chapter began with reflections on the early church and the importance that early church leaders placed on holding together belief and behavior, salvation and ethics. This has been important for Mennonites as well, whose Dutch leader Menno Simons is known for affirming an evangelical faith that is lived out in everyday life. While profile churches vary in their perspectives on a number of practices—from Bible reading to prayer to worship preferences—members of churches in the Global South in general indicate greater levels of Christian discipleship than do church members in North America. Older churches in the Profile tend to respond with more similarity—which may reflect when they received Eastern Mennonite Missions missionaries, maturation, or both.

# 6

# *Congregational Life*

> The enormous growth of Charismatic Christianity in Asia, Africa, and Latin America also means that it may continue to expand and influence all types of Christianity there and further afield. . . . In creative ways Pentecostals and Charismatics have promoted a globalized Christianity that has not lost touch with its local context. . . . This has become a phenomenon that preserves both global and local characteristics. . . . At least for the foreseeable future, the continued vitality of Charismatic Christianity is probably assured. The whole Christian church may be thankful that this is the case, for it may mean the salvation of Christianity itself in the next century from decline to eventual oblivion.[1]
> 
> —*Allan Anderson in* An Introduction to Pentecostalism

Despite theological differences between denominations in North America, congregationalism (i.e., the autonomy of the local congregation) remains a primary characteristic of Protestantism as it has evolved in the United States. While denominations in the

---

1. Anderson, 2004:286.

United States vary in their organizational patterns and tendency toward hierarchy or egalitarianism, congregationalism dominates, often making denominational unity difficult. Local congregations regularly differ from their denominations and often disregard denominational mandates or split away from the denomination altogether.

Unlike the state churches of Protestant Europe, the vitality and sustainability of local congregations depend on the engagement and interaction of the laity. In North America, most congregations are only as sustainable as their membership. When members disappear, the congregation dies. Not so in Europe, where congregations remain supported by funds from the state regardless of levels of membership.[2] The development of congregationalism in North America has meant that people in the pew wield substantial influence in shaping the direction of the local congregation. Most leaders serve—either directly or indirectly—at the favor of their members. When members desire a leadership change, it is typically granted. Such intense congregationalism has weakened American denominational structures in the last half of the twentieth century.

This evolution toward congregationalism has taken time and is related to historic developments in American religious history. Denominationalism flourished after the sixteenth-century Protestant Reformation. In North America, denominations became the vehicles of religious diversity as they acquired tolerance for other religious perspectives, a somewhat ambiguous identity, a de-emphasis on doctrine, acceptance of broader cultural values, low levels of religious commitment, and openness to ecumenical relationships.[3] It is arguable that the onset of denominationalism allowed the religious experiment in America to flourish without religious violence.

Most renewal movements begin with what social scientists often refer to as sect-like qualities. They are typically reacting

---

2. Christiano et al., 2008.
3. Wilson, 1959.

against more institutional and cumbersome religious forms. They tend to emphasize exclusive membership more than openness to all people and are relatively unwilling to make accommodations to the broader society of which they are part. Inevitably, however, sectarian groups in North America have moved toward the denominational qualities described above, accommodating the values and practices of the broader society, becoming more inclusive and inviting of all persons, and beginning to partner ecumenically with others in addressing goals and outreach to the world. Denominationalism leads groups to emphasize religious generalities and universal truths rather than unique beliefs and specific identities. In other words, most religious bodies and their adherents increasingly assimilate into the broader society and culture of which they are a part.

Denominations have weakened over time in North America, in large part because of the accommodating posture that is necessarily part of their nature. This has led to denominational switching by many members, who now see relatively little difference between denominations and little reason to retain denominational loyalty—evidence that denominations harbor within them the seeds of their own demise and loss of identity.

The decline of denominations in the United States since the 1950s has led to the increased importance of individual congregations in American religious life. Most church members today engage at the local level rather than at higher bureaucratic levels. To many lay members, the overarching denominational machinery has little relevance to the realities of their everyday lives and congregational experiences. Congregations as local communities of faith take on the greatest meaning in the lives of members. What occurs in these congregations and how they engage the world around them is a central sociological question.

The decline of denominations and the increasing status of congregations is also a byproduct of the decline of Christendom; as the historic structures of Christianity break down, the local context of faith gains importance in shaping identity and articulating vision.

138  *Winds of the Spirit*

Congregations in the United States have much greater autonomy than their European cousins did or do have. With its values of individualism, personal expression, and voluntarism—congregationalism has made sense within the cultural parameters of the United States. Congregationalism has not only meant that the congregation's sustainability depends on whether it has members or not; it also means that congregations hire and fire their leaders, decide their doctrinal positions and liturgy, and create their own membership guidelines.

Considering the importance of the local congregation, what follows focuses on the individual congregations that belong to the churches in the MNA Profile. We report member responses about their congregations and also reflect on the nature of congregations in the Global South. In addition, we address the question of differences between congregationalism in the Global North and the Global South.

## Organizational differences revealed in the MNA Profile implementation

The way in which churches conducted their profiles reveals differences in the ways they are organized. Certain groups in the Profile—including Amor Viviente Honduras, Happy Church Kenya, and FCA India—have fairly defined hierarchical models of leadership and quite efficiently completed the Profile data collection and data entry. Amor Viviente Honduras leaders asked their congregations to complete the Profile on a particular Saturday (the day of worship for Amor Viviente congregations), and nearly all did so. The Happy Church Kenya anchor created a PowerPoint presentation for regional leaders so that they could carry out the Profile. FCA India, which is organized with evangelists spread across various regions of India, gave several evangelists the responsibility of the Profile data collection; one alone logged nearly ten thousand kilometers carrying out the task.

Other churches had greater difficulty mobilizing their leaders at both regional and congregational levels to implement the Profile. In general, older and more established church bodies struggled more than younger churches. Churches facing the most challenges in carrying out the Profile were those in which local congregations and local leaders have high levels of autonomy, where there has been a history of division, and where there has been dependence on North American missionary presence and resources.

Organizational structures made a difference in the way the Profile was implemented in the different churches. Important factors influencing how local congregations responded to their denominational leaders included the general effectiveness of communication between leaders and local congregations, the level of authority assigned to denominational leaders, a church's origins relative to North American missionary presence, and the church's unity and cohesiveness. In addition, the more Pentecostal churches responded most readily to the Profile. Perhaps older, more traditional churches have become so laden with bureaucratic forms that they had trouble responding. On the other hand, churches that have been birthed in the freedom of the Pentecostal movement may be more flexible and responsive and may also attract members who give broad autonomy to apostolic-type leaders.

Interestingly, the size of a church, its growth trajectory, and the geographic spread of its congregations seemed to have little impact on the capacity of churches to carry out the Profile. For MKC Ethiopia—the largest church in the Profile—data collection was particularly challenging work, sometimes carried out at long distances from the central offices with only donkeys for transportation. Yet, participation rates were high among the Ethiopian churches, suggesting a strong central organization. FCA India also had strong participation from its leaders and members despite the challenges of geographic dispersion, strong recent growth, and concerns about giving out personal information in a context of Hindu oppression. Indian leaders were able to overcome such challenges, again reflecting the organization of their church body and the lower levels of congregationalist tendencies.

140   *Winds of the Spirit*

In sum, the churches that carried out the Profile most efficiently are those more indigenous in their beginnings, more Pentecostal, and less influenced by a direct North American missionary presence. Churches that had the most difficulty completing the Profile are the older churches with origins in the missionary efforts of fairly traditional Mennonites from the United States. They are the churches that are the least engaged in the Pentecostal movement and have the strongest denominational qualities discussed earlier in the chapter.

### Size of churches and congregations

Table 6.1 shows the number of congregations and members that each participating church reported at the outset of the Profile in 2008 (i.e., the population). It also shows the total number of congregations and members selected from each church to participate in the MNA Profile (i.e., the sample). The total number of congregations ranges from 20 (IMC Philippines) to 474 (MKC Ethiopia). The total membership of each church ranges from 771 (IMC Philippines) to 162,131 (MKC Ethiopia).

How and what kinds of numbers the churches report also reflects the organization of their denomination. For example, a leader of one church noted that they do not count membership very systematically, saying, "If you give money and come to our church, then you are a member." FCA India, however, clearly defines membership and restricts it to those who have experienced a rigorous discipleship program and have convinced their leaders that they are ready to faithfully follow Jesus. KMT Tanzania is less rigorous in this matter; when denominational leaders arrived at local congregations to carry out the Profile, they learned that some congregations had failed to provide their central offices with regular and accurate membership data. They generally found fewer attendees in congregations than was on record at the central offices.[4]

---

4. The average size of congregations was reported earlier in chapter 4 and varied from 34 in Vietnam to 342 in Ethiopia. The average of all twelve churches was 124 members.

Congregational Life 141

Table 6.1 Number of congregations and members for population and sample

| Church | Population Congregations | Population Members | Sample Congregations | Sample Members |
|---|---|---|---|---|
| Fellowship of Christian Assemblies | 43 | 2,497 | 25 | 1,566 |
| Persatuan Gereja-Gereja Kristen Muria Indonesia | 102 | 18,880 | 30 | 8,565 |
| Hoi Thanh Mennonite Viet Nam | 79 | 2,702 | 30 | 1,316 |
| Meserete Kristos Church | 474 | 162,131 | 29 | 9,549 |
| Kenya Mennonite Church | 98 | 8,814 | 25 | 2,477 |
| Happy Church Ministries International | 59 | 4,902 | 27 | 3,020 |
| Kanisa la Mennonite Tanzania | 126 | 19,129 | 35 | 5,850 |
| Organizacion Cristiana Amor Viviente | 32 | 8,642 | 15 | 5,522 |
| Iglesia Evangelica Menonita Hondurena | 136 | 4,753 | 40 | 2,012 |
| Iglesia Nacional Evangelica Menonita Guatemalteca | 105 | 12,000 | 35 | 3,990 |
| Integrated Mennonite Church of the Philippines | 20 | 701 | 20 | 701 |
| Lancaster Mennonite Conference | 167 | 15,951 | 39 | 4,011 |
| Total | 1,441 | 261,102 | 350 | 48,579 |

## Mission and outreach

Generally, members of all churches believe that their congregations are being faithful in engaging the world around them. An average of 92% of members in each church believe that their congregations have a clear mission and purpose. When asked if their congregation shares the message of salvation with those around them, positive responses are still high: the average positive response is 88%. A similar pattern emerges when members are asked if their congregation helps to meet the needs of the

142  Winds of the Spirit

community around them. An average of 87% of members in all churches respond in the affirmative—an overall level of agreement slightly lower than for the first question about mission and purpose. Apparently, while congregations strongly affirm the overarching purposes of their congregations, they are slightly less optimistic that their congregations are carrying out those purposes in mission to the communities around them.

Table 6.2 Percent who agree that their congregation has a clear mission and purpose

| Church | Believe |
| --- | --- |
| Fellowship of Christian Assemblies | 99% |
| Persatuan Gereja-Gereja Muria Indonesia | 94% |
| Hoi Thanh Mennonite Viet Nam | 99% |
| Meserete Kristos Church | 87% |
| Kenya Mennonite Church | 95% |
| Happy Church Ministries International | 95% |
| Kanisa la Mennonite Tanzania | 89% |
| Organizacion Christiana Amor Viviente | 96% |
| Iglesia Evangelica Menonita Hondurena | 95% |
| Iglesia Nacional Evangelica Menonita Guatemalteca | 90% |
| Integrated Mennonite Church of the Philippines | 96% |
| Lancaster Mennonite Conference | 89% |
| Total | 92% |

## Feelings about the local congregation

Members were asked about their feelings toward their own local congregations. Overall, they feel very positive. On average, 89% say that their congregation gives them many opportunities to use their spiritual gifts. An average of 92% agree that they feel personally supported by their congregation, with no less than 88% in any church agreeing with this statement. When asked whether their congregation helps them to feel connected to a community of believers, 93% agree. Interestingly, members are less likely to say that their congregations support the needs of elderly members (84%) than they are to indicate that their congregation values its children and young people (91%). Finally, a very high percentage overall—94%, with no church averaging less than 90%—state that a relationship with their congregation is very important to them.

## Comments from members about their churches

At the end of the Profile questionnaire, members were given an opportunity to say anything else about their church that they wished. The following responses—selections from several participating churches—give insight beyond the numbers regarding the relationship of respondents to their congregations. Differences in context, particularly between LMC United States and the churches in the Global South, are quickly revealed in these comments. Churches in the Global South face realities not known in North America that shape the relationships of members to local congregations. In addition, in contexts where there is great physical and material deprivation and few social services, the church is a center of spiritual and material assistance.

### MKC Ethiopia

- We need more biblical training.
- Our church is helping well the weakest.
- The Holy Spirit will give us strength.
- We have to grow up and be role models for others.
- There are not enough musical instruments—God is with us.
- We need ministers.
- We have no musical instruments and the house also isn't good.
- Our church has a good vision.
- Mission in the countryside is good—I am happy.
- We have to pray.
- I hope our church will reach a high position.

- There is a shortage of income—we have to help our church.
- Pray for God to help us.
- Drought and no highway.

## FCA India

- We need a church building.
- We are praying for a place to worship.
- Our church is good.
- If we have a place for worship more souls will come.
- I had pain in my leg, I went to church and God healed me.
- The sick were healed.
- I am spiritually growing.
- A witnessing church.
- Good fellowship in the church.
- I like to go to church—from church I am getting peace.
- I am getting power from the church.
- We have plot but no place of worship.
- No musical instruments.

## Happy Church Kenya

- People should promote holiness more than material gain.
- I would like God to continue helping me to worship in this church and to participate in any way.
- It is a fast growing church with a God fearing pastor—I am proud to be here.
- I love it. I would like to see it move to greater heights and have a massive, truthful congregation.
- The church should rise up to the level it is supposed to be.
- I am comfortable and spiritually fed in my church.
- My church has inspired me—I love to be a member here.

- It is a good church and has leadership—it is a place one can grow.
- I want to get saved, but I fear, please pray for me.
- I loved my church because it helped me to grow.
- All churches must know the welfare of its members.
- The church is good, worship is nice, but the majority of us don't take the work of God seriously.
- I do hope my church will represent Jesus in my nation.
- We should organize how we can see old people fit in our church; that is, use languages they can easily understand.
- It's a good church where everybody is somebody and Jesus is Lord.
- My church is ready to bring change to this country.
- We have enough room for growth and development.

## LMC United States

- I feel at home and I really appreciate our pastor.
- We have recognized a need to improve in some areas and are making an effort to grow and change.
- Stay biblical—not your own thinking of the Bible. Believe as it says.
- I have been welcomed by all members and invited to actively participate in the congregation.
- I love the closeness and comfort of attending our church.
- I think we need a revival in our church and teaching with meat and how to use God's word daily.
- Good group of Christians reaching out to our community—open door to those who are hurting.
- I am happy in my church—there is a family feeling.
- We are a good multi-ethnic congregation with very good leaders.
- I feel the Mennonite church is losing Christ as central focus. Lots of times I try not to even mention that I belong to a Mennonite church.

- We are a growing loving congregation.
- Our church is vibrant and receptive to the Holy Spirit.

## HTM Vietnam

- Pray that the church will be saved and experience salvation.
- Pray the Lord to open a way for His church to buy land and build a house of worship.
- One must be strong and gentle to witness in the grace of the Lord.
- A church that is growing in faith and all the believers are in harmony, equal to one another, and all helping one another.
- My church is growing and being lifted higher.
- I am very happy because the Lord provides blessings to my church.
- I have strong faith and I am proud of my church.
- My church . . . continually provides to me a basis of faith and belief in the Lord that is strong and stable.
- Please pray for us that we will have the means and finances to serve the Lord.
- Pray for us that we will have classes for the children.
- Pray for revival.
- Pray for the church to be saved.
- Pray that the church will grow, that we will have a house of prayer, and that members will have an income.
- I pray the Lord for enough to eat and to wear, and to have a house of worship.
- Please pray that our tribal and minority brothers and sisters will meet together with our lowlands majority people.

## KMT Tanzania

- We have to make sure that we find the face of the Lord.
- We shouldn't stop praying for those who are in need.

- God bless my church.
- Let us continue to pray to God so that he can give us peace.
- The church should promote evangelical service in order to spread the Church.
- We really need to spread our Church.
- We have to work together as a family and pray for orphans and those who don't come to church.
- Christians should sacrifice their heart in God's job and make sure that the church is in progress.
- The church needs to reform its old situation and Christians should work together as a team.
- The church should come up with new strategies on spreading the word of God.
- I love my church so much.
- What I think is we Christians need to stand firm in order to keep going on the same faith the church had before.

What follows are reflections about these comments and others that are not reported here but were also written down by Profile respondents:

1. Church members in the Global South express more physical and material needs than those in North America. Concerns about basic necessities, such as food and water, and church-related needs, such as musical instruments and a building, are absent in LMC United States responses. For churches in the Global South, the local congregation meets both spiritual and physical needs. In North America, the local congregational meets spiritual and emotional needs but is typically not seen as the source of material resources. This undoubtedly shapes the relationships of members to local congregations, making local congregations more central and important in members' lives in the Global South than in the Global North.

2. Regardless of church, Profile respondents express warm feelings for the experiences they are having in their local congregations and the sense of belonging found there.

3. North American Profile participants seem more focused on their denomination and issues of identity than respondents in the Global South. LMC United States members frequently express concerns about the direction of the larger church with which they identify, while participants in the Global South have much less to say about the broader church bodies to which their local congregations belong. This difference may be related simply to history—older churches have the opportunity to harken back to the way things were and to resist the way things are today, while newer churches without much history against which to react, focus on building their foundations.

4. Congregations in the Global South express more concerns about the young people and children in their churches than do North Americans, reflecting the larger number of children and young people in these churches.

5. In the comments section, many Profile participants in the Global South request prayer for immediate personal or congregational needs, indicating the importance of prayer for many of them.

6. There is more concern about witness and outreach in some Profile churches than in others, though all churches express a desire to be faithful in outreach. The most effective evangelistic activity is always local— occurring in time and space among real people with biographies and histories and social contexts. Thus, evangelism is more likely to occur when congregations are embedded in and identify with the local communities around them. The importance of locality for

Global South churches cannot be overlooked. In North America, where mobility and affluence allow members to avoid local engagements both in their congregations and in their communities, witness and outreach are often more abstract and focused on global needs instead of the immediate needs of those around the congregation.

## Waning denominationalism in the United States

Responses from the North Americans in the Profile suggest that denominationalism remains more present in North America than in the Global South. The effects of denominationalism in a post-Christendom world are seen in the heightened anxiety of members of LMC United States, who express concerns about their denomination, Mennonite Church USA. This anxiety makes sense. As churches move from sectarian positions to an established denominational identity (the history of denominations in North America), they become increasingly accommodating to the broader society and open to ecumenism. But in doing so, they inevitably begin to lose their identity. The angst produced by this common trajectory of church bodies in North America can be heard in the following responses from LMC United States members:

- I believe our church has our beliefs in line with God's word, but I am not convinced of the same thing of this larger organization Mennonite Church USA.

- I like the church body and its people, but coming from a small regional denomination of about thirteen churches, I have concerns about the larger conference it is part of.

- The broader Mennonite church: There's too much of a focus on peace. We should be more focused on people. . . . My church is foundational and has greatly inspired me to work with God.

- We have many new people coming. I like that a lot, but I also feel we are getting weak in the peace position.

- There are many in our congregation who are not aware of the many facets and affiliations of the broader church. Our leadership does not mention it.

- The Mennonite Church USA would profit from having less anxiety about numbers and giving more attention to spiritual renewal.

Such concerns are rarely expressed by church members in the Global South, where denominational distinctives and identities are less important. Although they periodically mention central offices or the larger church body, they rarely express anxiety about the direction of that church or about larger issues of theological identity. Instead, members are focused on issues of faithfulness and obedience, evangelism and outreach, and immediate physical and material needs—all concerns that are more local than denominational. From such responses it would appear that the churches in the Global South are growing without the kinds of concerns about theological identity or denominationalism that cling to the declining churches in the United States.[5]

## Conclusion

In their own periods of growth, it is likely that the churches of the West were also less focused on identity—since they were more exclusive and less accommodating in their origins—than is the case today. Churches in the Global South will likely move into their future without Protestant North America's denominational baggage. This means that local congregations, or congregationalism, will define the future of the church in the Global

---

5. Interestingly, the Pew Research Center's recent global survey of evangelical leaders showed that leaders from the North were much more pessimistic about the church's future than were Global Southern leaders.

South even more than it has in North America. This will lead to greater potential for diffusion and less likelihood that congregations will remain committed to a central denominational identity.

Does this mean that churches in the Global South are likely to divide and split from the denominational bodies to which they belong? Not necessarily. Where there is less tension at the central or denominational level, there is also less reason to leave that body. And, unlike many churches in North America, there is little historical evidence that the churches in the MNA Profile have the kind of DNA that would lead them to divide.[6] Despite their greater local orientation, to date the newer Anabaptist churches in the Global South have avoided the divisions that have plagued Anabaptists in North America. Perhaps the strong emphasis on congregationalism—without the umbrella of denominationalism as it developed in North America—allows congregations to stay connected to one another. Indeed, while the denominationalism that emerged from the Protestant Reformation may have created an accommodating context for religious diversity in North America, it may also be the best explanation for the divisiveness of Protestantism on the continent—including of Anabaptists. The churches of the Global South were birthed with a congregationalism indigenous to their own contexts that bypassed the phase of denominationalism so dominant in Christian history in North America. They are likely to exhibit less anxiety about denominational identity and focus more on the functioning and faithfulness of their local congregations. Perhaps this will become an area in which North American Anabaptists—now experiencing the loss of both Christendom and denominationalism—can learn and grow through their brothers and sisters in the Global South.

As Anabaptist churches in the Global South continue to be planted and prosper, it is safe to assume that they will be more

---

6. The fact that few historical divisions have occurred does not necessarily mean they will not in the future. Potential fault lines that could lead to division are leadership rivalries, developing doctrinal differences, as well as ethnic and tribal distinctions.

local than broad in their orientation, more concerned with meeting the spiritual and physical needs of their members than with shaping a particular theological identity, and more concerned with relationships in the local congregation and community than with denominational structures. As globalization occurs, the winds of change are working against denominationalism and in favor of local communities of faith where believers experience vibrant, warm, and nurturing relationships.[7] Since the first century, Christian communities have always expected that local congregations will be loving and compassionate communities that serve the church and the world and share the good news of Jesus Christ. Loving, serving, and witnessing sum up what it means to be a faithful local community of faith—and they are what we see in the data for all of the churches in the MNA Profile.[8] While concerns and emphases differ from church to church and context to context, all of the Profile churches give vibrant testimony to the blessing of belonging to a local Christian community.

---

7. Increasingly, global influences such as satellite television and the internet are having an effect on Global Southern churches, importing values and perspectives beyond those of the local culture and congregation. The long-term effects of these influences remain to be seen.

8. Guder, 1998.

7

# The Missionary Posture of Global Anabaptists

> Mennonites have long embraced the necessity for communicating the Gospel, but as I read it from the outside, it is often limited to the newest members of the community, that is to embracing the newly born of community members into the community, nurturing them, bringing them to faith, and discipling them. In many ways, it is a silent witness, a witness communicated through deeds much more than words. This may be a stereotype, but it strikes me that Pentecostals might be useful partners in the area of evangelism and mission when it comes to communicating the Gospel effectively by word.[1] —*Cecil M. Robeck Jr. in a presentation at Mennonite World Conference, 2006*

## Mission and the early church

In *The Change of Conversion and the Origin of Christendom*, Mennonite historian Alan Kreider suggests that a major difference

---

1. Robeck, 2006:15.

between the pre-Christendom church and the Christendom church is the local emphasis on God's mission in the former and the lack of such in the latter.[2] As mentioned in an earlier chapter, prior to the conversion of Constantine, the major societal distinctive was between pagan and Christian—those who chose to follow Jesus and those who did not. But after Christendom's establishment, the major difference in the church and society was between clergy and laity—those who were ordained and those who were not.

In Christendom, everyone was considered part of the church—except for the barbarians to the faraway North who still needed salvation. For many in the church and society, the need for local missionary outreach to neighbors, friends, and coworkers ceased to be relevant since all within Christendom were now considered "saved."[3]

As the impetus for local mission activity faded with the official church, the missionary movement of a Christendom church became a sending movement of missionaries to foreign contexts. Those who went—like the clergy who remained—were considered sacred and set apart in a way that was not the case prior to Constantine's conversion, when all believers were considered ministers and missionaries. Clergy and missionaries were now professionals, ordained and compensated. Ministry in Christendom was allocated to a few rather than to all. These few were to lead faithful and obedient lives, while expectations for lay members became minimal. Zeal for local missions disappeared along with standards of faithful discipleship.

Any local missionary movement after Constantine's conversion—at least in the Western church—was carried out by unregistered, underground believers churches.[4] Throughout

---

2. Krieder, 1999.

3. In reality, there continued to be followers of Jesus through the centuries who would from time to time stir local evangelistic activity, but they tended to be outside of the official church establishment.

4. It is too little recognized by Western church historians that there were always strong missional renewal movements around the official churches, whether within or without. Most frequently these impulses

European history, groups such as the Albigensians, Waldensians, Bohemian Brethren, and Anabaptists emerged as renewal movements with a missional edge, reaching out to their neighbors and inviting them to faith in Christ. Although these groups were typically discounted by the official church as heretics, they were in fact expressions of the early church's commitment to radical discipleship and Jesus' call to go into the world with the gospel. In the pre-Christendom church, baptism required both commitment to discipleship and evangelism. In Christendom, discipleship and evangelism were minimized and separated from one another—the call to follow Jesus was no longer Jesus' call to be sent out into the world. It became enough to believe in Jesus; mission activity was considered unnecessary and right behavior was optional. The radical movements of the Albigensians, Waldensians, Bohemian Brethren, and Anabaptists that emerged within Christendom were expressions of the same type of evangelical awakenings that would come later with the Baptists, Pietists, Methodists, and Pentecostals.

## Mission efforts among early Anabaptists

One can argue that the Protestant Reformation led by Luther, Zwingli, Calvin, and others primarily addressed reforms within the church. The reformers protested corruption, clergy abuses, and self-serving theology. But, in many ways, the changes that ensued were more about church forms and structures than they were about the "heart," which is usually so evident in renewal movements. For example, in the post-Reformation church, infant baptism rather than believers baptism, submission to the state rather than separation of church and state, retention of outer statues and iconography rather than a focus on the inner working of the Spirit, and the continued role of clergy as professionals rather than members of a priesthood of believers remained characteristic despite the break from Roman

---

were on the margins of the official churches since they were usually declared heretical by those churches.

156  *Winds of the Spirit*

Catholicism. But it was those leading the Radical Reformation, primarily the Anabaptists, who understood that such reforms were insufficient for renewing the church and transforming the world. Luther himself would later bemoan how little his efforts had wrought in changing the hearts and lives of ordinary German citizens—all too often, nominal Catholics simply became nominal Lutherans. Centuries later, Bonhoeffer would offer a similar lament: "If Protestantism had never become an established church the situation would be completely different. . . . [it] would represent an unusual phenomenon of religious life and serious thoughtful piety. It would therefore be the ideal form of religion. . . . [The church] must completely separate herself from the state."[5]

The Swiss Brethren and other Anabaptists demanded something much more radical than did Luther, Zwingli, or Calvin. Recapturing a pre-Christendom faith in which discipleship and evangelism went hand in hand, they called for obedience to Jesus and an experience with Christ that transforms hearts and lives. The Radical Reformers minimized distinctions between laity and clergy and engaged in local mission activity, which led to exponential growth despite persecution. In their radical call to follow Jesus, they reidentified the local missionary context. These reformers did not live with the Christendom pretext that everyone around them was Christian. Instead, they made it their responsibility to begin spreading the gospel in their local communities—despite the high cost of doing so.

While many Mennonites know about the first Anabaptist synod that took place on February 24, 1527, in Schleitheim, Switzerland, fewer are aware of a second gathering of Anabaptists that occurred in August of that same year in Augsburg, Germany. While the first synod defined the fundamental doctrines and practices of the new movement in the Schleitheim Confession, the second developed a program of mission for proclaiming these doctrines and practices, regardless of persecution. More than

---

5. Metaxas, 2010:55.

sixty individuals attended the second gathering. Missionaries were commissioned and sent out by twos and threes to places where Anabaptists were already emerging: Basel, Zurich, Worms, the Palatinate, Upper Austria, Franconia, Salzburg, and Bavaria. The missionaries were quite effective in their endeavor, with new congregations sometimes arising after only several hours of preaching. They were even accused of carrying magic potions to create spells for conversion. But the response of authorities was immediate, and some of the newly commissioned missionaries were apprehended before arriving at their destinations. The first two died at the stake on October 27, just two months after the Augsburg synod. Still others died later that year and the next by beheading, suffocation, and burning at the stake. In light of the threats they received, some recanted. Not one of them was able to carry on for long before either pressured to abandon their mission or put to death.[6]

For early Anabaptists, the radical call of Christian discipleship echoing so clearly from Schleitheim was necessarily connected to Jesus' radical call to take the gospel into a violent and dangerous world. For the Anabaptists, as for most participants in historic renewal, transformation of the heart led to a concern for and commitment to the transformation of the world.

## Mission in North America

The Radical Reformation and the believers church movement have inspired much of Christian mission over the past five hundred years of Christian history. But descendants of this initial sixteenth-century movement migrated to North America in the eighteenth century with less missionary zeal than the early reformers had. Persecution had taken its toll, and, as Robeck notes in the quote at the outset of this chapter, Mennonites became satisfied with limiting most of their evangelism to their own children. Any impetus for mission became a "silent witness," communicated more by deed than by word. In the

---

6. Hege, Christian and Harold S. Bender, 1957.

twentieth century, service projects, disaster relief, development efforts, and active peacemaking became the primary witness of North American and European Mennonites. From martyrdom to silence became the path of witness for many Anabaptists after the seventeenth century.

After Mennonites arrived in North America from Europe, it took nearly a century and a half for any sort of evangelical fervor to reemerge among them. It finally did so in the late nineteenth and early twentieth centuries, with the development of Sunday school and foreign mission involvements that would result in the birth of many of the churches in the MNA Profile. But the challenge for North American and European Mennonites to sustain their evangelistic voice continues. Juan Francisco Martinez, a Mennonite Brethren theologian, notes that Anabaptists have been called the "quiet in the land" for several different reasons: "One of them has been the inability to clearly define a mission of proclamation in the world or to clearly identify how one does evangelism and mission from a distinctively Anabaptist perspective." He suggests that conversation between Pentecostals and Anabaptists has the potential to allow the "Pentecostal evangelistic fervor" to rub off on Mennonites.[7]

Unfortunately, the evangelical nature of early Anabaptism is rarely remembered by Mennonites in North America and Europe today. We became a people who embrace our persecuted past but forget to embrace the call that led to the persecution in the first place. Perhaps the price our ancestors paid was so great, we determined to eliminate the risks of such a costly gospel. Or perhaps Anabaptist scholarship has selectively—intentionally or unintentionally—minimized the evangelical and pietistic nature of early Anabaptists. Jenkins suggests that Western scholars have long ignored the growth of Christianity in the Global South because they disdain or do not understand it; so perhaps some Mennonite scholars have revised history based on their own preferences.

---

7. Martinez, 2006:4.

Mennonite theologian Stephen Dintaman argues that post-World War II Anabaptist scholarship "gave only passing, nonpassionate attention to the work of Christ and the work of the Spirit in the inner transformation of the person."[8] The outcome, he says, is theological understanding without the fire to sustain it or pass it on to others effectively. He believes that a concern with right behavior without an emphasis on transformation through a personal relationship with Christ has left Anabaptists spiritually impoverished in a way that affects our missional engagement.

Because North American Mennonites have been so concerned with prescribing right behavior and detached from the transforming work of God's Spirit, we have difficulty connecting with broken people who are caught in addictions, dysfunction, and sin. With little to offer except the encouragement to do better, Mennonites have felt "frustrated and impotent when we met deeply troubled people who seemed incapable of change."[9]

## Mission and the church

Why were the early Anabaptists such effective evangelists, and why are their descendants in North America and Europe so barren in this ability? Simply put, the Radical Reformation recaptured the dynamism and faithfulness of the pre-Christendom church. Like all renewal movements since Christianity's inception, early Anabaptism readily crossed cultural boundaries. The gospel is at its core universal, emphasizing the love of a creator God who came to redeem the world and offer lost human beings a path toward wholeness, life, and light in Christ. The believers church—whether manifested as holiness or Methodist or Baptist or charismatic—is deeply aware of the universal application of the gospel. The believers church movement is a global movement—not Roman Catholic in its association with Rome, Lutheran in association with Luther, or Mennonite in its association with Menno

---

8. Dintaman, 1992:205.
9. Dintaman, 1992:206.

Simons. Rediscovering a limitless gospel, the Radical Reformation created a movement without boundaries.

These all-embracing renewal movements—so effective in crossing cultural boundaries and winning new converts—create a challenge for the Western church. Too often Western churches try to monitor and regulate missionary impulses by requiring an articulation of the gospel that will not threaten Enlightenment structures and rationality. A free-flowing, Spirit-led renewal threatens the status quo of the Christendom church, which too often reacts by trying to shut down mission engagement. Why, then, should we be surprised at the demise of the church in North America and Europe today? One could argue that the Spirit of God is dismantling the church in the West because it is getting in the way of God's mission, and that only the Enlightenment church's deconstruction will lead to renewal and new evangelical fervor.

George Ritzer, a social theorist, argues that Western society and the organizations of the twentieth century became precisely what Max Weber had feared—iron cages in which individuals were controlled by rational and efficient hierarchies. Values of predictability squashed spontaneity, control reigned in freedom, and quantity devalued quality.[10] North American and European churches are too often characterized by such values and their related structures, which have prevented the emergence of renewal and the movement of the Holy Spirit. Missionary outreach—local or global—inevitably challenges the church, but unless it is untethered from the constraints of the Western church, it will remain as unfruitful as that church too often has been. As long as the church restrains or controls the impulse of mission, it will be a dying church. But the church that releases its mission impulses will find itself freed as well.

### Mission and the Global South

Considering the MNA Profile churches, one is reminded of both the difference Christendom history has made in North

---

10. Ritzer, 2008.

America and Europe and the difference its absence has made in the Global South. Churches in the Global South, only indirectly influenced by Christendom (though in some contexts more than others), are radically aware of their local missionary context. Surrounded by Roman Catholics, Orthodox, Hindus, Buddhists, Muslims, and people of other faiths, those who choose to follow Christ immediately recognize that they are different from those around them who have not made that choice. Mennonites in the Global South do not share the evangelistic hesitation of their brothers and sisters in North America and Europe. While churches in the Global South show some variation, MNA Profile data reveal substantial differences in outreach and evangelism activity between them and North Americans.

The MNA Profile solicits responses regarding belief and engagement in activities such as personal evangelism, church planting and extension, ministries of social outreach, and intercultural witness. An illuminating portrait of current mission realities emerges from the data. For example, one question asked if Christians should do all they can to convert nonbelievers to Christ. All groups strongly agree. Other questions asked whether their congregation shares the message of salvation and helps meet the needs of the community. Again, all groups respond very positively. Differences between groups begin to appear, though, in responses to questions about personal commitments and practices.

Support for church planting varies among Profile churches. A high 97% of HTM Vietnam members say they would help plant new churches, and 50% of the members of Amor Viviente Honduras and MKC Ethiopia say they are willing to change locations to do so.[11]

---

11. On the question of church planting, respondents were asked to mark all of the categories that applied to them. In the Honduran Mennonite Church, those entering the data selected only one choice from each respondent for this question rather than allowing more than one choice, undoubtedly leading to fewer responses in other categories for this question.

## Table 7.1 Percent who agree that Christians should convert nonbelievers

| Church | Agree |
|---|---|
| Fellowship of Christian Assemblies | 98% |
| Persatuan Gereja-Gereja Muria Indonesia | 93% |
| Hoi Thanh Mennonite Viet Nam | 97% |
| Meserete Kristos Church | 85% |
| Kenya Mennonite Church | 95% |
| Happy Church Ministries International | 91% |
| Kanisa la Mennonite Tanzania | 91% |
| Organizacion Christiana Amor Viviente | 94% |
| Iglesia Evangelica Menonita Hondurena | 91% |
| Iglesia Nacional Evangelica Menonita Guatemalteca | 99% |
| Integrated Mennonite Church of the Philippines | 92% |
| Lancaster Mennonite Conference | 90% |
| Total | 91% |

Some of the older churches in the Profile exhibit less interest: LMC United States, KMT Tanzania, and KMC Kenya. In other churches, nearly everyone supports the idea of starting new churches: MKC Ethiopia, HTM Vietnam, and IMC Philippines.

Clearer differences between the Global North and South emerged when participants were asked whether they offer to share their testimony two or three times per month or more. The highest positive response is FCA India at 89%, and the lowest is LMC United States at 26%. All other groups range from 50% to 80%.

The range of response among individuals is similar when questioned if they lead others to faith two or three times per month or more. Here FCA India and KMT Tanzania rank highest at 77%, and LMC United States ranks lowest, with only 10% of respondents reporting such active evangelism efforts.

The Missionary Posture of Global Anabaptists 163

Table 7.2 Level of interest in church planting

| Church | Not Interested | Willing to Move within Country | Pray |
|---|---|---|---|
| Fellowship of Christian Assemblies | 4% | 14% | 38% |
| Persatuan Gereja-Gereja Muria Indonesia | 13% | 3% | 13% |
| Hoi Thanh Mennonite Viet Nam | 2% | 32% | 62% |
| Meserete Kristos Church | 2% | 20% | 20% |
| Kenya Mennonite Church | 29% | 21% | 26% |
| Happy Church Ministries International | 3% | 18% | 33% |
| Kanisa la Mennonite Tanzania | 19% | 7% | 20% |
| Organizacion Christiana Amor Viviente | 7% | 23% | 46% |
| Iglesia Evangelica Menonita Hondurena | 8% | 18% | 49% |
| Iglesia Nacional Evangelica Menonita Guatemalteca | 8% | 19% | N/A |
| Integrated Mennonite Church of the Philippines | 2% | 22% | 48% |
| Lancaster Mennonite Conference | 18% | 18% | 36% |
| Total | 6% | 19% | 32% |

On the question of whether or not they invite people to attend worship services two or three times per month, FCA India and HMC Honduras rank highest at 71%, and LMC United States participants come in lowest at 16%.

## 164  Winds of the Spirit

**Table 7.3 Percent of members who share their testimony at least two to three times a month**

| Church | Share Testimony |
|---|---|
| Fellowship of Christian Assemblies | 69% |
| Persatuan Gereja-Gereja Muria Indonesia | 56% |
| Hoi Thanh Mennonite Viet Nam | 79% |
| Meserete Kristos Church | 63% |
| Kenya Mennonite Church | 77% |
| Happy Church Ministries International | 74% |
| Kanisa la Mennonite Tanzania | 63% |
| Organizacion Christiana Amor Viviente | 50% |
| Iglesia Evangelica Menonita Hondurena | 57% |
| Iglesia Nacional Evangelica Menonita Guatemalteca | 65% |
| Integrated Mennonite Church of the Philippines | 62% |
| Lancaster Mennonite Conference | 26% |
| Total | 64% |

**Table 7.4 Percent of members who lead others to faith in Christ two to three times a month or more**

| Church | Lead Others to Faith |
|---|---|
| Fellowship of Christian Assemblies | 77% |
| Persatuan Gereja-Gereja Muria Indonesia | 55% |
| Hoi Thanh Mennonite Viet Nam | 65% |
| Meserete Kristos Church | 67% |
| Kenya Mennonite Church | 71% |
| Happy Church Ministries International | 63% |
| Kanisa la Mennonite Tanzania | 77% |
| Organizacion Christiana Amor Viviente | 65% |
| Iglesia Evangelica Menonita Hondurena | 74% |
| Iglesia Nacional Evangelica Menonita Guatemalteca | 69% |
| Integrated Mennonite Church of the Philippines | 30% |
| Lancaster Mennonite Conference | 10% |
| Total | 64% |

For most of the non-Western participants, it is clear that "mission" is something they are experiencing in their own backyards. They are inviting people to church, witnessing to them, and leading them to faith in Christ. This missional fire is most evident in the younger churches and seems to wane in older churches, though mission organizations in older churches tend to maintain missional zeal for intercultural outreach after the local zeal that gave them birth has lessened.

Giving evidence of an older church presence, mission boards, departments, and agencies that send people from country to country are located in the United States and Indonesia. Increasingly, though, they are found in places like Honduras and Ethiopia, as vibrant churches became mature enough to look beyond their national borders. An important question for churches as they institutionalize their mission efforts is whether doing so will cause them to focus less on local mission or lose energy for their own missionary contexts.

Table 7.5 Percent of members who invite non-Christians to worship services two to three times a month or more

| Church | Invite Others |
| --- | --- |
| Fellowship of Christian Assemblies | 71% |
| Persatuan Gereja-Gereja Muria Indonesia | 36% |
| Hoi Thanh Mennonite Viet Nam | 68% |
| Meserete Kristos Church | 53% |
| Kenya Mennonite Church | 69% |
| Happy Church Ministries International | 61% |
| Kanisa la Mennonite Tanzania | 70% |
| Organizacion Christiana Amor Viviente | 62% |
| Iglesia Evangelica Menonita Hondurena | 71% |
| Iglesia Nacional Evangelica Menonita Guatemalteca | 60% |
| Integrated Mennonite Church of the Philippines | 46% |
| Lancaster Mennonite Conference | 16% |
| Total | 58% |

## Political engagement and mission

During the last several decades, Western, postmodern conversations have begun to probe more deeply the legacy of Constantine. How much affirmation by the state and integration of church and state can the church handle before it compromises its witness to the world? Is even being affirmed by the state dangerous to the vitality of the church? These questions are crucial for the emerging evangelical movements of Asia, Africa, and Latin America as they have been in the United States where the integration of church and political activity has been detrimental to the church's witness. Ultimately, these questions must be answered by the churches themselves—not by Western thinkers whose history has been shaped by age-old struggles between the registered and unregistered churches of Europe and the civil-religious context of the United States.

While all the churches in the Profile are oriented to differing degrees to the propagation of their faith—locally, globally, or both—their perspectives on political engagement as part of their mission vary widely; it would be hard to isolate any part of the Profile that shows more diversity than this. Of particular interest are the answers to a question that is perhaps particularly Mennonite: Is it always wrong to run for political office? Fewer than 10% of respondents from LMC United States and GKM Indonesia answer yes. Yet, 70% or more of the respondents in INEM Guatemala and HTM Vietnam believe it is wrong. Between these two extremes there is great variation among the other Profile churches.

One could easily conclude that the global church simply doesn't know what it thinks about political engagement, and that may well be the case. At least in this group of Anabaptist churches, there is no unanimity. There seems to be no clear pattern or correlation between particular political systems and attitudes about political engagement. For example, in both Honduras and Kenya, the two Profile churches in each of these countries respond differently regarding political engagement. In Honduras, one-third of Amor Viviente Honduras respondents say it is always wrong to run for political office, whereas nearly two-thirds of IEM Honduras respondents said it is always wrong. Amor Viviente Honduras is far more urban: Are urban Christians more likely to opt for political engagement? One could also consider the origins of these churches, which are quite different. IEM was birthed out of the work of LMC United States missionaries in the 1950s, and Amor Viviente came nearly two decades later as a youth movement during the second wave of the Pentecostal movement.

Table 7.6 Percent who believe running for political office is always wrong

| Church | Believe It Is Always Wrong |
|---|---|
| Fellowship of Christian Assemblies | 21% |
| Persatuan Gereja-Gereja Muria Indonesia | 9% |
| Hoi Thanh Mennonite Viet Nam | 77% |
| Meserete Kristos Church | 44% |
| Kenya Mennonite Church | 53% |
| Happy Church Ministries International | 23% |
| Kanisa la Mennonite Tanzania | 34% |
| Organizacion Christiana Amor Viviente | 34% |
| Iglesia Evangelica Menonita Hondurena | 60% |
| Iglesia Nacional Evangelica Menonita Guatemalteca | 69% |
| Integrated Mennonite Church of the Philippines | 25% |
| Lancaster Mennonite Conference | 7% |
| Total | 40% |

In Kenya, Happy Church Kenya—in which 23% of respondents say it is wrong to run for office—has more members of the politically dominant tribal group than KMC Kenya, 53% of whose members say it is wrong to run for office. Most of KMC Kenya's members are part of a tribe that is less dominant politically. Does tribal affiliation affect theology? Or is it a matter of origin? Like IEM Honduras, KMC Kenya was formed from the witness of North American Mennonites in an era when most were against political engagement. Does the missionary DNA continue to impact that particular church? Both the sociological and the theological factors may well be influential.

How important is social standing in giving rise to different convictions about Christian political engagement? One thesis is that the lower one's social status, the less one affirms using the political system as part of Christian mission. This thesis seems to hold for Profile churches in Honduras and Kenya. A look at the history of LMC United States also corroborates this thesis. Perhaps the more wealthy and highly educated the church becomes, the more it assimilates into the larger culture around it and the more convinced it becomes that political engagement is a positive good. The two groups whose respondents say most strongly that it is acceptable to run for political office (LMC United States and GKM Indonesia) are the churches most heavily invested in the power structures of their nations, both in their wealth and their levels of education.

It is not surprising that different parts of the global church have different theologies of political engagement that are formed to a significant extent by their social status, origins, and other demographic factors. The Western church is becoming more acutely aware of both the strengths and the perils of Constantinian privilege at the very moment we are losing it. As the evangelical church grows in Africa, Asia, and Latin America, it faces the simultaneous challenges of how to use the new privileges it has gained through numerical strength and how to remain faithful in the midst of increased status and wealth.

The nature of a church's mission work is shaped by political engagement or the lack of it. At the height of Western power, the "managerial mission enterprise" of Europe and the United States resulted in the churches in this Profile. The new churches growing from that mission movement will challenge and reinvigorate global missions, changing both its politics and its theological formulations.

### Global or local mission?

Can a church focus simultaneously on its global and local mission, or does one always detract from the other? One could make a case from the data of this intercultural profile that global and local ministries are rarely found with equal intensity in the same church. Profile data also suggest that a focus on global mission reflects older churches, while a focus on local mission characterizes younger churches.

The Profile data suggest that there might be a natural missional life cycle in a church, beginning with a local perspective and activity, continuing with a movement toward the global, and returning once again to local outreach for revitalization and reengagement. Using this trajectory, FCA India could be described as first-stage (local), Amor Viviente Honduras and Ethiopia as second-stage (movement to global), and LMC United States as third-stage (global moving back toward local). At the same time, the cycle may not apply to the history of all churches. For example, the trajectory of a church's mission movement might be from local to national and back to local, without the global dimension at all—it is too early to tell the exact trajectory of most of the MNA Profile churches.

## Observations about Profile churches in the Global South

MNA Profile findings reveal the greatest differences between LMC United States and the churches in the Global South in the areas of evangelism and outreach. The following are several observations about the Global South in particular:

**Profile churches in the Global South are missional in origin, vision, and character.** They were born out of mission, and their missional character is never far beneath the surface. For example, profile churches in India, Vietnam, East Africa, and Central America are bursting with grassroots growth. In HTM Vietnam and FCA India, the mean of membership in the church is only five years. Of all Profile churches, only LMC United States has a mean membership of more than seventeen years. Most of the Profile participants in the Global South simply have not been in their churches very long.

With such youthfulness and growth, Profile churches in the Global South are asking for leadership training, discipleship programs, and economic development. Simultaneously, they are both interested and engaged in evangelism and local outreach. As some of these churches move into their second and third generations, intercultural mission is beginning to emerge more strongly, giving evidence to the fact that evangelism, church planting, and mission are part of their DNA.

**The churches in the Global South practice holistic ministry** without distinction between word, deed, and being. In the context of mission, the three are one seamless package. In one breath they speak of starting a dozen new congregations, and in the next they link this to meeting the human needs of people with HIV/AIDS, creating economic infrastructure, feeding the hungry, or sheltering the homeless. Their attitudes and ministries show that they have been largely spared Western debates over the primacy of word or deed, which are the product of the Enlightenment and Christendom.

**Church founders continue to shape church life in the Global South.** The identity of Profile churches in the Global South is closely linked to their founders. KMT Tanzania, for example, was founded by North American Mennonite missionaries in the 1930s. Now seventy years old, KMT Tanzania still possesses distinct traditional organization and leadership structures of the North American Mennonite churches of that period. Amor Viviente Honduras, founded in the 1970s by North American Mennonite missionaries Ed and Gloria King, reflects the equally distinct charismatic imprint of their founders. The influence of founders remains strong, both in the memory of the current leaders and in the shape of the church.

In at least three cases, church founders are still present and active in their denominations. P. C. Alexander, a missionary from South India who identifies with Anabaptist Christianity, still leads FCA India, and the choices he makes shape that fellowship of churches in powerful ways. Similarly, shared leadership in HTM Vietnam between former North American missionaries and Vietnamese pastor Trung are molding the patterns of the church. In HCM Kenya, founder Joseph Kamau leads a church that reflects both his more cosmopolitan and charismatic personality. As noted above, these three churches report the lowest mean years of membership (five years for FCA India and HTM Vietnam and seven years for HCM Kenya), revealing that they are, in fact, still being founded.

**Profile churches in the Global South are expanding their outreach, both in other cultures and locally.** MKC Ethiopia and Amor Viviente Honduras in particular are involved in intercultural mission. Strikingly, the members of these two groups scored the highest on percentage of members willing to move to another country for church planting: 31% and 28%, respectively. Amor Viviente Honduras runs a mission school that is preparing students for ministries in Spain, Italy, and Israel. Discussing this program, one of their leaders said, "We start with the individual's sense of calling [and] send them back to their congregation, so that it is actually the congregation that 'owns' the mission and sends them. In fact, *only* the local church sends missionaries; our task is to help *equip* missionaries and their congregation."

Foreign mission is not the only focus for Amor Viviente Honduras. The church's leadership understands the close connection between intentional discipleship and local mission outreach, and all members undergo seven years of discipleship training at three different levels. One leader explains, "The main people doing the real work is not the leaders, it's the young people. . . . Most members are in work teams; everyone has a team. This opens up the circle of impact to include lots and lots of young people." Young people are integral to Amor Viviente Honduras ministries.

Interestingly, the two churches with the highest levels of personal evangelism also have experienced the greatest persecution for their faith. Perhaps this is because opposition to one's faith creates opportunities to witness more frequently, one's motivation to witness is greater when under fire, or outspoken witness creates persecution. Whatever the case, the churches in the MNA Profile reveal substantial differences in their practice of outreach and evangelism—even though all embrace the idea that a gospel witness is important. Growing congregations show greater evidence of evangelistic practices than churches that are declining in membership. While growth and decline of a church may not necessarily be evidence of faithfulness or the lack thereof, it should be no surprise that congregations reaching out to others with the good news of Jesus will experience growth through the fresh breath of new converts who have found life and hope in Christ.

In Profile data, the outspoken witness of sixteenth-century Anabaptism is more strongly represented in the churches of the South, especially in locations where opposition to Christian faith is greater. Although our sample of contemporary North American Anabaptism is too narrow to draw conclusions, the "Anabaptist DNA" of evangelism and witness appears to be less apparent among LMC United States members than it is in the rest of the sample churches. This finding is consistent with Conrad Kanagy's 2006 profile of Mennonite Church USA, which reported that racial/ethnic members (many who are immigrants from Asia, Africa, and Latin America) are much more likely to report active evangelistic activity and outreach than are Caucasian Mennonites.[12] It would be easy to doubt the high levels of witness and testimony among many of the MNA Profile churches, particularly when compared to those of LMC United States. But other researchers have found that Pentecostals often share their faith on a weekly and even daily basis, in "stark contrast to the religious traditions from which converts are typically being attracted."[13]

## Conclusion

In this chapter we have argued that the Radical Reformers rediscovered the fundamentals of embracing the gospel—fervent love

---

12. Kanagy, 2007.
13. Miller, 2009:285.

for Jesus, experience of personal transformation, movement of the Holy Spirit, and commitment to mission and evangelism. We tracked changes that occurred as Mennonites migrated from Europe to North America, particularly their abandonment of missionary zeal. Worn out from persecution, they became content to rest and accept a quiet space where they were unthreatened and unafraid. Evangelistic activity was mostly restricted to deed rather than word. Anabaptism came to be defined in terms of right behavior rather than in terms of spiritual renewal or personal transformation.

Nonetheless, the Anabaptists of the Global South have rediscovered the zeal of the early Anabaptists. Emphasizing personal transformation through a personal relationship with Christ, experiencing the presence and movement of the Holy Spirit, embracing the charismatic gifts, and actively proclaiming the good news—these Anabaptists of Asia, Africa, and Latin America have the potential to reawaken the church in the West to the spiritual realities that have always been part of the Anabaptist movement. If not awakened, the Western church must face the likelihood of its demise in the coming generations. If the Enlightenment "leapfrogged" the Global South, as Donald Miller asserts, history just might reveal that the radical nature of Anabaptism in sixteenth-century Europe also leapfrogged North American Mennonites.

# 8

# Anabaptism from Sixteenth-Century Europe to the Twenty-First-Century Global South

> Perishing communities (and ideas) produce historians and sociologists and academic conferences. Flourishing communities produce preachers, missionaries, and prayer meetings. Right now the Anabaptist Vision is producing lots of the former, few of the latter. Unless there is some way to put Pentecost into the Anabaptist Vision its creative role in the Mennonite churches is exhausted.[1]
> —*Stephen Dintaman, Mennonite theologian*

Anabaptism represents the believers church movement of the European Protestant Reformation, with origins in the early sixteenth century—just a few years after Luther nailed his ninety-five theses to the Wittenberg church door.[2] Early Anabaptists are

---

1. Dintaman, 1992:12

2. January 21, 1525, marks the beginning of the Anabaptist movement as several of its early leaders baptized one another on this day.

sometimes referred to as "Radical Reformers" and their movement as the "third way" of the Protestant Reformation. Also identified as a "believers church" because they baptized adult believers, these followers of Jesus were radical because they wanted not simply to reform the church but rather to restore it to a New Testament simplicity. They were a third way because of their distinctiveness from both Catholicism and Protestantism in refusing to accept the protection of the state or embrace the power and privilege the state might offer. Some have suggested that the early Anabaptists were in fact the first advocates for the separation of church and state.

The entire Western evangelical missionary movement of the past three hundred years owes much to the faithfulness, persistence, and suffering witness of the Anabaptists. The believers church took root in many parts of Europe and particularly in North America, and later Protestant groups—including Baptists, Friends, and Methodists in England—adhered to many believers church principles. A still later expression of the believers church is the Pentecostal movement of the twentieth century. Like other renewal movements, the Radical Reformation was characterized by "energy, vision and direction because their adherents were people who loved the Lord with an unquenchable passion." Such passion, says Adrian Chatfield, is a "defining feature of all Pentecostal spirituality."[3] The early Anabaptists, she argues, were "ancestors of the Pentecostal tradition" in their love for the Lord.[4]

Prominent features of early Anabaptist Christianity include (1) an outspoken witness, (2) a willingness to suffer for the sake of Christ, (3) a commitment to one another as brothers and sisters, (4) dependence on the Word and the Spirit, and (5) an emphasis on discipleship and holiness of life. These qualities were manifested in Anabaptists' refusal to bear arms even in self-defense, which set them apart from other Christians of their

---

3. Chatfield, 1997:96.

4. Chatfield, 1997:96.

time. Their commitments also occasionally led to the practice of sharing possessions. Taking the Scripture literally and highlighting the words of Jesus in the Gospels, they demonstrated love for their enemies, refused to utter oaths, declined taking others to court, and rejected divorce. Christocentric in their reading of the Scriptures, the Gospels, and particularly the Sermon on the Mount in Matthew 5–7 were important to their understanding of what it means to follow Jesus.

## Anabaptism's development in North America

Anabaptism has evolved significantly in North America since the first immigrants landed in Philadelphia in the early eighteenth century and today is far removed from the Anabaptism of Europe during the Radical Reformation. As with most social movements, the charisma of early Anabaptism gradually faded and was virtually gone by the time it came to North America. Along with this loss of charisma, by the mid-seventeenth century missionary zeal and spiritual fervor had also been abandoned.[5] Several forces further contributed to the loss of spiritual vitality and evangelical commitment in the North American Anabaptist church. Mennonites settled into the peace and prosperity of their eastern Pennsylvania surroundings and focused on farming, raising their families, and establishing local congregations. Some have suggested that it was the persecution in Reformation Europe that caused early Mennonites in North America to abandon evangelism. Sociologists would argue that all social movements in one way or another eventually become routinized or institutionalized, and their original vitality is replaced by policies, procedures, and structures intended to sustain their earlier vision. Over time, the vision tends to be lost for the sake of sustaining the organizations and institutions that were supposed to serve it.

In the late nineteenth and early twentieth centuries, however, evangelical renewal movements in the United States began

---

5. Showalter, 1995:16.

to impact Mennonites. Evangelical fervor emerged among young people, who showed particular interest in evangelism and mission. Before long, Mennonites in North America became part of the global mission-sending movement. In addition to engaging in new, vigorous local outreach, Mennonites began to commission foreign missionaries to Asia, Africa, and Latin America. They experienced the excitement of connecting with a broader world that they had largely avoided until that time. One LMC United States member, who was a small child when this was occurring in the 1950s, recalls:

> The sending of missionaries to Tanganyika united congregations in the mission endeavor. Faith was strengthened as God answered prayers for the protection of these pioneering family members and a sense of stewardship was heightened. Glowing reports of Africans coming to faith in Jesus stirred enthusiasm. Regular air-mail forms came to my childhood home . . . as my mother faithfully corresponded with her sister. . . . I recall the bus trip in the early 1950s with my parents and friends to New York harbor to bid farewell [to departing LMC United States missionaries]. . . .[6]

But just as missional zeal was being renewed among Mennonites in North America, several other forces influenced their faith and worldview and ultimately affected their mission activities: World War II; Harold S. Bender's essay, "The Anabaptist Vision"; and Mennonites' broad embrace of higher education.[7]

Bender's essay, published in 1944, provided Mennonite scholars and church leaders with a template of what it meant to be Anabaptist that would be used for decades. Rather than creating his own Anabaptist vision, Bender accurately tapped a broad understanding among Mennonites in the United States about what it meant to be Anabaptist in the twentieth century.

---

6. Interview, Mary Ellen Shertzer, 2010.
7. Bender, 1944.

In doing so, he reinforced and solidified an Anabaptist identity for generations to come. In sociological terms, "The Anabaptist Vision" became a social fact, or part of the taken-for-granted reality of North American Mennonites for the remainder of the twentieth century.

In "The Anabaptist Vision," which was presented at the annual meeting of the American Society of Church History, Bender attempts to identify the seminal commitments of early Anabaptists. First, he says, Anabaptists perceived Christianity as discipleship. By this Bender means that Anabaptists recognized that all of life has been transformed by Christ. Faith in Christ is more than belief—it is action, obedience, or "an outward expression of an inner experience." Second, Bender asserts that Anabaptists redefined church as those who voluntarily believe and enter fellowship together—rather than belonging because of birth or by law and force. Third, he says, Anabaptist understandings of Christ demanded a response of love and nonresistance in the face of conflict, war, and violence. In part due to Bender's work, nonconformity, a believers church, and nonviolence became the defining characteristics of Anabaptists.

The shortcoming of Bender's articulation of the Anabaptist vision, as critiqued by some, is that it creates a context for right behavior and holy living without connecting such holiness to a personal relationship with Christ or to the power of the Holy Spirit.[8] By focusing primarily on Swiss Anabaptism and ignoring other Anabaptist impulses of the sixteenth century (such as that of southern Germany), Bender downplays the pietism, mysticism, and spiritualism of early Anabaptists, portraying them more for their ascetic commitments than for anything else.[9] Discipleship according to Bender is evidenced in doing good or denying self rather than by receiving divine grace,

---

8. For further critique of Bender's "Anabaptist Vision," see Dintaman (1992 and 1995) and Showalter (1995).

9. For a helpful discussion of historic streams of Anabaptist spirituality and mysticism, see Snyder, 2004.

as taught in Roman Catholicism; through the inner experience of grace communicated in Lutheranism; or by means of the mystical grace emphasized by the Pentecostal movement. Against these grace-oriented definitions of discipleship, Bender asserts that Anabaptists emphasize the following of Christ in everyday life in contrast to the institutionalism, mysticism, and piety of other traditions.[10]

While Bender accurately identified three elements that were important to early Anabaptists, he failed to recognize the fullness of what it meant to be Anabaptist in the sixteenth and seventeenth centuries. His self-acknowledged focus on the Swiss Brethren as his primary source for interpreting the Anabaptist vision led him to discount other manifestations of Anabaptist expressions that were more explicitly pietistic, mystical, and spiritualist in nature. Bender's vision failed to connect right behavior with the heart religion of renewal movements and with the Spirit's power evident in the early Anabaptist movement.[11] It failed to offer the good news of the Holy Spirit's transforming presence to the generations that follow.

Bender, as well as scholars who would follow him, tended to take early Anabaptist emphases on peace, justice, and community and lifted them out of the fullness of the Radical Reformation. While it is true that these were salient features of the movement, they were no more significant than the mystical dimension of the sixteenth-century reformers' faith. Indeed, one could argue that the pietistic and pre-charismatic elements were most fundamental and affected how the Radical Reformers articulated peace, discipleship, and the nature of the church. Historian C. Arnold Snyder writes,

---

10. Bender, 1944.

11. Even early Anabaptist leaders such as Menno Simons, who explicitly rejected spiritualist and prophetic streams, still emphasized the power of the Spirit for regeneration and new birth in Christ. This emphasis on the Holy Spirit was minimized, however, in the ongoing development of Anabaptist theology over the following centuries such that Anabaptists today by and large have no substantive pneumatology.

It is not an overstatement to say that early Anabaptist pneumatology was the *sine qua non* of the movement. The appeal to an active working of the Holy Spirit in believers was the bedrock on which rested anticlericalism and anti-sacramentalism. . . . Likewise the "letter of the scripture" remained a "dead letter" if it were not interpreted in the power of the Holy Spirit. And again, the life of discipleship which led to salvation rested on the regenerative activity of the Holy Spirit, which made discipleship possible. . . . The emergence of Anabaptism as a church renewal movement would not have taken place apart from the pneumatological rationale and impulse that underlay its more "visible" features.[12]

Too often, the heart and soul of the Radical Reformation has been missing in Mennonites' scholarly discussions, and the relative decline of the North American Mennonite church could be seen as one outcome. Says Dintaman,

The verdict of history will be that the Anabaptist Vision was essentially a one-generation phenomenon. . . . the Anabaptist Vision no long offers us significant resources for the renewal and sustaining of a vital Christian life. . . . The children of the Anabaptist Vision will not find in it what their parents found. They will either maintain a Mennonite identity based on social service ideals . . . or abandon faith. . . . Or they will find their way back to the primal Christian truths that were assumed but not expressed in their upbringing.[13]

At the very time that Bender articulated his vision, Mennonites in North America were walking a pathway that would make them solidly middle class within just two generations. Until World War II, during the time Bender was writing, Mennonites were largely rural farmers and relatively few went on for higher education. But Mennonites living after World War II changed that. In part, the

---

12. Snyder, 1994:389.
13. Dintaman, 1995:10.

shift was due to many Mennonites' exposure to the broader world during their time as conscientious objectors, when they chose alternative service instead of military engagement. To fulfill their service obligations, they dispersed throughout the United States and Canada into hospitals, camps, and other assignment locations. When these men and women returned, they recognized in new ways the need for and usefulness of higher education, particularly if they were going to faithfully articulate the major themes of the Anabaptist Vision.

Over the next several decades, with the Anabaptist Vision in view, young Mennonites would embrace higher education at levels exceeded by only a few other denominations (i.e., Presbyterians, Reformed Jews, and Anglicans).[14] Today, nearly 40% of Mennonites in the United States have a four-year degree. Mennonites have moved from farms to suburban and urban areas and from agricultural and blue-collar occupations to professional ones. In two generations, Mennonites in North America have transitioned from the American cultural shadows firmly into the social and political American middle. For few other denominations in the United States has the ascent from working class to middle class been so quick and the consequences so dramatic.[15]

Bender's articulation of what it means to be Anabaptist—focused on peacemaking and social justice without connecting to issues of the heart and spirit—created a Mennonite ethos that felt compatible with their embrace of higher education and rational view of God and society. Bender's vision of Anabaptism and the new social status of Mennonites reinforced one another. Educated individuals, with their liberalized and critical perspective, had no problem with a vision of right behavior focused on social concerns detached from the pietistic, pre-charismatic expressions of the early Anabaptists. Even the most enlightened could embrace Bender's vision.[16]

---

14. Kanagy, 2007.

15. Kanagy, 2007.

16. It is true that the impact of Bender's writing would vary among Mennonites—those in more rural regions of the U.S. and less connected

What few seemed to sense at the time was the eventual deterioration that is inevitable when a religious identity is supported both by a strong cultural identity and by an enhanced social status but lacks a heartfelt relationship with Christ. Educated Mennonites who promoted peacemaking began to align themselves with other activists, regardless of their faith commitments or relationship with Christ. Peacemaking and social justice became disconnected from Christocentric theology. Notes Dintaman,

> We discovered that nonviolence, which Mennonites had historically rooted in Christology, eschatology and piety, can also express itself as political strategy. But progressively the language of eschatology and piety became strange to us and nonviolence came to be explained and understood within the framework of political strategy.[17]

This interpretation of Anabaptist history does not deny the importance of peacemaking as part of following Jesus. Peacemaking has had an important place historically in all renewal movements. An authentic experience of the Holy Spirit's presence should always lead one to a peacemaking position—but a commitment to peacemaking alone will not necessarily lead to an embrace of the Lordship of Christ or to submission to the Spirit's movement and power. But, as a movement loses its Christocentric focus, the power to live as a peacemaker is also lost. Too many Mennonites in the last half of the twentieth century have become comfortable with connecting their peace concerns to those of others who do not embrace a Christian perspective on peacemaking.[18]

While it is true that an increasing number of North American theologians and representatives of other Christian

---

to the denomination were less likely to be characterized or to embrace certain elements of "The Anabaptist Vision."

17. Dintaman, 1992:4.

18. For a recent assessment of the change in attitudes about peacemaking and the movement from traditional nonresistance to social activism, see Stutzman, 2011.

traditions have recently been attracted to Anabaptist theology, it is not uncommon to hear the surprise of such individuals when they learn how little this theology is operationalized or evident in Mennonite congregations. Often, those who are attracted to Anabaptist theology come from traditions already deeply grounded in clear commitments to Jesus and even the embrace of the Holy Spirit. For these individuals, the Anabaptist focus on ethics makes sense because they hear it within the context of their own connection to Jesus. But for too many contemporary Mennonites, the separation of ethics from evangelical impulses has led to a spiritual dryness that may account for the decline of many of our North American congregations.

### Anabaptism and the global Christian movement

Anabaptists in the Global South, however, are neither constrained by nor products of Bender's vision. And they have not embraced higher education with the zeal of their North American cousins. The dominant social and spiritual force that has shaped them is the Pentecostalism of the Global South. Indeed, as noted earlier, these Mennonites are even more concerned about right belief than the descendants of Bender's vision; the bar for right behavior is much higher in the Global South than in the Global North. At the same time, the emphasis on holiness in Asia, Africa, and Latin America is an outcome of a personal relationship with Christ and a life empowered by the Holy Spirit. Holy living, intimacy with Jesus, and movement of the Holy Spirit are central to the Christianity of Mennonites in the Global South. North American Mennonite emphases on right behavior have meant less commitment to evangelism as proclamation. But witness in both word and deed is as characteristic of Mennonites in the Global South as it was of early Anabaptists.

Because of their holy living, transformed lifestyles, and proactive evangelical witness, members of Global South churches—at least those in the Multi-Nation Anabaptist Profile—have more in common with sixteenth-century Anabaptists than with contemporary Mennonites in North America or Europe today.

This proximity to the Radical Reformers reflects several realities. First, neither Reformation Anabaptists nor Global South Mennonites experienced the direct effects of the Enlightenment and Industrial Revolution. This created an openness to the supernatural in general and more specifically to the movement of the Holy Spirit. Such openness in both Europe and North America was dimmed by the Enlightenment's focus on the empirical. Second, both groups emerged in sociocultural contexts where poverty, oppression, and persecution were much more common than they were for Mennonites in Europe and North America. These difficult contexts led to more literal interpretations of the Scripture and an understanding of the biblical narrative that is more consistent with its writers' intentions, since they were often writing from similar sociocultural situations.[19] The affluence, education, upward mobility, and emphasis on civil liberties in Europe and North America since the Enlightenment have too often resulted in a critical reading of the Scripture that minimizes its authenticity and meaning and dampens the expectancy of supernatural engagement in one's life and community. Anabaptism as it has evolved from Europe to North America has little in common with the social conditions of the Global South. Without renewal, it may one day be seen as an anomaly—with little connection to the Anabaptism of its forbearers or to the emerging Anabaptism of the Global South.[20]

In many respects, the entire Pentecostal movement in both the Global North and the Global South has substantive roots in sixteenth-century Anabaptism. The Profile churches in the Global South have a double claim on sixteenth-century Anabaptism: first, because of the heritage they inherited from North American and

---

19. Jenkins, 2002.

20. This is comparable with Jenkins's argument that the Christianity of the Global South has more in common with its medieval past than with European and North American contemporary Christianity While Jenkins is arguing this as a "catholic" writer, this same comparison is easily defensible for the believers church tradition (including Anabaptist/Mennonites) in the North and South.

European Mennonite missionaries, with their historic Radical Reformation expressions, and second, because of their connection to the Pentecostal movement of the Global South. Given the connections between the Radical Reformation and the Pentecostal movement, one should expect to find "Anabaptist-like" movements in the Global South that are not formally connected to Anabaptism but reflect Anabaptist values and are drawn to Anabaptist commitments. In many churches in the Global South—not just Mennonite—one finds a combination of evangelism, charismatic expression, and concern for social justice that reflects the values deeply embedded in the historic Anabaptist movement. This should be no surprise; the Anabaptist reformation and its values are not entirely unique but rather reflect commitments shared by all true renewal movements among followers of Jesus.

The question remains as to whether North American and European churches can accept the Anabaptism of the Global South as a genuine expression of the gospel, given its close identity with the Pentecostal movement. In our conversations with North American Mennonites, it is not uncommon for them to ask whether the churches in our sample truly represent Anabaptism—reflecting some skepticism as to their Anabaptist legitimacy. At the same time, those in the South are sometimes heard asking the whereabouts of the Holy Spirit in Anabaptist churches in the North.

The work and results of the MNA Profile convince us that Mennonites in the Global South identify with the Pentecostal movement in a particular way that is rooted in their Anabaptist commitments. Being Anabaptist in theological orientation necessarily makes them comfortable with Pentecostalism, and being Pentecostal in their commitments makes them feel at home with Anabaptism. In other words, Pentecostalism is a carrier of Anabaptist commitments in Asia, Africa, and Latin America. Pentecostalism has made it possible for Christians in the Global South to identify with being Anabaptist in ways that they could not without it (e.g., if they looked exactly like European or North American Mennonites). In sum, the Pentecostal movement in the Global South has created a pathway for the continued development and evolution of historic Anabaptism.

## Findings among MNA Profile churches

Most but not all of the groups in the MNA Profile consider themselves Mennonite. All of them, however, identify theologically with the commitments of the Anabaptist movement. Since each church body in the MNA Profile was selected from groups of churches that are Anabaptist by conviction and connection, the question "How Anabaptist are we?" was both embedded in the MNA questionnaire and arose repeatedly in our analysis and discussions with church leaders at the 2010 consultation in Thika, Kenya. Has the European expression of sixteenth-century Anabaptism survived in the DNA of these groups? How diverse are these groups in their expressions and understanding of what it means to be Anabaptist? To what extent is an Anabaptist identity of concern to leaders and members of these churches? Following are a number of our findings.

**Religious identity.** The MNA Profile questionnaire presented members with a set of "religious identity" categories from which to select those that best describe them. The categories were Christian, Anabaptist, Mennonite, Pentecostal, and Evangelical, among others. In the results, members of church bodies with the word "Mennonite" in their name are most likely to choose that term: HTM Vietnam, KMC Kenya, LMC United States, IMC Philippines, INEM Guatemala, IEM Honduras, and KMT Tanzania. Those most likely to identify as Anabaptist are GKM Indonesia, KMC Kenya, KMT Tanzania, IEM Honduras, IMC Philippines, and LMC United States.

A number of churches identify closely with evangelicalism, including Amor Viviente Honduras and the IEM Honduras. Only one church, FCA India, ranks high in its self-identification with Pentecostalism.[21]

---

21. Our argument in this book is that the charismatic nature of the Profile churches emerges not from their self-identity as Pentecostal or

## Table 8.1 Religious identity of members

| Church | Mennonite | Anabaptist | Evangelical | Charismatic |
| --- | --- | --- | --- | --- |
| Fellowship of Christian Assemblies | 1% | 11% | 43% | 75% |
| Persatuan Gereja-Gereja Muria Indonesia | 1% | 22% | 34% | 3% |
| Hoi Thanh Mennonite Viet Nam | 45% | 13% | 38% | 4% |
| Meserete Kristos Church | 32% | 16% | 8% | 6% |
| Kenya Mennonite Church | 66% | 32% | 7% | 5% |
| Happy Church Ministries International | 2% | 12% | 18% | 18% |
| Kanisa la Mennonite Tanzania | 63% | 39% | 26% | 7% |
| Organizacion Christiana Amor Viviente | 11% | 15% | 77% | 13% |
| Iglesia Evangelica Menonita Hondurena | 62% | 25% | 61% | 8% |
| Iglesia Nacional Evangelica Menonita Guatemalteca | 84% | 5% | 8% | 2% |
| Integrated Mennonite Church of the Philippines | 74% | 56% | 29% | 9% |
| Lancaster Mennonite Conference | 73% | 64% | 27% | 6% |
| **Total** | **35%** | **20%** | **31%** | **13%** |

**Peace and social justice.** We have noted that, in addition to their outspoken witness, early Anabaptists had a prominent commitment to peacemaking, even in the face of injustice and persecution. They taught that true Christians should expect to suffer and experience opposition and should always respond with love and forgiveness. Most early Anabaptists taught that Christians should not resort to violence either on behalf of the nation or in self-defense.

---

charismatic or from historic connections to such churches, but rather from a self-expression manifested in worship and evangelistic activity that is consistent with historic renewal movements. Thus, it should be no surprise that most do not respond to Pentecostalism as a religious identity.

## Anabaptism from Europe to the Global South

### Table 8.2 Percent who believe Christians should practice peacemaking

| Church | Believe |
| --- | --- |
| Fellowship of Christian Assemblies | 99% |
| Persatuan Gereja-Gereja Muria Indonesia | 97% |
| Hoi Thanh Mennonite Viet Nam | 97% |
| Meserete Kristos Church | 87% |
| Kenya Mennonite Church | 93% |
| Happy Church Ministries International | 95% |
| Kanisa la Mennonite Tanzania | 88% |
| Organizacion Christiana Amor Viviente | 95% |
| Iglesia Evangelica Menonita Hondurena | 90% |
| Iglesia Nacional Evangelica Menonita Guatemalteca | 99% |
| Integrated Mennonite Church of the Philippines | 93% |
| Lancaster Mennonite Conference | 97% |
| **Total** | **92%** |

Several Profile questions addressed one's commitment to values that have been historically important to Anabaptists. The percentage of members that believe Christians should do all they can to promote social justice ranges from 84% to 99%. The percentage supporting the idea that "Christians should do all they can to practice peacemaking" ranges from 87% to 99%. Indeed, churches in the Profile reveal little variation in endorsing these two historic Anabaptist positions.

Several other questions asked members specifically about their attitudes regarding certain activities that have long been important to Anabaptists. One such question was, "Is it wrong for Christians to fight in any war?" The individuals most likely to say yes to this statement are in HTM Vietnam, KMC Kenya, Happy Church Kenya, KMT Tanzania, IMC Philippines, and LMC United States—60% or more of each of these churches respond in this manner. Those least likely to categorically dismiss participating in war are members of the three Central American churches (INEM Guatemala, Amor Viviente Honduras, and IEM Honduras) and MKC Ethiopia, with percentages ranging between 39% and 49%.

190  Winds of the Spirit

Table 8.3 Percent who believe it is wrong to fight in any war

| Church | Believe |
|---|---|
| Fellowship of Christian Assemblies | 57% |
| Persatuan Gereja-Gereja Muria Indonesia | 55% |
| Hoi Thanh Mennonite Viet Nam | 74% |
| Meserete Kristos Church | 49% |
| Kenya Mennonite Church | 63% |
| Happy Church Ministries International | 70% |
| Kanisa la Mennonite Tanzania | 68% |
| Organizacion Christiana Amor Viviente | 47% |
| Iglesia Evangelica Menonita Hondurena | 45% |
| Iglesia Nacional Evangelica Menonita Guatemalteca | 39% |
| Integrated Mennonite Church of the Philippines | 71% |
| Lancaster Mennonite Conference | 73% |
| Total | 55% |

Table 8.4 Percent who believe it is always wrong to file a lawsuit

| Church | Believe It Is Always Wrong |
|---|---|
| Fellowship of Christian Assemblies | 15% |
| Persatuan Gereja-Gereja Muria Indonesia | 77% |
| Hoi Thanh Mennonite Viet Nam | 27% |
| Meserete Kristos Church | 21% |
| Kenya Mennonite Church | 34% |
| Happy Church Ministries International | 55% |
| Kanisa la Mennonite Tanzania | 40% |
| Organizacion Christiana Amor Viviente | 78% |
| Iglesia Evangelica Menonita Hondurena | 63% |
| Iglesia Nacional Evangelica Menonita Guatemalteca | 14% |
| Integrated Mennonite Church of the Philippines | 50% |
| Lancaster Mennonite Conference | 40% |
| Total | 40% |

Another belief that sometimes led to early Anabaptists' disenfranchisement from the broader society was their refusal to file lawsuits. "Is it all right for a Christian to file a lawsuit?" asks the MNA Profile. The strongest set of negative responses to this question come from INEM Guatemala, FCA India, and MKC Ethiopia, in that order. Two other groups, HTM Vietnam and KMC Kenya, join them, with more than 60% of members saying no. In eight of the twelve groups, at least 50% of members say no. Regarding swearing an oath in court—another Anabaptist teaching—50% or more members of eight of the twelve groups state that it is not acceptable to swear an oath in court. The greatest opposition to swearing oaths is in MKC Ethiopia and FCA India.

In each of these cases (swearing of oaths, lawsuits, and fighting a war), a majority of members in two-thirds of the participating groups agree with the historic Anabaptist position. In no case, however, does the strongest support for any of these particular Anabaptist positions come from North America. Some of the greatest evidence of Anabaptist commitments in terms of these practices are evidenced in two groups—MKC Ethiopia and FCA India.

Table 8.5 Percent who agree that they feel personally supported by their congregation

| Church | Agree |
| --- | --- |
| Fellowship of Christian Assemblies | 99% |
| Persatuan Gereja-Gereja Muria Indonesia | 96% |
| Hoi Thanh Mennonite Viet Nam | 96% |
| Meserete Kristos Church | 89% |
| Kenya Mennonite Church | 93% |
| Happy Church Ministries International | 94% |
| Kanisa la Mennonite Tanzania | 88% |
| Organizacion Christiana Amor Viviente | 90% |
| Iglesia Evangelica Menonita Hondurena | 92% |
| Iglesia Nacional Evangelica Menonita Guatemalteca | 90% |
| Integrated Mennonite Church of the Philippines | 96% |
| Lancaster Mennonite Conference | 95% |
| Total | 92% |

**Commitment to the fellowship of believers.** An outstanding feature of Anabaptism is congregations' commitment to caring for one another in community. The Profile questionnaire asked several questions to elicit the extent of this commitment. Other questions explored the feelings of members about their relationship with their congregations. Across the board, members feel good about their congregations and their connectedness to the congregations. For example, 88% or more of members in every church body say they feel personally supported by their congregation. And 87% or more agree that their "congregation helps them to feel connected to a community of believers."

Table 8.6 Percent who agree that their congregation helps them to feel connected

| Church | Agree |
| --- | --- |
| Fellowship of Christian Assemblies | 99% |
| Persatuan Gereja-Gereja Muria Indonesia | 97% |
| Hoi Thanh Mennonite Viet Nam | 98% |
| Meserete Kristos Church | 87% |
| Kenya Mennonite Church | 94% |
| Happy Church Ministries International | 96% |
| Kanisa la Mennonite Tanzania | 90% |
| Organizacion Christiana Amor Viviente | 95% |
| Iglesia Evangelica Menonita Hondurena | 94% |
| Iglesia Nacional Evangelica Menonita Guatemalteca | 90% |
| Integrated Mennonite Church of the Philippines | 96% |
| Lancaster Mennonite Conference | 97% |
| Total | 93% |

**Dependence on the Word and Spirit.** The Anabaptists were the sixteenth-century forerunners of contemporary believers churches, which emphasize both the authority of Scripture and dependence on the Holy Spirit. Profile findings on the Holy Spirit are covered in detail in another chapter; we only note in passing here that most participants in the study strongly emphasize the charismatic gifts of the Holy Spirit, though there is substantial variation in the experiences of those gifts. Members of LMC United States are least likely to have had such experiences.

Since how we read the Bible has been of importance to Anabaptists historically (they have emphasized the New Testament and particularly the Gospels), Profile churches had the option of asking their members several questions about their understanding of the Bible.[22]

The additional, optional questions about the Bible are as follows:

1. In your view, which Testament in the Bible has the highest authority?

2. Which part of the New Testament has influenced you the most?

Seven churches chose to answer these questions. LMC United States is the only church in which a majority answer the "New Testament" in response to the first question. MKC Ethiopia and IMC Philippines respond "New Testament" at 34% and 20%, respectively. These two churches also have relatively higher percentages answering "Old Testament": 10% in MKC Ethiopia and 9% in IMC Philippines. In all churches but LMC United States, a majority answer that the New Testament and Old Testament have equal authority.

The fact that members of Global South churches are more likely than North Americans to answer that the Old Testament has the highest authority is consistent with what others have noted about the Bible in Asian, African, and Latin American contexts: the stories of God's deliverance of his people resonate profoundly in the contexts of oppression, poverty, and persecution in which these churches are located. The prophetic words

---

22. In some ways this is a more contemporary Anabaptist question, not truly out of the sixteenth century. For the Anabaptists, the question was not "Which Testament has the greatest authority?" but "What is the lens through which you read the whole Bible?" When asked that question the early Anabaptists would have said that it was Jesus.

of Isaiah, Jeremiah, and others calling for justice for the poor, the widow, and the fatherless ring clear among those who for so long have been victims of global injustice.[23]

Table 8.7 Testament with the highest authority

| Church | New Testament | Old Testament | Both |
|---|---|---|---|
| Fellowship of Christian Assemblies | N/A | N/A | N/A |
| Persatuan Gereja-Gereja Muria Indonesia | N/A | N/A | N/A |
| Hoi Thanh Mennonite Viet Nam | 5% | 1% | 95% |
| Meserete Kristos Church | 34% | 10% | 56% |
| Kenya Mennonite Church | N/A | N/A | N/A |
| Happy Church Ministries International | N/A | N/A | N/A |
| Kanisa la Mennonite Tanzania | N/A | N/A | N/A |
| Organizacion Christiana Amor Viviente | 11% | 4% | 83% |
| Iglesia Evangelica Menonita Hondurena | 13% | 4% | 83% |
| Iglesia Nacional Evangelica Menonita Guatemalteca | 9% | 3% | 89% |
| Integrated Mennonite Church of the Philippines | 20% | 9% | 71% |
| Lancaster Mennonite Conference | 52% | 1% | 47% |
| Total | 24% | 6% | 70% |

Responding to the second question (Which part of the New Testament has influenced you the most?), a majority in all

---

23. See Martin, 2002:27 and Jenkins, 2002.

churches except LMC United States answer, "All parts equally." In LMC United States, 37% respond, "The Gospels," a much higher percentage than in any other church. The emphasis of LMC United States on the New Testament and on the Gospels in particular reflects strong teaching in recent years among North American Anabaptists regarding the teachings of Jesus and a Christocentric view of the Bible—a view that arguably interprets all of Scripture through the lens of the Gospels. This teaching is less prevalent among Mennonites in Asia, Africa, and Latin America, and there it also competes with the attractiveness of an Old Testament narrative of deliverance for the oppressed and judgment for the oppressors. The decline of liberation theology in the Global South has not meant a diminishing awareness of the social and economic inequities and injustices that continue to define the global church—rather, Pentecostalism has become a means of addressing these issues.

Profile members were also asked about the extent to which they read and study the Bible. In only three groups do more than 50% of the members report that they read or study the Bible daily. These churches are FCA India, HTM Vietnam, and INEM Guatemala, in descending order. The remaining churches range between 30% and 42%.

The three churches whose members report daily Bible reading have some of the lowest educational levels and highest levels of illiteracy among the Profile churches. They also have histories of physical persecution. Do groups with lower levels of reading ability actually read the Bible more? If so, how can this be? Western Christians' traditional emphasis of daily "reading the Bible" may skew our understanding of what is most important. Such a practice makes sense among a people with high literacy and ready access to the written Scriptures. However, most Christians in most generations have either been illiterate or have had limited access to the written Scriptures.

Historically, Christians accessed Scripture through memorization, meditation, and communal discourse. Paintings and other art forms have also played a significant role in communicating Scripture; icons, for example, have been important to the Eastern and Oriental churches. Believers memorized large sections of Scriptures, either through hearing it repeated by others or with occasional access to the written text. (It is well known that people who are illiterate tend to have greater capacity for retention of what they hear than those who are literate.) Memorization, in turn, gave rise to meditation. And Christian gatherings were filled with Scripture readings and recitation. Whereas the Western, highly literate church has emphasized discourse about the Scripture in preaching and teaching, the more traditional, illiterate church focused on reading and reciting Scripture itself, both in the celebration of the Eucharist and in the singing of psalms.

Table 8.8 Part of the New Testament with the most influence

| Church | Gospels | Epistles | Acts | Revelation | All Equally |
|---|---|---|---|---|---|
| Fellowship of Christian Assemblies | N/A | N/A | N/A | N/A | N/A |
| Persatuan Gereja-Gereja Muria Indonesia | N/A | N/A | N/A | N/A | N/A |
| Hoi Thanh Mennonite Viet Nam | 7% | 3% | 7% | 3% | 80% |
| Meserete Kristos Church | 12% | 13% | 6% | 17% | 52% |
| Kenya Mennonite Church | N/A | N/A | N/A | N/A | N/A |
| Happy Church Ministries International | N/A | N/A | N/A | N/A | N/A |
| Kanisa la Mennonite Tanzania | N/A | N/A | N/A | N/A | N/A |
| Organizacion Christiana Amor Viviente | 18% | 8% | 3% | 9% | 62% |

| Church | Gospels | Epistles | Acts | Revelation | All Equally |
|---|---|---|---|---|---|
| Iglesia Evangelica Menonita Hondurena | 15% | 7% | 3% | 10% | 66% |
| Iglesia Nacional Evangelica Menonita Guatemalteca | 6% | 3% | 2% | 5% | 84% |
| Integrated Mennonite Church of the Philippines | 11% | 4% | 5% | 7% | 73% |
| Lancaster Mennonite Conference | 37% | 12% | 2% | 4% | 46% |
| Total | 14% | 9% | 5% | 11% | 61% |

The contemporary global church has begun to rediscover the importance of orality in both the spread of the church and in discipleship. A high percentage of the global population—and the global church—is either illiterate or marginally literate. Must they learn to read in order to become devoted disciples of Jesus? A traditional Western understanding is yes, Christians must learn to read in order to be "good Christians." Otherwise, how can they know the Bible? But, as noted in our comments about memorization, meditation, and communal discourse, there are many other ways to do so. Whole congregations of illiterate people, often with illiterate pastors, exist in many parts of the world today.

For much of Christian history, a vast majority of Christians could not read or write and yet found ways to learn the Scripture and be disciples of Christ. Christianity has also thrived in the absence of Bibles due to persecution and government intervention. In Vietnam, for example, the government sometimes confiscated Bibles and hymnbooks. As mentioned earlier, one African leader chided LMC United States about their rates of daily Bible reading, failing to understand how a church so rich in books and literature could score so low in Bible reading: "What is the point of writing so much literature?" he asked.

198  Winds of the Spirit

Table 8.9 Percent who read or study the Bible daily

| Church | Read or Study the Bible Daily |
|---|---|
| Fellowship of Christian Assemblies | 84% |
| Persatuan Gereja-Gereja Muria Indonesia | 41% |
| Hoi Thanh Mennonite Viet Nam | 61% |
| Meserete Kristos Church | 42% |
| Kenya Mennonite Church | 39% |
| Happy Church Ministries International | 37% |
| Kanisa la Mennonite Tanzania | 39% |
| Organizacion Christiana Amor Viviente | 33% |
| Iglesia Evangelica Menonita Hondurena | 33% |
| Iglesia Nacional Evangelica Menonita Guatemalteca | 53% |
| Integrated Mennonite Church of the Philippines | 30% |
| Lancaster Mennonite Conference | 33% |
| Total | 43% |

Considering Christian history, the correlation between illiteracy and the reading of the Scriptures that we discovered is less surprising. Scripture is valued more by those who have less access to it. Where the written Word is scarce, those who can read and have Bibles do so assiduously, not only for themselves but also for all those around them who cannot. As noted earlier, groups with greater degrees of persecution tended to be more outspoken witnesses. Here it appears that they also read the Bible more faithfully. Although North Americans are the most highly educated church members in the Profile, only one group scored lower on Bible reading than LMC United States.

**Devotional life.** Profile respondents are asked how often they pray privately outside of corporate worship and prayer at meals. Responses vary dramatically, from 40% in KMC Kenya praying daily to 92% in HTM Vietnam. Levels of prayer tend to be higher in the Asian churches—all with more than 70% of their members praying daily. In INEM Guatemala and LMC United States, the percentages of members praying daily also exceed 70%.

### Table 8.10 Percent who pray daily

| Church | Pray Daily |
| --- | --- |
| Fellowship of Christian Assemblies | 73% |
| Persatuan Gereja-Gereja Muria Indonesia | 77% |
| Hoi Thanh Mennonite Viet Nam | 92% |
| Meserete Kristos Church | 52% |
| Kenya Mennonite Church | 40% |
| Happy Church Ministries International | 63% |
| Kanisa la Mennonite Tanzania | 65% |
| Organizacion Christiana Amor Viviente | 59% |
| Iglesia Evangelica Menonita Hondurena | 59% |
| Iglesia Nacional Evangelica Menonita Guatemalteca | 88% |
| Integrated Mennonite Church of the Philippines | 70% |
| Lancaster Mennonite Conference | 76% |
| Total | 63% |

Prayer is clearly an important part the ethos of churches in the Global South. Profile anchors enriched our data with stories of prayer activities in their churches. In FCA India, a group of women pray four hours daily, five days per week, in support of the church's ministries. The prayer group is in its sixteenth year. In KMC Kenya, a system of prayer focuses on deliverance from demonic activity. According to a Kenyan leader, this kind of prayer was not part of the practices brought to Tanzania and Kenya by LMC United States missionaries, whom he called "quiet and humble." Church leaders have since recognized the need for a different type of prayer to address demonic powers.

## MKC Ethiopia: an example of Anabaptism in the Global South

MKC Ethiopia exemplifies how Anabaptist churches in the Global South both reflect and differ from Anabaptists in Europe and North America. MKC Ethiopia has been actively involved in global Anabaptist fellowship and activities, including the leadership of Mennonite World Conference. When it first organized, one of the issues facing church leaders—both missionaries and Ethiopians—was what to name the church. Should it include the name Mennonite or not? Eventually "Meserete Kristos" was chosen. Drawing on 1 Corinthians 3:11, "Meserete Kristos" means "Christ Foundation." The selection of this verse was not coincidental; rather, it was chosen because it was the favorite verse of Menno Simons. So, while early MKC Ethiopia leaders were attuned to their Anabaptist roots, they also wanted to create an Ethiopian name that would give the church authenticity as an "evangelical church."[24]

Studying the similarities and differences between MKC Ethiopia's confession of faith and other Mennonite confessions, former MKC executive secretary Bedru Hussein found much in common. There are several differences, however, that he cited. The MKC Ethiopia confession of faith places more emphasis on angels, Satan, child dedication, and prayers for the sick. In addition, Hussein noted that the MKC confession gives less attention to peace, justice, and nonresistance to war than other Mennonite confessions of faith.[25]

Although MKC Ethiopia grew from seeds planted by Mennonite missionaries, the Pentecostal movement that swept across Ethiopia in the 1960s radically transformed the church—as it did other denominations in the country and throughout the Global South. While MKC Ethiopia is intentionally Anabaptist, it also reflects both the influence of the global Pentecostal movement and its own unique social and cultural context. In some ways, the Pentecostal movement has had a leveling effect in Ethiopia and other places in the Global South by removing theological and doctrinal distinctives and creating commonalities across denominations. Although many aspects of MKC Ethiopia reflect its particular context, its malleability to the global charismatic movement is not unique. Many churches in the MNA Profile share this experience.

---

24. Hege, Nathan, 1998.
25. Beyene, 2003.

## Family matters

As stated earlier, the Anabaptism expressed by MKC Ethiopia and the other Profile churches in the Global South cause some Mennonites in North America and Europe to question the Anabaptist authenticity of their brothers and sisters in the South. This concern emerges for several reasons:

1. Most churches in the Global South do not have a direct genealogical connection to Mennonites of Reformation Europe. This connection has been very important to Swiss and Dutch Mennonites in North America, who are often known to play the "Mennonite game," tracking common ancestry to discover genealogical relationships. Those who join Mennonite churches in North America often feel excluded by the ethnic lines that remain quite clear in these Anabaptist immigrant churches. Lacking a similar ethnic line of Swiss/German or Dutch descent, it is difficult for some Europeans and North Americans to accept the authenticity of Anabaptists in the Global South.

2. Global South churches may not state their commitment to peacemaking and nonresistance to war as strongly as do North American churches. For North American and European Mennonites, commitment to peacemaking has become the litmus test of Anabaptism. Any failure to embrace this as the gold standard of Anabaptism—even though many members in North American Mennonite congregations do not prioritize it themselves—leads to questions about one's Anabaptist commitment.

3. The Pentecostal nature of churches in the Global South leaves many in North America and Europe uneasy. As mentioned earlier, Mennonite theology and doctrine in Europe and the United States largely rejected pietist and spiritual streams in favor of an Anabaptism that

focuses on nonconformity and separation from the world—despite ample evidence of spiritualist elements among early Anabaptists as noted by C. Arnold Snyder:

> It is not an overstatement to say that early Anabaptist pneumatology was the sine qua non of the movement. The appeal to an active working of the Holy Spirit in believers was the bedrock upon which rested anticlericalism and anti-sacramentalism. . . . Likewise the "letter of the scripture" remained a "dead letter" if it were not interpreted in the power of the Holy Spirit. And again, the life of discipleship which led to salvation rested upon the regenerative activity of the Holy Spirit, which made discipleship possible. . . . The emergence of Anabaptism as a church renewal movement would not have taken place apart from the pneumatological rationale and impulse that underlay its more "visible" features.[26]

Not only are North American and Europeans Mennonites unfamiliar in their experience with Pentecostalism, they are also part of a long history of explicitly minimizing, if not rejecting, that movement.

## Conclusion

Despite concerns about identity within the Anabaptist family and differences between Anabaptists of the Global North and South, the data also show similarities in identity and commitment to certain expressions of Anabaptism. It is possible that God is using the offspring of North American and European Mennonites in the Global South to return the older churches to their original vibrancy and commitments—to rediscovering their roots as radical followers of Jesus—and to redefining contemporary Anabaptism.

The major historical concerns of Anabaptist Christianity are reflected to varying degrees in the beliefs and practices of MNA

---

26. Snyder, 1994:389.

Profile churches. Those that are most like the sixteenth-century Anabaptists in many of their qualities are younger churches in places where the church is growing rapidly and where converts often face hostile opposition to following Jesus. The churches most aware of questions of Anabaptist identity and most concerned that churches and individuals identify themselves as Anabaptist are the older churches that are struggling to be faithful to that identity after three or more generations of existence. In general, they are growing more slowly.

# 9

# The Holy Spirit's Movement among Global Anabaptists

> Pentecostalism is in our century the closest parallel to what Anabaptism was in the sixteenth: expanding so vigorously that it burst the bonds of its own thinking about church order, living from multiple gifts of the spirit in the total church while holding leaders in great respect, unembarrassed by the language of the layman and the aesthetic tastes of the poor, mobile, zealously single-minded.[1] —*John Howard Yoder, Mennonite theologian*

By now our assertion should be clear: one cannot appreciate the growth of Anabaptist Christianity in the Global South without considering the dramatic expansion of Pentecostalism that has shaped its expression. When considered a unified movement, Pentecostalism has been the fastest growing segment of Christianity in the past century, with membership estimates

---

1. Yoder, 1967.

ranging between 250 and 500 million members.[2] Pentecostalism has forever changed the face of the global church—including the Mennonite segment of that church.

The North American Pentecostal movement originated in the midwestern United States in the early twentieth century. In 1905, the teaching of Charles Parham in Houston, Texas, was overheard through a half-open door by an African American preacher named William Seymour. Seymour resonated with Parham's views of the baptism of the Holy Spirit. In 1906, Seymour became the pastor of an African-American Holiness church in Los Angeles. While locked out of his church for preaching that speaking in tongues is a sign of the Holy Spirit's baptism, Seymour and others experienced the baptism of the Holy Spirit manifested in being slain in the Spirit and speaking in tongues. When the home where they were worshiping began to overflow with both white and black participants, they rented a building on Azusa Street in Los Angeles. Meeting daily, participants prayed, worshiped, and experienced the presence of the Holy Spirit, and for three years Azusa Street remained the center of the new movement of the Spirit.[3]

From the beginning, the Pentecostal movement was holistic in its presentation of the gospel. The interracial makeup of participants—exceptional for the time—highlighted the radical and countercultural nature of the movement. Allowing women in leadership, focusing on social needs and the poor, and embracing pacifism further illustrated the barrier-breaking nature of the Spirit's arrival in the early twentieth century. Focusing from the outset on evangelism and mission, those who experienced the Azusa Street revival moved across the globe with the message of the Holy Spirit's fresh anointing. Known as the first wave of Pentecostalism, the movement eventually developed into several different Pentecostal denominations, including the Assemblies of God. A second wave of the

---

2. Miller and Yamamori, 2007.

3. Anderson, 2004.

Pentecostal movement developed in the 1960s and 1970s and swept across many Protestant denominations, as well as Roman Catholicism. More recently, a third wave of Pentecostalism has developed, identified with independent and other churches that embrace more expressive worship styles and create freedom for the expression of charismatic gifts.

## Explaining Pentecostalism

Pentecostalism emerged in the early twentieth century among those on the ecclesiastical and sociological margins of North American society, reflecting the fact that most renewal movements—including the Radical Reformation—originate on the periphery. In addition to emerging on the margins, Paul Pierson argues that renewal movements share the following:

- They are concerned about both the church and the world.

- Methods of selecting leaders are less institutional and more lay oriented.

- The Bible is rediscovered.

- The social arrangement of the movement is more egalitarian then hierarchical.

- The movement reaches out to society's neglected with ministries to address their needs.

- The Holy Spirit is manifested in unusual ways, such as healings, visions, tongues, and other miracles.[4]

As we have shown in the last chapter, both early Anabaptism and Pentecostalism share many of these renewal qualities.

Numerous hypotheses have emerged to explain the rapid growth of Pentecostalism over the past century, particularly in the Global South. In 1995, Harvey Cox attributed the growth to

---

4. In Lorenzen, 2005.

what sociologists commonly call the deprivation hypothesis. In other words, the poor and oppressed are attracted to a brand of religion that promises other-worldly rewards if they are faithful in this life. This hypothesis, which assumes that deprivation is a motivation for conversion, is a functionalist argument, in which religion is seen as providing hope and comfort to those on society's social and economic margins. Karl Marx also held this perspective. Writing in Germany in the mid-nineteenth century, Marx argued that religion is nothing more than an "opiate" or drug to dull the wits of the poor, keeping them from feeling their pain and revolting against the structures that oppress them. Regarding Pentecostalism, the deprivation argument assumes that those who are disadvantaged economically and socially and are living on the margins of society find the promises of health and wealth of some brands of Pentecostalism appealing.

Minimizing the strength of this argument, however, is the fact that Pentecostalism's appeal today is not solely among the poor but also increasingly among the middle class.[5] Not only are members of the middle class being attracted, there is ample evidence that Pentecostalism is also creating economic improvement among the poor in many countries and expanding the middle class. Pentecostalism, then, both attracts the poor and lifts them out of their marginal existence. Rather than being simply satisfied with promises of health and wealth in heaven (i.e., an other-worldly perspective), Pentecostalism creates a this-world orientation, much in the same way that Max Weber found in an earlier Christian renewal stream among the Puritans of the northeastern United States.[6] The deprivation hypothesis no longer seems like an adequate or full explanation for the rapid growth of Pentecostalism in the Global South.

Another suggestion made by some is that the Pentecostal movement is African in nature. Identifying it as such, scholars are suggesting similarities between Pentecostalism and indigenous

---

5. Miller and Yamamori, 2007.

6. Weber, 1904.

religions—such as ecstasy and possession—that make the Pentecostal movement more palatable and acceptable in Global South contexts than in North America and Europe. In other words, because many indigenous religions in the Global South acknowledge active intervention of the supernatural in daily life, Pentecostalism is particularly appealing, since it too advocates the direct movement of God's Spirit through miraculous acts (e.g., speaking in tongues, healing, visions, prophetic words, resurrection from the dead, exorcisms). In addition, a Pentecostal expression of Christianity is attractive because it offers freedom from and empowerment over evil forces, which are a dominant part of many indigenous religions. While it acknowledges evil and spiritual warfare, Pentecostalism promises its converts new power over such forces through faith in Jesus Christ and the presence of the Holy Spirit. Profile anchors in Kenya report that exorcisms and freedom from demonic oppression are often an entry point for many to become Christians; as individuals see their friends and neighbors delivered from fear of evil forces, they too are attracted to the gospel.

David Martin argues that Pentecostalism's expansion is related to the conditions of the modern world, which have created soil in the Global South that is ripe for Pentecostal conversion. The transitory nature of globalization and movements within and between countries and societies has made individuals and people groups more amendable and ready for transition and change. Martin writes,

> The question of what niches may favor Pentecostalism is ... bound up with the radical disturbance of roots, including traditional sources of authority and social control, and the accelerating compression of time and space in contemporary global society as people move about and become aware of new horizons and the options realistically open to them. ... the key lies in religious 'movement' accompanying and facilitating the movement of people.[7]

---

7. Martin, 2002:23.

Martin is adamant that Christianity is "chosen" and not "received" in today's global religious context, and, with the power of global migration to diffuse ideas and technology, it now thrives without the need for a missionary presence. In his view, Christian conversion in the global religious marketplace represents true indigenization of the gospel rather than the imposition of neocolonial forces.[8]

The idea of movement is important here, because the emergence of Pentecostalism has occurred within the context of a century of social, political, economic, and demographic change. Pentecostalism develops in places where there is openness to movement between the local and universal, traditional and postmodern, marginalized and middle class. Pentecostal conversion becomes a link that enables or reinforces transition for individuals caught in the winds of change. Using Martin's rationale, the rapid growth of Pentecostalism in the past one hundred years should be seen in part as an outcome of globalization.

Still others suggest that Pentecostalism's spread is due to its unusual fluidity across cultures.[9] These scholars assert that Pentecostalism's qualities, such as freedom of expression and a focus on one's individual relationship with God, allow it to enter new cultures in forms that are less constraining and less likely to be institutionalized than other Christian traditions. As a Christian renewal movement, Pentecostalism focuses on the core beliefs and practices of Christianity. Less tethered by doctrines, dress codes, and historical contexts than religious traditions that are closely tied to European or North American cultural identities, it can be adapted or contextualized more readily. In fact, in much of the Global South, Christianity prospered only after political independence and postcolonialism led to the departure of Western missionaries. Only then was the gospel able to indigenize and take on local forms and adaptations.[10]

---

8. Martin, 2002.
9. Vasquez, 2009.
10. Jenkins, 2002.

Rather than being the product of neocolonialist forces, the contemporary Pentecostal movement has its own internal energy and represents a "a repertoire of religious explorations . . . [occurring] within a Christian frame and apt for adaptation in a myriad indigenous contexts."[11] Unbounded by the centuries of tradition found in other denominations, Pentecostals are free to move wherever the Spirit leads.

Since its origins, Christianity has proved its ability to move across cultural boundaries with ease. This has not meant that it does so without carrying cultural baggage that is often destructive and oppressive. Christianity's ability to cross cultural boundaries has often resulted in syncretism, which occurs when the gospel as presented by missionaries or church leaders becomes integrated with other religious beliefs and rituals that are not Christian in origin. The differences between syncretism and the contextualization, however, are not always clear. Amos Yong, a Pentecostal theologian, cites an example from northern Luzon in the Philippines: an Assemblies of God missionary suggests that one group's practices are syncretic—including prayers for the dead and the slaughtering of animals at weddings and funerals. Yong, however, argues that the difference between syncretism and contextualization (i.e., indigenization) is more complex than the missionary allows. He suggests a continuum, with syncretism on one side and indigenization on the other.[12] Revealing a concern about syncretism, MNA Profile anchors shared worries about church members who continue to engage in indigenous practices with which they feel uncomfortable. They were very interested in including questions in the Profile about practices such as being present at ancestral worship, eating food offered to idols, performing non-Christian religious ceremonies, and believing in good luck.

One possible explanation for Christianity's permeable boundaries and the ease with which it flows across cultures is the

---

11. Martin, 2002:6.
12. Yong, 2005.

universalism of its message—a loving Creator God who offers salvation to a rebellious people. It may also be due to the fact that Christianity rose between cultures. Rooted in Judaism, Christianity emerged as a Jewish sect after Jesus' ascension to heaven. But, powered by persistent evangelism, the gospel soon took root in Gentile communities and forced early Jewish leaders to make critical decisions about the flexibility and permeability of their sectarian faith. At the Jerusalem Council and in other contexts, these leaders agreed that the gospel should not be limited by race, ethnicity, or culture, but rather should be able to contextualize as it spread. Less important than the early decisions these leaders made about circumcision and food offered to idols was the principle of contextualization that they represented—a principle that almost immediately embedded in the Christian faith tradition. Because of these factors, Christianity emerged as a missionary movement with permeable boundaries. The principle of permeability has much to do with the rapid growth of the church today outside of Europe and North America.

While sociological arguments must be considered, the question remains for some about whether or not the Pentecostal movement taps into a real transcendent presence. Miller and Yamamori—both Christian but neither Pentecostal—are unwilling to discount the movement of God's Spirit in the rapid growth of Pentecostalism around the world (even while acknowledging that this assertion is outside their investigation as social scientists).[13] As Christians who come from an older, charismatic Anabaptist tradition who have witnessed and worshiped in Pentecostal churches in the North and in the Global South, the authors of this text agree with Miller and Yamamori that one must be open to the possibility of a transcendent presence at work in Pentecostalism. Indeed, we would argue that God's Spirit is the primary dynamo in the Pentecostal movement, as it has been in other Christian renewal movements as well. Acceptance of this possibility does not discount sociological explanations of

---

13. Miller and Yamamori, 2007.

Pentecostalism but rather puts them in a larger, sovereign frame. This position acknowledges that social, cultural, and economic forces are all part of God's creation and the context in which God has always moved.

## Pentecostalism and liberation theology

Some argue that Pentecostalism has replaced liberation theology in the Global South as the leading edge of Christianity, expanding from the same energy that birthed liberation theology.[14] Miroslav Volf has suggested that, while the emphases of each are different, with liberation theology focusing on changed structures and Pentecostals on changed individual lives, both are concerned with material outcomes of salvation as compared to the nonmaterial focus of classic Pentecostalism. While Volf may be correct, there is relatively little interest today in the Global South in a gospel motivated by the political concerns of liberation theologians.[15] Liberation theologians appeal to the poor, inviting them to revolt against the structures of power that are perceived to be responsible for their oppression. The challenge for liberation theology, however, is that it often has been promoted more by religious elites and scholars than by those at the grassroots. And its solution has often been a costly political one—inviting the poor who are already powerless to challenge powerful structures from which it is difficult to imagine ever finding freedom. In many ways, liberation theology remains an ideology of the elites—the imagination for the change it promotes has been slow to infiltrate the masses. As one theologian from Argentina has noted: "Liberation theology opted for the poor and the poor opted for Pentecostalism."[16]

A limitation of liberation theology is its assumption that those on the margins are powerless, when in fact they sometimes

---

14. Jenkins, 2002.
15. Volf, 1989.
16. Miller, 2006.

find creative ways to co-opt those in power and resist oppression. As explained earlier, conversion to evangelical or charismatic expressions of Christianity over the last two decades should be seen less as a result of Western imperialism and more as a form of resistance by those on the margins. As Karl Marx noted (to whom liberation theology owes much in terms of assumptions about power and societal conflict), a revolution from the grassroots is difficult unless the consciousness of the poor is transformed. Liberation theology, nurtured by elites and largely articulated by them, did not readily win the imaginations of the poor. Pentecostalism has been much more successful at doing so, and its gains are much more likely to be sustained.

With the decline of liberation theology in the 1980s, Pentecostalism very quickly began to fill the ideological void. But Pentecostalism's definition of the problem of the poor and its solution could not be more different than that of liberation theology. Pentecostals approach the world's problems not as structural and collective but rather as moral and individual, and their answer is supernatural instead of political or economic. The promise is that each person can be empowered through the forgiveness of sin and the filling of the all-powerful Holy Spirit and bring about individual transformation now and the promise of heaven and eternal life later.

Pentecostalism as it is being manifested in much of the Global South is empowering members to be engaged in the political processes of their societies and to see politics as an avenue for greater freedoms and upward mobility. Pentecostals in the Global South tend to embrace capitalism, but in doing so they also teach the poor that, being made in God's image, they have inherent value and can be contributors to a better society. In contrast to the overt and radical nature of liberation theology, Pentecostalism's approach to social changes is more understated but also appears much more likely to bring about sustained social and economic change. Miller and Yamamori argue that Pentecostalism leads to upward mobility, entrepreneurism, and the development of skills that can be used in the secular world—thus accounting for a Pentecostalism that is thoroughly this-worldly, even as it promotes and creates opportunities for transcendent worship experiences. According to Miller and Yamamori, instead of creating greater differences between haves and have-nots, as capitalism is often expected to do, Pentecostalism is fostering a kind of egalitarianism that will be good for public citizenship. They are highly optimistic that the presence of Pentecostals will lead to greater civic engagement. The egalitarian quality of these churches makes them especially appealing to those who wish to cross status lines and become upwardly mobile.[17]

## Anabaptists and the Pentecostal movement

What are the beliefs and practices of MNA Profile churches regarding the work and movement of the Holy Spirit? Answers to this question are important because of the divide in North American Christianity between charismatic and evangelical expressions of faith. For example, for decades the two major associations of mission agencies in North America have been distinguished from each other in part by their different postures on the work of the Holy Spirit.[18] This question also deserves attention because of the relative lack of Pentecostal expression among Mennonites in North America and Europe over the last several centuries.

The Anabaptist family of churches has natural affinities with the Pentecostal movements of the twentieth century: Anabaptists have been described as the Pentecostals of the sixteenth century because of their mystical and pietistic emphases.[19] However,

---

17. Miller and Yamamori, 2007.

18. CrossGlobal Link (formerly IFMA) and The Mission Exchange (formerly EFMA) are these two associations. The first does not accept charismatic or Pentecostal member agencies; the second does. Both are evangelical and often meet together for resourcing mission leaders. EMM is a member of The Mission Exchange.

19. Williams, 1962.

North American Mennonites of the twentieth century reacted to the rise of the Pentecostal movement in much the same way as other conservative evangelicals. Only with the coming of the charismatic renewal to traditional Protestant and Catholic churches in the second half of the century did some Mennonites begin to self-identify as both charismatic and Mennonite. As a result, some elements of the Mennonite church became more open to the gifts of the Holy Spirit as interpreted by charismatic Christians.

Eastern Mennonite Missions, the mission agency of LMC United States, became one of the vehicles of charismatic renewal among North American Mennonites. Its connections with many of the growing Anabaptist churches in the Global South that participated in this study strengthened that charismatic focus. Furthermore, even before the charismatic renewal, Eastern Mennonite Missions had been influenced by the East African Revival Movement through its missionaries in Tanzania and Kenya.[20]

In these two ways, missionary engagement through LMC United States Mennonite Conference in the twentieth century was tied to significant movements of the Holy Spirit. The East African Revival defined itself more strongly in terms of reconciliation with others and a continual experience of cleansing through the blood of Jesus than it did as charismatic or Pentecostal. The charismatic movement, on the other hand, focused on the baptism of the Spirit. Both emphasized being led by the Holy Spirit and having a strong personal relationship with Jesus.

These renewal movements affected local church life in LMC United States as well as its missionary expressions. One objective of the Profile was to develop a clearer understanding of the embrace of the work of the Holy Spirit in its charismatic expressions among LMC United States as well is in its partner churches globally. Much like Miller found, we learned that Profile churches most explicitly embracing a Pentecostal

---

20. MacMaster and Jacobs, 2006.

approach are also engaged in trying to alleviate the economic suffering and marginalization of their people.

## Examples from Mennonite churches

In their study of Pentecostal churches in the Global South, Miller and Yamamori describe the leaders they observe as charismatic but not necessarily trained to lead organizations or interested in spending time creating bureaucracies. They are humble but at the same time risk-takers and entrepreneurs. "Many of the people who founded . . . programs were not trained to run major organizations. Nor was there any blueprint when they responded to what they viewed to be was God's calling on their life. Instead, they launched out, inevitably making mistakes and running into roadblocks . . . and then humbly regrouped and began again."[21] These are precisely the kinds of individuals leading the more Pentecostal churches in the MNA Profile.

In the San Pedro Sula district of IEM Honduras, district leader Melvin Fernández is a classic example of one whose charismatic perspective has empowered him to become increasingly entrepreneurial in the marketplace. As a way of offering an economic opportunity for those in his churches, Fernández developed a network of bilingual and trilingual schools throughout his district. The founding school is on his church's property and currently has nearly three hundred students in pre-kindergarten through twelfth grade. Attendance at the school is not inexpensive, as parents are expected to pay for tuition, books, and uniforms for their children. Students learn English and French as part of their education, and education in upper grades is entirely in English. Those who graduate to seventh grade make a two-week trip to the United States to visit other Mennonite churches, tour national sites, and attend a Mennonite school. Fernández speaks often of his expectation that this experience in the United States will offer his students an alternative to the poverty and oppression that is part of their everyday lives. He believes that such a change of

---

21. Miller and Yamamori, 2007:128.

perspective will position them to be leaders in their home country and around the world. The school slogan that children learn quickly is, "We are high level leaders who will transform Honduras and seduce the nations with love!" Throughout the surrounding villages, Fernández is organizing similar schools that will serve as a foundation from which to launch missionaries and professionals for Honduras and for the broader world. Although converted by earlier Mennonite missionary activity that was not charismatic, Fernández's faith has evolved so that he now fully embraces the charismatic movement of the Holy Spirit in his own life and in his congregation. Vibrant worship, speaking in tongues, prophetic words, and being slain in the Spirit are part of what characterizes worship at his church on a typical Saturday evening.

Fernández is not alone in promoting the educational and economic well-being of his churches. P. C. Alexander, founder of the Pentecostal-oriented FCA India, also constructs schools in villages where his pastors plant new churches. These schools are open not only to Christians but to Hindus as well. In addition, his leaders strongly encourage their young people to consider political careers, attempting to create a Christian alternative that challenges the rapid growth of radical Hinduism in the Indian political system.

The churches of Melvin Fernández and P. C. Alexander work closely with converts who come from poverty and oppression to provide them with economic improvement and upward mobility; other MNA churches focus largely on the middle class. Amor Viviente Honduras has drawn the bulk of its members from the growing middle class in Honduras. Its congregations are largely urban, upwardly mobile, and Pentecostal in worship and their embrace of the charismatic gifts. The church was birthed during the second wave of charismatic renewal in the United States and founded by a missionary who had been deeply influenced by that renewal. His encouragement of youth gatherings in coffee shops, "Jesus rallies," and work among local high school students kick-started a movement that would eventually develop into its own church. The movement was particularly attractive to Catholic youth who were restless with the formalities of Roman Catholicism and looking for a vibrant religious experience and fellowship.

A second example of a charismatic church that is drawing on upwardly mobile converts is Happy Church Kenya, begun by Kenyan leader Joseph Kamau. In the United States in the late 1970s to prepare to be a medical doctor, he felt called to become a church planter. Changing his education plans, he attended a Mennonite Bible school in Ohio and then returned to Kenya. Once home, Kamau organized a series of outdoor renewal meetings, out of which grew a church that is largely urban, highly educated, multiethnic, and charismatic—all qualities different from KMC Kenya, which was indirectly planted by Mennonite missionaries from the United States.

These examples show that Mennonite churches in the Global South are drawing from the lower classes and working to provide economic opportunities for their converts while also attracting members from the growing middle class in their countries.

## The gifts of the Spirit among MNA churches

In every Profile church except one, two-thirds or more of the members believe that the charismatic gifts are genuine gifts of God's Spirit. Only 65% of KMT Tanzania members affirm this statement—the lowest level of any church. This is not surprising, since it was the first church initiated by LMC United States missionaries, during a season of Mennonite life when the Pentecostal movement was most strongly resisted. It is to be expected that the North American Mennonite spiritual DNA from the first half of the twentieth century is more strongly represented there.[22] The Profile provides evidence that this is the case.[23]

---

22. Lancaster Conference missionaries went to Tanzania in 1933. At that time the renewal streams among eastern Pennsylvania Mennonites were linked most strongly to the evangelical revivals of the nineteenth century typified by such leaders as D. L. Moody. Resistance to "the Pentecostals" was high.

23. For example, the Tanzanian Mennonite Church, at 61% of the members, ranked well above all other participating groups in the

Table 9.1 Percent who believe that the charismatic gifts are genuine

| Church | Believe |
| --- | --- |
| Fellowship of Christian Assemblies | 90% |
| Persatuan Gereja-Gereja Muria Indonesia | 95% |
| Hoi Thanh Mennonite Viet Nam | 95% |
| Meserete Kristos Church | 75% |
| Kenya Mennonite Church | 81% |
| Happy Church Ministries International | 79% |
| Kanisa la Mennonite Tanzania | 65% |
| Organizacion Christiana Amor Viviente | 91% |
| Iglesia Evangelica Menonita Hondurena | 89% |
| Iglesia Nacional Evangelica Menonita Guatemalteca | 97% |
| Integrated Mennonite Church of the Philippines | 83% |
| Lancaster Mennonite Conference | 76% |
| Total | 83% |

Most other churches are very positive about the charismatic gifts, with the most positive Profile response regarding these gifts coming from INEM Guatemala (97%). The English version of the questionnaire used the term *charismatic*, which may have resulted in lower scores than would have been generated by using the word *Pentecostal*. In MKC Ethiopia, for example, only 75% of its members respond affirmatively to this question. Given that they are commonly known as *Pentes* in their local setting, it may be that a reference to "charismatic" gifts was confusing to some.

The bellwether question on the Holy Spirit in the Profile was "Have you experienced the charismatic gifts?" The three strongest responses (all above 90%) come from FCA India, KMC Kenya, and HTM Vietnam. More than two-thirds of the members of all other groups gave a positive response, with the exception of two: IMC Philippines (64%) and LMC United States (54%).[24]

---

percentage who feel very positive about hymns with four-part harmony. This was a strong worship conviction of the Lancaster Mennonite Conference in the early to mid-twentieth century.

24. On the questions of experience with the charismatic gifts,

Table 9.2 Percent who have experienced the charsimatic gifts

| Church | Have Experienced Gifts |
|---|---|
| Fellowship of Christian Assemblies | 97% |
| Persatuan Gereja-Gereja Muria Indonesia | 74% |
| Hoi Thanh Mennonite Viet Nam | 91% |
| Meserete Kristos Church | 77% |
| Kenya Mennonite Church | 92% |
| Happy Church Ministries International | 90% |
| Kanisa la Mennonite Tanzania | 88% |
| Organizacion Christiana Amor Viviente | 73% |
| Iglesia Evangelica Menonita Hondurena | 76% |
| Iglesia Nacional Evangelica Menonita Guatemalteca | 68% |
| Integrated Mennonite Church of the Philippines | 64% |
| Lancaster Mennonite Conference | 54% |
| Total | 80% |

The difference between LMC United States and all of the other groups in the survey is striking. Only slightly more than half of the North American participants believe they have experienced the charismatic gifts. In contrast, the average of those from the Global South is 82%. This is one of the significant contrasts we find between the churches of the North and the South; although the differences between the Global North and Global South in *belief* about the Holy Spirit are not substantially different, it is clear in this study that there are differences in experience and practice. There are also differences among the churches of the Global South themselves.

It became obvious that the way the presence of the Holy Spirit is experienced varies markedly. For example, the number of members who report having experienced deliverance from demons varies from more than 50% in FCA India and HTM Vietnam to fewer than 10% in INEM Guatemala and KMT

---

respondents were asked to mark all of the categories that applied to them. In the Honduran Mennonite Church, those entering the data selected only one choice from each respondent for these questions rather than allowing more than one choice, undoubtedly leading to fewer responses in other categories for these questions.

Tanzania. Those who report speaking in tongues vary from more than 50% in FCA India and HTM Vietnam to fewer than 5% in GKM Indonesia and INEM Guatemala.

The experience of healing as reported by the churches produces a notable exception to the general distinction between the Global North and Global South. Surprisingly, 42% of the members of LMC United States report experiences of divine healing, while only 14% of the members of MKC Ethiopia report this. Yet this difference is an anomaly, as the highest percentages of affirmative responses belong to the churches of the Global South, with HTM Vietnam (72%), Happy Church Kenya (68%), FCA India (67%), and IEM Honduras (67%) indicating the most experience with divine healing.

Table 9.3 Percent who have experienced specific charismatic gifts

| Church | Deliverance from Demons | Speaking in Tongues | Prophecy | Resurrection from Dead | Healing |
|---|---|---|---|---|---|
| Fellowship of Christian Assemblies | 55% | 58% | 32% | 7% | 67% |
| Persatuan Gereja-Gereja Muria Indonesia | 26% | 4% | 1% | 1% | 45% |
| Hoi Thanh Mennonite Viet Nam | 53% | 55% | 40% | 47% | 72% |
| Meserete Kristos Church | 33% | 24% | 8% | 4% | 14% |
| Kenya Mennonite Church | 35% | 9% | 8% | 7% | 64% |
| Happy Church Ministries International | 30% | 48% | 31% | 9% | 68% |
| Kanisa la Mennonite Tanzania | 8% | 17% | 19% | 15% | 61% |
| Organizacion Christiana Amor Viviente | 16% | 33% | 17% | 4% | 61% |

# The Holy Spirit's Movement among Global Anabaptists

| Church | Deliverance from Demons | Speaking in Tongues | Prophecy | Resurrection from Dead | Healing |
|---|---|---|---|---|---|
| Iglesia Evangelica Menonita Hondurena | 20% | 23% | 16% | 6% | 67% |
| Iglesia Nacional Evangelica Menonita Guatemalteca | 4% | 1% | 16% | 2% | 43% |
| Integrated Mennonite Church of the Philippines | 35% | 11% | 2% | 10% | 33% |
| Lancaster Mennonite Conference | 6% | 18% | 17% | 1% | 42% |
| Total | 28% | 28% | 16% | 8% | 46% |

## MKC Ethiopia: A case study

The history of the Meserete Kristos Church (MKC Ethiopia)—the largest Mennonite church body in the world—provides a window through which to examine in more detail the dynamics of mission, Anabaptism, and Pentecostalism that we have been exploring.

**Origins of the church.** MKC Ethiopia was birthed after the arrival of Eastern Mennonite Missions missionaries from eastern Pennsylvania in 1947.[25] The missionaries founded a relief center and hospital in Nazareth, in central Ethiopia. The missionaries quickly found favor with Emperor Haile Selassie and were granted permission to conduct mission work in areas outside of Orthodox Christian territory. By and large, education and health care were the primary emphases of these early missionaries, who saw little response among Ethiopians to the brand of Christianity they were proclaiming. Finally, ten believers were baptized in 1951.

---

25. Mennonite relief work began in Ethiopia in 1945.

**A movement of the Spirit begins.** Growth in the new church was slow. Missionaries remained the overseers of the church, establishing expectations and control that provided stability likely appreciated by church members at the time. But in the 1960s, the winds of revival began to touch Ethiopia through the arrival of Finland Pentecostal Mission and the Swedish Philadelphia Mission. The movement gained impetus with the activity of a Kenyan Pentecostal evangelist, through whom people were filled with the Holy Spirit and began to speak in tongues. The movement faced resistance from both the Orthodox Church and Protestant churches in the country.

In 1962, a youth movement began in Nazareth in close association with the Eastern Mennonite Missions missionaries. The group began to refer to themselves as "Heavenly Sunshine" and became active in prayer, fasting, and evangelism. The group developed a relationship with the larger Pentecostal movement in Ethiopia, from whom they received guidance and instruction on being filled with the Holy Spirit, speaking in tongues, healing, casting out of demons, and prophetic revelations.

**Dispersion of the movement.** The Orthodox Church eventually began to rigorously oppose the Pentecostal movement, and in 1972 the Full Gospel Chapel in Addis Ababa was closed and many members were detained and fined. As persecution flared against Pentecostals, they began to disperse and join local churches—bringing with them their convictions, songs, and worship styles. In this way, Pentecostalism gradually seeped into the content and worship styles of diverse churches, slowly changing the character of most denominations in the country.

Some time earlier, the Heavenly Sunshine group had begun to distance itself from the larger Pentecostal movement in Ethiopia. Even though MKC Ethiopia continued to relate to the group, Heavenly Sunshine members were hesitant to reciprocate out of concern that doing so would cause them to lose their vitality—they believed that MKC Ethiopia was a church without life and the baptism of the Holy Spirit. Nonetheless, by 1974, following the persecution of Pentecostals nationally, Heavenly

Sunshine members joined MKC Ethiopia. Their influence began to change MKC Ethiopia, bringing with it tension between the more charismatic youth and those who were accustomed to their traditional worship styles. Despite conflict, membership swelled and tithing increased as lives were changed. Witness and active evangelism accompanied healing services and the filling of the Holy Spirit. Existing church buildings could not contain the new crowds.

**Political turmoil and persecution.** Even as Pentecostal winds were sweeping Ethiopia, so were other winds of change brought about by political agitation among university students against Emperor Haile Selassie. Mobilizing around sympathies toward Karl Marx, Lenin, Mao Tse Tung, and others, the protests grew to include the working class. In 1974, the armed forces toppled the government and established a Marxist government. Interestingly, both the Pentecostal and Marxist movements developed at the same time and competed for young supporters.

Hesitating to persecute Muslims or Orthodox, the new government began to oppress evangelical Christians, including MKC Ethiopia, and closed all MKC churches in 1982. Leaders were jailed, bank accounts closed, and all activities banned. Without access to their churches, MKC Ethiopia members began to meet quietly in homes as cell groups. The church became self-reliant, since North American missionaries had been forced to leave the country. For the first time in the church's history, the entire leadership was from the charismatic stream.

**Deliverance and emergence as a charismatic church.** In 1991, after the removal of the Marxist government, MKC Ethiopia was once again formally recognized. It was a time of rejoicing, and thousands flooded to church services. MKC Ethiopia had fourteen congregations with five thousand members at the time it was closed, but amazingly, it reemerged with fifty-three congregations and thirty-four thousand members. The newly visible church had a clear charismatic orientation that included singing contemporary worship songs, raising hands and clapping in worship, healing through the laying on of hands, anointing with oil, speaking in tongues, and offering prophetic words.

MKC Ethiopia's story illustrates several characteristics that other scholars have cited about the growth of churches in the Global South over the last several decades. First, its numerical growth occurred especially after North American Mennonite missionaries gave control to local leaders and then left the country. Second, political independence and postcolonialism created space for the indigenization of Christianity in many societies around the world.[26] Third, although the origins of MKC Ethiopia were decidedly not Pentecostal in nature, the Spirit's movement in the country overcame any resistance that may have been linked to its beginnings. Indeed, the growth of Pentecostalism over the past several decades has washed across geographic and denominational divides like few other Christian movements have ever done. Fourth, the growth of the church and its renewal was rooted in the youth of the church, who have so often been the primary carriers of the new wind of the Holy Spirit in the last century. As a youth movement, it created tension with the leaders of the established church. Fifth, the oppression and persecution of the church resulted in its sudden growth—reflecting the fact that persecution has repeatedly generated growth throughout Christian history.

## Reasons for the North/South contrast

Why is there such a difference in our findings between the Global South churches (only one that explicitly identifies itself as Pentecostal) and the one representative from North America— LMC United States? This finding of hemispheric differences among Mennonites is in broad strokes the same conclusion that Philip Jenkins reaches: the emerging Christendom of the Global South is more strongly oriented to the experience of the Holy

---

26. Jenkins, 2002.

Spirit than is the older Christendom of the North.[27] What factors produce this contrast? The answer is complex, but we identify here a few significant factors:

**1. The emerging churches of the Global South are closer to their roots in the traditional religions of the world, in which the belief in good and evil spirits is powerful.** In contrast, the older churches of the North and West have tended to substitute the worldview of the Bible with one profoundly influenced by the Enlightenment and modern science. The Western scholarly community either denies or is agnostic about, for example, the existence of evil spirits, while the traditional cultures of Africa, Asia, and Latin America are deeply grounded in such belief. As a result, the Christianity that has taken root in these traditional cultures acknowledges a power encounter between the Holy Spirit of God and the demonic spirits that hold people in bondage. The very existence of the Christian church in the Global South is grounded in a lively embrace of the presence and power of the Holy Spirit to replace the power of the evil spirits.

**2. The new churches of the Global South have emerged in an era in which a leading edge of Christian renewal in the West has been the Pentecostal and charismatic movements.** While other renewal movements have occurred in the West, none have had the pervasive, widespread effect of Pentecostalism. Although historians trace its beginnings to the first decade of the twentieth century in the United States, it quickly became a global movement with powerful expressions in Europe and on other continents as well. Since mission is tied so closely to movements of Christian renewal, it is natural to expect that the renewal that was most vital in the West would be reproduced in the younger churches of the Global South.

**3. The traditional churches of the West are more dependent on their history, traditions, and intellectual wealth than on the explicit work of the Holy Spirit.** Overt experiences with the power of the Holy Spirit are more sporadic in traditional

---

27. Jenkins, 2002.

churches in the West than among their brothers and sisters in the Global South. Furthermore, because such experience is lacking, even Christian theology in these churches suggests unbelief in the movement of the Spirit.

**4. The churches of the Global South are *new*.** New, organic entities are full of energy; this is a principle of all life. Such entities are also more prone to radical experimentation and a new understanding of what distinguishes them from the more fossilized traditions from which they come. The newness of the church of the Global South makes it more likely that they will embrace the very essence of the Christian faith with abandon. The apostle John refers to this reality as the "first love" (Rev. 2:4). Jesus spoke of the importance of placing new wine in new wineskins. It may well be that when these new churches attain the age of two or three hundred years, they will be challenged by the same tendency toward traditional fossilization that plagues their sister churches in the North.

**5. Anabaptists in the Global South are closer to the sixteenth-century Radical Reformation than they are to Anabaptist expressions in North America or in contemporary Europe.** Being Anabaptist makes Mennonites in the Global South particularly comfortable with Pentecostalism, and Pentecostalism in the Global South may ensure the continued development and evolution of historic Anabaptism. It may be through Anabaptists in the Global South that Mennonites around the world begin to recognize and experience the affinities between these two Christian movements with origins in the sixteenth-century Radical Reformation.

## The future of Anabaptism and the charismatic movement

What does the future hold for global Anabaptists—and for the charismatic movement with which so many of them connect in some way or another? We have already suggested that the rapid growth of Mennonites in the Global South should not be taken for granted or assumed necessarily indefinite. Over time, most renewal movements become organized and structured in ways that minimize the freedom of expression and creativity of the earlier movement. Stable, sustainable, and predictable behaviors and structures begin to dominate, and early innovative leaders are replaced with those who are socialized in a set of practices and beliefs that over time become relatively uniform. In the United States, for example, the frontier revivals of the eighteenth century were routinized in Methodism, and the Azusa Street revivals were routinized in various Pentecostal denominations, including the Assemblies of God and the Church of God (Cleveland).

The question of whether such routinization will take place in the Global South is debated. While the reality of routinization is now a taken-for-granted assumption of sociologists, there is no reason to assume that Pentecostalism's course in the Global South will be the same as that of Christianity in the West. Social and economic contexts as well as historic social developments are quite different in the two hemispheres. While most Christian traditions in the West have been routinized, the Pentecostal movement in the Global South is simply too new to offer substantive critique about its possible tendencies toward routinization. Pentecostalism represents a kind of universal renewal movement, and hence it may not be routinized in the same way as other brands of Christianity have been.

Jenkins argues that the churches the Global South are sect-like in comparison to the church of the West—the former being emotional and spontaneous, supportive of mystical experiences, and fundamentalist.[28] Sects, he says, tend to rely on conversion of new members, while churches depend on reproduction (their own children) for the next generation of new members. Sects experience God as intimate and close, while for churches God is more remote and distant.[29] Most of the churches in the MNA Profile—with the exception of LMC United States and perhaps

---

28. Jenkins, 2002.
29. Jenkins, 2002.

the older mission churches GKM Indonesia, KMT Tanzania, and KMC Kenya—fit Jenkins's profile of sectarian groups. The question for scholars of religion is whether the churches of the Global South will evolve from sect to church—as has been the case in North America—or retain many of the qualities of sectarian faith because of their unique "pre-Christendom" contexts.

It may be that the Pentecostal nature of the churches in the Global South will effectively resist the kind of routinization that is expected in the church-sect thesis. It is possible that an emphasis on charisma invites continued renewal and the expectation of new manifestations of spiritual life and expressions of supernatural power. Perhaps charisma will prevent the iron cage of rationality that Weber predicted would come with routinization.

Cecil Robeck seems to embrace the idea that the Pentecostal movement may well resist the iron cage of modernity:

> After a century, one would logically expect to find a degree of institutionalization in the movement, and institutionalization is present in many parts of the Pentecostal world. But always the home of independent individualists and entrepreneurs claiming that they are following the voice of the Holy Spirit, the Pentecostal movement remains very much a movement without a rigid center, a multitude without any overarching hierarchy or governing board.[30]

Like many social movements, Pentecostalism may hold within it the seeds that predetermine its future. Some argue that capitalism holds the seeds of its eventual self-destruction through the abuse of natural resources and the creation of monopoly capitalism. Others suggest that the Protestant Reformation had the seeds of its own division embedded within it, now expressed in hundreds of Christian denominations and groups. Pentecostalism may hold the seeds of its own renewal

---

30. Robeck, 2006:4.

through the movement of the Holy Spirit that resists routinization and continually sprouts renewal and growth. The fluidity, porosity, and adaptability of Pentecostalism, along with the spiritual and cultural space for its growth in the Global South may well defy historical pressures toward routinization and rationalization.

## Conclusion

Without Pentecostalism in the Global South, it is possible that Anabaptism as a movement would deteriorate, since its trajectories in Europe and North America are so clearly downward. But as Pentecostalism and Anabaptism combine in the Global South, it is likely that Anabaptism will be sustained in a form that is much closer to the sixteenth-century Radical Reformers than the Anabaptism of Europe and North America. Anabaptism in the West is waning not for lack of a doctrine or a rich history but rather because it is so far removed from the context of social and religious oppression that first birthed it. [31]

---

31. This argument would be consistent with Jenkins (2002) who argues that, in general, the Christianity of the Global South has more in common with its medieval past than with European and North American contemporary Christianity.

10

# Emerging Visions of Anabaptism in the Global South

What does it mean for the future of Christianity that its centre of gravity continues to move south and east? Three areas can be mentioned briefly here. (1) Southern Christians will interpret and critique Northern Christianity's recent dominance in theology and ecclesiology by producing their own reflections and by looking back to the earliest Christian centuries, when they were in the majority. (2) The dominant languages of Christianity are shifting south. . . . (3) Christians are in increasingly close contact with Muslims, Hindus, and Buddhists. This will potentially intensify both conflict and dialogue."[1] —*Todd M. Johnson and Kenneth R. Ross, leading scholars of world Christianity*

For many reasons, it is understandable that Harold Bender's articulation of the Anabaptist Vision in 1943 has nothing to say about Anabaptists outside of Europe and North America.

---

1. Johnson and Ross, 2009:10.

Indeed, in many places of the Global South, Mennonite missionary efforts were just beginning at that time. What is less excusable is his selective reliance on certain historical elements of Anabaptist history to the exclusion of the more explicitly pietist and spiritualist streams that were also part and parcel of the same movement. To suggest a singular Anabaptist vision was to ignore the plurality of Anabaptist expressions that emerged in the renewal movements of the sixteenth century. Fortunately, the growth of Mennonite communities in the Global South over the last several decades has the potential to correct this omission and to redirect Mennonites back to their early pre-charismatic impulses.

Echoing this sentiment, Mennonite theologian Robert Suderman, who has been visiting and teaching among Anabaptist churches in the Global South, concludes,

> An Anabaptist focus is no longer something that comes from the North. . . . The church in the North is learning very much, and needs to learn even more from the Southern churches. For example, in Africa and Latin America there is a new awareness that Pentecostal fervor is not contradictory to Anabaptism. Anabaptists in the South have shown and reminded us that Anabaptism at its roots is Pentecostal. We in the North have shied away from, even scoffed at certain aspects of the Pentecostal stream. It is important to find ways of understanding Anabaptism through a Pentecostal lens.[2]

In this chapter, we will suggest some forces that we believe are shaping emerging Anabaptist visions or identities of Mennonites in the Global South. We are less interested in defining the nature of these identities than with outlining the sociological and spiritual influences upon them, based on findings from the MNA Profile. There are many reasons to believe that ongoing expressions of Anabaptism will be shaped largely by Mennonites in the Global South, and we should not necessarily expect that their

---

2. Suderman, 2011–12:9,14.

*Emerging Visions of Anabaptism in the Global South* 235

positions will replicate those of Mennonites in the last several centuries. While the twentieth-century statements of Bender, Yoder, and others shaped North American Anabaptism, future Anabaptist expressions from the Global South will be formed by the experiences of brothers and sisters in very different historical, socioeconomic, political, and religious contexts.

This perspective will likely raise questions among North American and European Anabaptists—questions we have heard as we report MNA Profile data. Skepticism exists among North Americans who have come to understand Anabaptism in a way that excludes certain historic elements of Anabaptist theology and practice while emphasizing others. It is quite likely that sixteenth-century Anabaptists would have less difficulty accepting the Anabaptism of the Global South than North American and European Anabaptists do today; the contexts of sixteenth-century Europe and the contemporary Global South are simply more similar than anything experienced by Europeans and North Americans since the Enlightenment and Industrial Revolution. Regardless of concerns in the Global North, barring unforeseen growth in North America and Europe, Anabaptists in the Global South will have the last word in describing what it means to be both Christian and Mennonite in the present century.

Anabaptist visions from the Global South will be decidedly more straightforward and less cerebral than those crafted in North America during the twentieth century. Anabaptist identities from the Global South will be articulated in barrios, shantytowns, and villages more than in the scholarly confines of universities and denominational offices in North America and Europe. Because the church in the Global South is much less influenced by the forces of the Enlightenment, its visions will be shaped in the everyday contexts of work, ministry, and family. Because educational levels are lower than in North America and Europe, the visions of Anabaptism that emerge from the South will have a strikingly grassroots feel—so much so, they may create discomfort among many in the North who wish to ignore or outright reject them for their simplicity, piety, and spirituality. Of course, the latter qualities are precisely those to which the Spirit of God has historically been drawn and from which renewal movements develop. Pentecostalism is a prime example of this.

Absent in most formulations of Anabaptism by twentieth-century Europeans and North Americans is a thorough treatment of the Holy Spirit or the recognition of one's powerlessness to embrace a radical vision of discipleship without the transforming presence of the Spirit. As noted earlier, the work of the Holy Spirit has received scant attention from Mennonites since the Radical Reformation. While Mennonites have written many books about Jesus, few Anabaptist materials exist about the Holy Spirit. Perhaps, in our zeal to be Christocentric, we have minimized the Spirit who transforms us into Christ's image and who Christ himself sent to empower us to faithfulness. Perhaps, in our focus on a historic Jesus, we have rejected the present power of Jesus as manifested in his death, resurrection, and the sending of the Spirit at Pentecost. Embracing the work of the Spirit will not make Anabaptists less Christocentric, but rather will make them more so, as the life and teaching of Jesus find fuller expression in current realities and experiences.

## A missionary context

As Kreider notes, the early church existed within a missionary context where the differences between pagan and Christian were strikingly clear to Christian converts. Those who were called out from their cultures of origin had a new master and Lord and immediately became witnesses to their new allegiance.[3] The same is true for many Anabaptists in the Global South; in following Christ, they step away from their old identities as Roman Catholic, Orthodox, Muslim, Hindu, or Buddhist and assume their new identity in Christ. Family and friends often fail to understand or appreciate their decision and may openly oppose them. Living in a context with clear distinctions between

---

3. Kreider, 1999.

*Emerging Visions of Anabaptism in the Global South* 237

Christian and non-Christian adds sharpness to one's faith and practice that does not exist when the definitions of who is in and who is out are blurred—the latter still being largely true in the declining post-Christendom context of North America.

Although early Anabaptism developed in a similar missionary context that included resistance, oppression, and persecution, Mennonites in North America have been immune to such experiences. In the midst of the Christendom context of North America, the idea of pagan versus Christian has been largely absent, and Mennonites have been distinguished more for their cultural expressions than for being Christian in a non-Christian context.[4] Because of the lack of distinction between pagan and Christian, Anabaptism in North America is less radical than the Christianity of the early church or the Anabaptist faith in the sixteenth century. Today, the kind of Anabaptism that exists in North America is not far removed in some respects from that of mainline Protestantism—an argument made by John Howard Yoder.[5] Indeed, when one compares the demographic and belief profiles of contemporary Mennonites in North America today, they are in many ways more like mainline Protestants than like North American evangelicals or charismatics.[6]

In the Global South, a missionary context is an assumed reality in many places. Christianity is springing up in communities and regions where it has not existed before, where most are not Christian. In the contexts of many MNA Profile

---

4. During the major wars of the twentieth century, Mennonites often felt isolated from the values and commitments of the broader culture. In fact, some Mennonites suffered both physical and emotional hardship for choosing conscientious objector status. For the last four or five decades, however, Mennonites have become increasingly accommodating to the broader culture, and young persons today are much less likely to feel the same kind of cultural isolation that some of their grandparents and great-grandparents experienced.

5. Yoder, 1970.

6. Kanagy, 2007.

churches, evangelical Christians are a religious minority. When P. C. Alexander, the leader of FCA India, was asked whether new converts are trained as evangelists, he noted that such training is less important in contexts where these new believers are among the only Christians in their villages. In coming to Christ, they recognize immediately that their lives are a testimony to the gospel. The distinction between Christian and nonbeliever is so clear that neither is confused about their relationship vis-à-vis the other.

Being in a minority status immediately creates a greater sensitivity to one's missionary context. In both Europe and the United States, centuries of Christendom have created ambivalence about whether or how to engage in local mission. The impulse to pray for the salvation of one's neighbors and friends or to consider those individuals "lost" has been minimized. Fortunately, however, the dissolution of Christendom in the West may be clearing up some of this ambiguity and may once again lead to crisper lines between those who are in the church and those who are not. Then Christians may again begin to recognize their responsibility to their neighbors, friends, and coworkers.

The missionary context of Christians in the Global South also means they must create dialogue with other religious traditions while faithfully representing Christ. Such dialogue has the potential to strengthen convictions and faithfulness while creating greater sensitivity to others. In Indonesia, a country with some of the harshest religious restrictions in the world, Mennonites are learning how to walk alongside Muslim neighbors, coworkers, and family members. Eruptions of violence and attacks against Christians—including Anabaptists—require the church to practice the life and teaching of Jesus in ways not pressed by Mennonites in Europe and North America. The kind of Anabaptism that is emerging in Indonesia will look different than North American and European Anabaptism because of Indonesia's interreligious tensions and missionary context. Indeed, perhaps Anabaptism can only be birthed and authentically thrive in a missionary context where the distinction between pagan and Christian is clearly defined. Whatever the case, expressions of Anabaptism that emerge from the Global South will be shaped in a missionary context where Christians are keenly aware of their minority status and feel deeply the resistance and oppression of majority religious groups.

## Oppression and persecution

Prior to Constantine's conversion, many new believers faced martyrdom. In fact, it was largely persecution that drove the early church so rapidly across Asia and Asia Minor, as it simply was not safe to settle down. Anabaptists of the sixteenth century also experienced intense persecution, which again accounted for the rapid growth of the believers church movement as converts remained on the run. Today, persecution and oppression are real for many of the Anabaptists in the Profile. Here are some of the trials Profile church members documented:

### Ethiopia

- Rejection by my family
- Rejection by my friends
- Put in prison
- Rejected by my office boss
- My husband was fired.
- Exposed to poverty
- Separated from my parents
- For one month my husband rejected me.
- Rejected by Muslim society
- The Orthodox believers rejected me.
- Beating
- Injured on the street

### India

- Hindus harass me.
- Persecution from my community

- I was beaten by some people.
- Hindrances to attend worship
- People mocked me for changing religions.

## Tanzania

- I was isolated by my community.
- When I decided to move from Islam to Christian I was isolated by my family.
- I was forced to follow bad cultural practices.
- I was beaten when I decided to go to Church.
- I was attacked by demons but I was cured when I ask God.
- I was attacked by diseases but God help me.
- My parents refuse me.
- I suffered from some of my property being stolen and my house was burned.
- I had suffering within my marriage because my husband was not Christian.
- Society hates me.

## Vietnam

- Those who were not of the same faith harassed me.
- My father and my family often harassed me.
- My family are Buddhist. I am regarded as a traitor to my faith.
- I was taken to the Security Police station and interrogated but not detained.
- They forbade us from witnessing and worshiping the Lord.
- I/We were taken to the Police station, and made to sign promises to change; fired from my/our jobs. Fined heavily many times.
- In 1993 as a teacher, I was forbidden to bring my Bible into the school (because of these difficulties I quit teaching). In 2003 I was arrested/written up and forbidden to go to worship 2 times.

- I was imprisoned. The Vietnamese authorities always looked for every means to disturb the lives of those who served the Lord.

The responses from Profile churches indicate variation from church to church regarding the kinds of oppression and persecution experienced. Interestingly, even in North America respondents talked about a sense of isolation from non-Christians. The level of persecution in North America, however, pales in comparison with some of the Profile examples of Christians losing their livelihoods, homes, and families.

In the early church, the level of persecution varied, but "every Christian knew that persecution, because of imperial edict or local crisis, could break out with community engulfing virulence. So they passed down the acts of the martyrs and celebrated the anniversaries of their deaths. . . . They knew that 'every Christian by definition was a candidate for death.'"[7] The expectation of persecution and oppression creates a level of faithfulness in following the demands of Christ that disappears without it. In such circumstances, the church is limited to those who will count the cost of being a disciple of Jesus; they know their decision may result in the loss of all they hold dear. Again, however, this was the context in which Anabaptism grew and flourished, and it may be the only context for true faithfulness to Christ.

Thus, as new Anabaptist visions emerge from the Global South, we should expect to hear in them themes of radical discipleship and faithfulness to Jesus. These themes will sound alien to Western ears, where counting the cost of Christian discipleship has become irrelevant. But, as Suderman concludes about Mennonites in the Global South, "These churches help us regain a sense that there are some things that are worth suffering for; that suffering is indeed integral to discipleship. It's something that we in the North find hard to learn."[8]

---

7. Kreider, 1995:6.
8. Suderman, 2011–12:14.

## Emphasis on discipleship

Because Christendom downplayed right behavior and focused on the greater importance of belief and belonging, it should be no surprise that right behavior is again emerging as important in contexts of the Global South that have not experienced Christendom. When anchors presented the results of Profile findings about moral practices to other church leaders at the Thika consultation, many expressed concern whenever they saw their members deviating from normative expectations. Although the percentages of deviants were often quite small, these leaders showed little tolerance. As findings from LMC United States were reported—often exhibiting greater diversity than any other church in the Profile—its leaders were silent and apparently unsurprised by the findings. In addition to the cultural assimilation of the church in North America and Europe, another outcome of Christendom is a declining expectation that members will behave differently than the society around them. North American leaders now take for granted that their members will vary greatly on issues that only a few decades ago would have garnered nearly unanimous agreement. As in the early church and early Anabaptism, it is arguable that Anabaptists in the Global South are more concerned about right behavior than in North America or Europe.

Why such a concern for right behavior in the Global South? Churches there are well aware of their minority status and recognize the importance of socializing (i.e., discipling) new converts in right practices and behaviors. These leaders understand that they are constructing a new reality for their members, and the extent to which new converts truly convert will affect the long-term sustainability of their emerging churches. In creating this new reality—just as in the first centuries of the early church—leaders are intentional about teaching new believers the norms, values, beliefs, and behaviors expected of new Christians.

An example of this intentionality is FCA India, where new converts are discipled until the leadership is sure that he or she has truly abandoned their besetting sins in order to follow

Jesus. In addition, FCA India churches do not baptize Muslim or Hindu converts until they are eighteen years old in order to mitigate conflict with the broader culture. In a similar vein, MKC Ethiopia requires new believers to undergo three months of discipleship training before they are baptized and received as new members.

The commitment to right living and behavior seen among Anabaptists in the Global South should not be considered an anomaly. Rather, it is consistent with high expectations of the early church and with sixteenth-century Anabaptists. Both the Schleitheim Confession and the Dordrecht Confession require deep commitment from Anabaptist followers of Jesus. Bender's articulation of the Anabaptist vision emphasizes this component of the Christian life; if we are going to believe in Jesus we must live like him. But, as Kanagy documents in his 2006 profile of Mennonite Church USA, Anabaptists in North America are much less concerned about right behaviors and practices than in the past, tolerating much greater differences than was imaginable just a few decades ago.[9]

Pentecostalism also places a particular emphasis on personal transformation and discontinuity from the convert's former society and relationships. The rupture or break with the culture that comes with conversion is continually reinforced by the Pentecostal experience.[10] Baptisms, exorcisms, and miraculous interventions—also part of the early church's experience—separate believers from the satanic influences and forces of darkness that belong to a former identity. In addition, defining a new way of life that includes the rejection of behaviors identified with one's former life creates a sense of discontinuity and rupture. The abandonment of alcohol, tobacco, sexual immorality, and cultural and religious rituals identified with one's pre-conversion identity serves to reinforce one's new commitments and belonging. In societies where the perceived distance is

---

9. Kanagy, 2007.
10. Robbins, 2002.

greatest between Christian and pagan cultural identities, there is likely more need for discontinuity and rupture. Without such, the risks of returning to one's former self are likely higher and the chances of true transformation lower. The church's interest in socializing new converts and discipling them, then, is strongest in contexts where the social distance between Christians and others is greatest.

Even as it reinforces cultural discontinuity and rupture among converts, Pentecostalism tends to reinforce the reality of the world from which converts have come. The reality of evil and the devil are taken for granted rather than rejected as mere fantasy.[11] But, as Pentecostal believers, individuals gain power over the world from which they came. Again, it is likely that such reinforcement of belief in Satan and evil is greatest in societies where the distinction between Christian and non-Christian is greatest. When converts see little difference between their new reality and that of the broader world around them, they have less need to spend time imagining a devil.

Pentecostalism's expression and shape is always local, because it is tied to the context from which converts emerge.[12] While the broad themes of Pentecostalism are universal, its operationalization always engages and takes root in indigenous contexts. The contextualizing power of Pentecostalism is found in its twofold nature as both universal and local. Pentecostalism takes seriously the cosmic story of God's grace and the Spirit's power but also applies those realities to local settings where a particular people are walking from darkness into light.

As Anabaptist visions emerge from the Global South, often in contexts of marginality and persecution, we should expect to see them grappling with and calling for closer obedience to Jesus and a higher standard of moral faithfulness. Relative to Mennonites in North America and Europe, we will likely see them identifying themselves against the world rather than with

---

11. Robbins, 2002.
12. Robbins, 2002.

it. And, unlike Anabaptists in the North, Anabaptists in the Global South will recognize the impossibility of fulfilling the hard demands of Christ without the fullness of the Holy Spirit.

## A holistic gospel

Pentecostals are often criticized by non-Pentecostals for a gospel message that minimizes social transformation and material well-being, with some suggesting that their salvation message is largely nonmaterial or spiritual in nature. Some complain that Pentecostal notions of salvation are too vertical, emphasizing only one's relationship with God and failing to acknowledge the social and cultural dynamics of human reality.[13] But evidence is growing that contemporary Pentecostals, and particularly those in the Global South, are embracing a Christianity that is more holistic than has often been the case with mainline Protestantism or evangelicalism.[14] For these Pentecostals, the salvation message of Jesus and the kingdom necessarily include physical and material dimensions. The impression that Pentecostal expressions of salvation are only "spiritual" and ignore social and structural concerns can no longer be upheld.[15]

Anabaptists in the Global South are likely to feel quite at home among such Pentecostal expressions, for this emphasis on holism has been central to Anabaptist understandings of the gospel since the movement's origins. Profile data provide overwhelming evidence that Anabaptists are concerned about both pietistic obedience to Jesus and effective response to social, economic, and other material needs in their churches and local communities. In fact, for many MNA Profile churches, building social institutions has a threefold importance: (1) it allows them to address social and economic needs of their members; (2) it creates an opportunity for witness to non-Christians who benefit

---

13. Volf, 1989.
14. Miller and Yamamori, 2007.
15. Volf, 1989.

from their presence in local communities; and (3) it creates a buffer between the Christian community and the larger culture and society from which converts come—further socializing them and emphasizing their separation from their former life.

In places of great physical and material need, the debate over the importance of "spiritual" versus "material" expressions of salvation, often heard among Christians in the United States and Europe, is simply irrelevant. The luxury of time to argue over such theological differences does not exist in congregations and communities characterized by poverty, sickness, natural disasters, famine, and persecution. Future expressions of Anabaptism as they develop in the Global South will likely converge with very early expressions of Christian discipleship, such as that of early Dutch Anabaptist leader Menno Simons who taught that "true evangelical faith" is not merely vertical in relationship to Christ, but expresses itself outwardly by caring for the poor and those on the margins.[16]

### The movement of the Holy Spirit

Anabaptist visions that emerge from the Global South in the next several decades will certainly reflect the Pentecostal movement in the midst of which many of these churches are growing. These expressions will sometimes feel foreign to North Americans and European Mennonites, who by and large have not engaged Pentecostalism or been shaped by it. But Pentecostalism will strengthen Anabaptism rather than diminish it. In fact, by connecting Anabaptists with pre-charismatic streams of their history, Pentecostalism may save Anabaptism as a distinct identity in both the Global North and the Global South.

The Pentecostal nature of Anabaptists in the Global South, however, will challenge the established Mennonite churches of North American and Europe, confronting the realities they take for granted and their long accepted understandings of what it means to be Mennonite. David Martin argues that charismatic

---

16. Simons, 1539.

Christian expressions do not readily integrate with establishment religions, and that establishment religions do not nurture a soil favorable to charismatic or experimental expression. Such movements, he says, are always on the edges of the historic religions whose structures, institutions, and rational ways of functioning are barriers to the free movement of the Holy Spirit.[17] This means that charismatic congregations or individuals that belong to established Christian churches will necessarily feel restricted and trapped within these churches' structures and spiritual streams. Simultaneously, Martin explains, historic religious traditions will feel threatened by the freedom exhibited by those embracing a Pentecostal experience and will often marginalize these impulses even more than they already are.

Martin's argument has proven to be true in North America over the past century, as Mennonites have consistently left their denominations when they have felt stifled and prevented from embracing the work of the Spirit. In doing so, they have created numerous networks of churches that have some affinity to Anabaptism but are often pulled more fully into evangelical Protestant streams. Mennonites in North America might have experienced less decline in the last several decades had we found a way to embrace those in our churches who were touched by the movement of the Holy Spirit in the second and third waves of the Pentecostal movement. Those who are most zealous for the Spirit's work are often most zealous for the mission of God. Where the former is excluded, energy for the latter typically wanes. Failure to fully embrace the Spirit's movement must account in part for the decline of Mennonite congregations in North America and Europe.

The inability of North American Mennonites to integrate those who are touched by the Pentecostal movement should serve as a caution to the global Anabaptist family. A sign that North American power has been truly redistributed throughout the global church will appear when the charismatic and

---

17. Martin, 2002.

Pentecostal impulses of the Global South are free to move unfettered across the entire global church. But, if these impulses are restrained and churches in the Global South are encouraged to replicate North American and European churches, global Anabaptism's future may be short-lived, regardless of the strength of current demographic trends. Because the impulse to move with the Spirit is so much greater in the Global South, any repression of that impulse will result in an exodus of members and congregations to other churches that allow and embrace the Spirit's movement. On the other hand, as mentioned earlier, the embrace of Anabaptist visions that are Pentecostal in nature may well be the key to preserving an Anabaptist witness in both the North and the South.

The historic and sociological motivations for congregations in the Global South to remain in their broader churches may be even lower than for North Americans. These bodies are more congregational than those in the Global North, and they are less grounded in the denominational and historic identities that shaped North American and European Mennonites. The Mennonite cultural identity is less important in the Global South than it was for centuries in North America. The dominance of Pentecostalism in the Global South will continue to put pressure on these churches to embrace the work of the Holy Spirit, but if the global Anabaptist church—particularly in North America and Europe—cannot do so, it may lead to a diminishment of the global Anabaptist communion.

The Anabaptist vision as it has been articulated in North America over the past century has been decidedly Christocentric, and rightfully so. But Mennonite expressions of Christocentrism have sometimes created too little space for the one Christ left in his place—the Holy Spirit. Without room for the Spirit, Christocentrism produces a historical Jesus who taught an important ethic of love but failed to provide a way for us to express that love in our lives and to the world. Any articulation of Anabaptist visions today, if they have integrity in reflecting the global Anabaptist church as a whole, will necessarily recognize the presence and movement of the Holy Spirit. Doing so will lead to a holistic Gospel, whereby Christ is recognized as the one who brings salvation to spiritual and physical ills and redemption for both individual and structural sin.

## Conclusion

Anabaptist identities that form in the Global South in the coming decades will look distinctly different than their earlier European and North American counterparts from the twentieth century. Differing from the Global North, the spiritual and sociological conditions of the Global South involve (1) a missionary passion and context that distinguishes Christian from non-Christian, (2) persecution and oppression, (3) a concern for discipleship and faithful living, (4) an emphasis on a holistic gospel, and (5) an embrace of the Holy Spirit. These factors will lead to expressions of Anabaptism that feel unfamiliar to many in North America and Europe. And yet, if one looks carefully, one will recognize that these expressions have much in common with the themes and emphases that emerged in the early church and in the sixteenth-century Radical Reformation.

What will the global Anabaptist church look like in the future? If Christendom continues to decline in the West, we might expect a North American and European church that is more marginalized, persecuted, focused on discipleship, and committed to mission in its local contexts than it has been over the last several centuries. At the same time, the forces of secularization—put into play by the Enlightenment and Industrial Revolution—may lead to a church that simply becomes less and less relevant as individualism, consumerism, and pluralism overwhelm the more radical Christian impulse that has been given space to emerge in post-Christendom. Or perhaps the church will split between those who choose a radical call to follow Jesus and those who increasingly join the culture and eventually disappear into it.

On the other hand, what will happen in countries in the Global South where Christianity, and Pentecostalism in particular, becomes the dominant religious presence? Will a kind of mini-Christendom lead to the same consequences that the church experienced under European Christendom, with less influence culturally and socially? Reflecting on the possibility of becoming the dominant religion, Miller notes,

> The old Colonial model of domination is being broken; globalization is having its revenge, and with it are changes in the locus of Christianity. No longer do Pentecostals in the Global South see themselves as marginal to Christianity; rather they view themselves as carriers of Christian tradition, while liberal Episcopalians, for example, are viewed as the deviant minority.[18]

What will happen when economic growth propels the masses in the Global South into a middle class, where the temptations of consumption and materialism overwhelm the radical tendencies of the Christian message resulting in what Miller and Yamamori call "Pentecostal ethic"?

There is ample evidence that, in the last fifty years, Christendom has fractured and lost its hegemony in Europe and the United States. Once-powerful denominations have declined in influence, and many local congregations are shutting their doors—unable to pay clergy or the costs of building maintenance or without members to justify keeping the doors open. The foreign mission budgets of major denominations have shrunk, and the expensive infrastructure sustaining these denominations has run dry of cash. Layoffs, budget shortfalls, and membership declines are typical. This loss of Christendom in the Global North may create a convergence with the South, as the Anabaptist movement globally becomes more grassroots and less reliant on denominational centers and rationalizing structures. As a post-Christendom missionary context reappears in the North, it may create opportunities for shared conversations across hemispheres about missionary engagement and faithfulness to God's mission.

Anabaptism in its truest form cannot survive or thrive

---

18. Miller, 2009:283.

*Emerging Visions of Anabaptism in the Global South* 251

within the iron cage of Enlightenment rationality. It is a charismatic movement that in its purest form always threatens the structures that surround it. While Anabaptism over the past three hundred years in the United States has become routinized, Anabaptist expressions in the Global South provide a fresh wind of the Spirit once again reminding us of our origins. What the early Anabaptists practiced and believed was not original but rather the product of radical obedience to Jesus that can spring up wherever people are committed to following Jesus and to the movement of the Holy Spirit.

Anabaptism first emerged in the context of the temporary breaking up of Christendom during the Reformation, when space was created for a radical response to following Jesus. It is possible that a return to early Anabaptism will only occur when there is similar flux and change, when Christendom as it was reformulated after the Reformation again falls to its knees. Is it possible that the Spirit of God is dismantling the church in the West in order for another radical response—a charismatic response in the classic Weberian sense that results in the destruction of the iron cages that constrain the Spirit's movement?

While it is easy to despair as a Christian believer in the European and North American context, it is helpful for us to remember the biblical story of God's people in the sixth century BC. Forgetting that they were called and created to be a blessing to the world and focused more on their own wealth and well-being, God's people were taken into exile by neighboring Babylon. Jeremiah and other prophets had predicted that day—chastising the people for their disobedient and rebellious hearts that had abandoned the poor among them in exchange for a self-righteous religiousness that found no favor with God. In describing this tragedy, Jeremiah makes it clear that God has not abandoned or forgotten them and that God is still very much in control. In fact, Jeremiah suggests that the exile is not so much a punishment as an opportunity to be a blessing—a source of shalom—to enemies to the east (Jeremiah 29). As hard as it was for them to believe, God's people had been taken into exile and the sacred places of their faith had been destroyed so that they could again see their call to be a blessing to the world. Babylon was a missional opportunity for the people of God, and embedded within Jeremiah's words are the promise that if God's people offer shalom to a broken world, shalom will come right back to them.

This story reminds us that the dismantling of Christendom may be more a blessing than a tragedy. Stripped of resources that gave us security and legitimation, the church in North America and Europe may now be in a position to think seriously about partnering with the church in Asia, Africa, and Latin America. Stripped of its status, the Western church has a new opportunity to both be and receive a blessing. The church has always thrived where it is on the margins of society. The fall of Christendom and the growth of the church in the Global South have begun to create a more marginal position for Christians in the Global North where new Anabaptist visions may even begin to emerge. New visions from the margins of the Global North are likely to have more in common with those emerging in the Global South than with anything that appeared among Mennonites in North America during the nineteenth and twentieth centuries.

Perhaps the Pentecostal movement, particularly as it is manifested in the Global South, will consistently resist routinization and institutionalization. Some will celebrate this, while others—particularly Anabaptists in North America—will likely remain skeptical of whether or not a truly Anabaptist faith can take root and prosper in contexts without strong denominations and Anabaptist identities. At its historical core, however, Anabaptism has always been less about formal identity and structures (these were later imposed on the movement within the cultural contexts of Europe and North America) than it has been simply about a way of following Jesus faithfully in daily life and embracing the Spirit of Jesus. Wherever we see this happening—whether in denominations with strong Anabaptist ties or in local congregations in the Global South with minimal understanding of Anabaptist theology—it should be celebrated.

# Bibliography

Anderson, Allan. 2004. *An Introduction to Pentecostalism*. UK: Cambridge University Press.

Baecher, Claude, Neal Blough, James Jakob Fehr, Alle G. Hokema, Hanspeter Jecker, John N. Klassen, Diether Gotz Lichdi, Ed van Straten, and Annelies Verbeek. *Testing Faith and Tradition*. John A. Lapp and C. Arnold Snyder, eds. *The Global Mennonite History Series*. Intercourse, PA: Good Books.

Barrett, David. 2001. "The Worldwide Holy Spirit Renewal" in *The Century of the Holy Spirit: 100 Years of Pentecostal and Charismatic Renewal*. Nashville: Thomas Nelson Publishers, 381–83.

Bellah, Robert N., Richard Madsen, William M. Sullivan, Ann Swidler, and Steven N. Tipton. 1985. *Habits of the Heart: Individualism and Commitment in Everyday Life*. Berkeley, CA: University of California Press.

Bender, Harold. 1944. "The Anabaptist Vision." *Mennonite Quarterly Review*, 18(April): 67–88.

Berger, Peter. 1999. *The Desecularization of the Word: Resurgent Religion and World Politics*. Grand Rapids, MI: Eerdmans Publishing Company.

Beyene Kidane, Tilahun. 2003. *The Impact of the Pentecostal/ Charismatic Movement on the Meserete Kristos Church* (MKC).
Brusco, Elizabeth E. 1995. *The Reformation of Machismo.* Austin: University of Texas Press.
Camp, Lee C. 2003. *Mere Discipleship.* Grand Rapids, MI: Brazos Press.
Chatfield, Adrian. 1997. "Zealous for the Lord: Enthusiasm and Dissent, Lovers and the Beloved: Brides of Christ," *Journal of Pentecostal Theology*, 11:95–109.
Checole, Alemu, Samuel Asefa, Bekithemba Dube, Doris Dube, Michael Kodzo Badasu, Erik Kumedisa, Barbara Nkala, I.U. Nsasak, Siaka Traore, and Pakisa Tshimisa. 2006. *Anabaptist Songs in African Hearts.* John A. Lapp and C. Arnold Snyder, eds. *The Global Mennonite History Series.* Intercourse, PA: Good Books.
Christiano, Kevin J., William H. Swatos, and Peter Kivisto. 2008. *Sociology of Religion: Contemporary Developments* (2nd ed.). New York: Rowan and Littlefield Publishers, Inc.
Clark, Mathew S. 2004. "Pentecostalism's Anabaptist Roots: Hermeneutical Implications." *The Spirit and Spirituality: Essays in Honor of Russell P. Spittler.* Wonsuk Ma and Robert P. Mensies, eds. London: T & T Clark International.
Dintaman, Stephen F. 1992. "The Spiritual Poverty of the Anabaptist Vision." *The Conrad Grebel Review*, 10(2):205–08.
Dintaman, Stephen F. 1995. "The Pastoral Significance of the Anabaptist Vision" in *Refocusing a Vision: Shaping Anabaptist Character in the 21st Century.* John D. Roth, ed. Mennonite Historical Society. http://www.goshen.edu/mhl/Refocusing/ DINTAMAN.htm
Durkheim, Emile. 1912 (2008). *The Elementary Forms of Religious Life.* New York: Oxford University Press.
Epp, Robert O. 1975. *One Hundred Years of Bethesda Mennonite Church.* Henderson, NE: Centennial Committee of the Bethesda Mennonite Church.
Greeley, Andrew and Michael Hout. 2006. *The Truth about Conservative Christians: What They Think and What They Believe.* Chicago: University of Chicago Press.

Guder, Darrell L. 1998. *Missional Church: A Vision for the Sending of the Church in North America*. Grand Rapids, MI: Eerdmans Publishing Company.

Hege, Christian and Harold S. Bender. (1957). "Martyrs' Synod." *Global Anabaptist Mennonite Encyclopedia Online*. Retrieved 06 July 2011, from http://www.gameo.org/encyclopedia/contents/M378595.html.

Hege, Nathan. 1998. *Beyond Our Prayers: An Amazing Half Century of Church Growth in Ethiopia*. Scottdale, PA: Herald Press.

Jenkins, Philip. 2002. *The Next Christendom: The Coming of Global Christianity*. New York City: Oxford University Press.

Jenkins, Philip. 2006. *The New Faces of Christianity: Believing the Bible in the Global South*. New York City: Oxford University Press.

Johnson, Todd M. and Kenneth R. Ross. 2009. *Atlas of Global Christianity*. Edinburgh: Edinburgh University Press.

Kanagy, Conrad L. 1990. "The Formation and Development of a Protestant Conversion Movement among the Highland Quichua of Ecuador." *Sociology of Religion*, 51 (2):205–17.

Kanagy, Conrad L. 2007. *Road Signs for the Journey: A Profile of Mennonite Church USA*. Scottdale, PA: Herald Press.

Kreider, Alan. 1995. *Worship and Evangelism in Pre-Christendom*. Cambridge, UK: Grove Books Limited.

Kreider, Alan. 1999. *The Change of Conversion and the Origin of Christendom*. Harrisburg, PA: Trinity Press International.

Linder, Eileen W., ed., 2011. *Yearbook of American and Canadian Churches 2011*. USA: National Council of Churches.

Lorenzen, Jay. 2005. "Factors in Revival and Renewal Movements by Dr. Paul Pierson." http://onmovements.com/?p=42.

MacMaster, Richard K. and Donald R. Jacobs. 2006. *A Gentle Wind of God: The Influence of the East African Revival*. Scottdale, PA: Herald Press.

Martin, David. 2002. *Pentecostalism: The World Their Parish*. Malden, MA: Blackwell Publishing.

Martinez, Juan Francisco. 2006. "When Anabaptists Relate to Pentecostals." *Courier* (1&2), Mennonite World Conference.

Marx, Karl. 1844. "Contribution to Critique of Hegel's Philosophy of Right." *Deutsch-Franzosische-Jahrbucher*. Paris.

Mennonite World Conference. http://www.mwc-cmm.org.

Metaxas, Eric. 2010. *Bonhoeffer: Pastor, Martyr, Prophet, Spy*. Nashville, TN: Thomas Nelson Publishers.

Miller, Donald E. 2006. Interview by the Pew Forum on Religion and Public Life. http://pewforum.org/Christian/The-New-Face-of-Global-Christianity-The-Emergence-of-Progressive-Pentecostalism.aspx.

Miller, Donald E. and Tetsunao Yamamori. 2007. *Global Pentecostalism: The New Face of Christian Social Engagement*. Berkeley, CA: University of California Press.

Miller, Donald E. 2009. "Progressive Pentecostalism: An Emergent Trend in Global Christianity." *Journal of Beliefs and Values*, 30:275–87.

Noll, Mark A. 2009. *The New Shape of World Christianity: How American Experience Reflects Global Faith*. Downers Grove, IL: IVP Academic.

The Pew Forum on Religion and Public Life, 2011. "Global Survey of Evangelical Protestant Leaders." http://pewforum.org/Christian/Evangelical-Protestant-Churches/Global-Survey-of-Evangelical-Protestant-Leaders.aspx.

Prieto, Jaime, 2010. *Mission and Migration*. John A. Lapp and C. Arnold Snyder, eds. *The Global Mennonite History Series*. Intercourse, PA: Good Books.

Ritzer, George. 2008. *The McDonaldization of Society*. Fifth Edition. Thousand Oaks, CA: Pine Forge Press.

Robbins, Joel. 2004. "The Globalization of Charismatic and Pentecostal Christianity." *Annual Review of Anthropology*, 33:117–43.

Robeck, Cecil M., Jr. 2006. "Introducing Mennonites to Pentecostals." Presented at a gathering of Mennonite World Conference, Pasadena, CA.

Roth, John D. "'The Anabaptist Vision and Mennonite Reality' Revisited" in *Refocusing a Vision: Shaping Anabaptist Character in the 21st Century*. John D. Roth, ed. Mennonite Historical Society.

Ruth, John, 2001. *The Earth Is the Lord's: A Narrative History of the Lancaster Mennonite Conference*. Scottdale, PA: Herald Press.
Sanneh, Lamin. 1993. *Encountering the West: Christianity and the Global Cultural Process*. Maryknoll, NY: Orbis.
Shertzer, Mary Ellen. 2010. Interview.
Showalter, Richard. 1995. "The Spiritual Poverty of the Anabaptist Vision: A Critical Assessment." *The Conrad Grebel Review*, 13(1):14–18.
Simons, Menno. 1539 (1956). Why I Do Not Cease Teaching and Writing in *The Complete Writings of Menno Simons*. John C. Wenger, ed. Scottdale, PA: Herald Press.
Snyder, C. Arnold. 1994. *An Introduction to Anabaptist History and Theology*. Kitchener, ON: The author.
Snyder, C. Arnold. 2004. *Following in the Footsteps of Christ: The Anabaptist Tradition*. Maryknoll, NY: Orbis Books.
Stutzman, Ervin. 2011. *From Non-resistance to Justice: The Transformation of Mennonite Peace Rhetoric, 1908–2008*. Scottdale, PA: Herald Press.
Suderman, Robert J. (Jack). 2011–12. "Cultivating an Anabaptist Identity." Mennonite World Conference: *Courier*.
"United States Religious Landscape Survey." 2008. Pew Forum on Religion and Public Life. http://religions.pewforum.org/reports.
Vasquez, Manuel A. 2009. "The Global Portability of Pneumatic Christianity: Comparing African and Latin American Pentecostalisms." *African Studies*. 68(2):273–86.
Volf, Miroslav. 1989. "Materiality of Salvation: An Investigation in the Soteriologies of Liberation and Pentecostal Theologies." *Journal of Ecumenical Studies*, 26(3):447–67.
Walls, Andrew F. 1996. *The Missionary Movement in Christian History: Studies in the Transmission and Appropriation of Faith*. Maryknoll, NY: Orbis.
Weber, Max. 1904 (2008). *The Protestant Ethic and the Spirit of Capitalism*. New York City: W.W. Norton and Company.
Williams, George Huntston. 1962. *The Radical Reformation*. Philadelphia, PA: Westminster Press.

Wilson, Bryan. 1959. "An Analysis of Sect Development." *American Sociological Review*, 24:3–15.

World Values Survey. http://www.worldvaluessurvey.org.

Wuthnow, Robert. 2010. *Boundless Faith: The Global Outreach of American Churches*. Berkeley, CA: University of California Press.

Yoder, John Howard. 1967. "Marginalia." *Concern* pamphlet, (15):77–80.

Yoder, John Howard. 1970. "Anabaptist Vision and Mennonite Reality," in *Consultation on Anabaptist-Mennonite Theology*, A. J. Klassen, ed., Fresno, CA.: Council of Mennonite Seminaries.

Yong, Amos. 2005. *The Spirit Poured Out on All Flesh: Pentecostalism and the Possibility of Global Theology*. Grand Rapids, MI: Baker Academic.

# The Authors

Conrad L. Kanagy is professor of sociology at Elizabethtown College, Pennsylvania, where he has taught since 1993. From 2000–2005 he was lead pastor of Elizabethtown Mennonite Church and since October, 2011, has again been serving in that role. Conrad was born in Covington, Kentucky, and grew up in Belleville, Pennsylvania. His undergraduate degree is from Wheaton College in Illinois and his MS and PhD degrees are from Penn State University. From 2005–2007 Conrad was director of the Mennonite Member Profile of Mennonite Church USA and authored *Road Signs for the Journey* (Herald Press) as a result of that project. In 2008 he conducted a study of Mennonite church planters in the U.S. and in 2010 the Global South profile described here in *Winds of the Spirit*. Conrad and his wife, Heidi, live in Elizabethtown, Pennsylvania. They are parents of one adult son.

Tilahun Beyene is the coordinator of the International Missions Association, affiliated with Eastern Mennonite Mission.

He was born in Deder, Ethiopia, and received his high school education at the Mennonite-run Bible Academy in Nazareth, Ethiopia. In the late 1960s, he studied business administration at the Haile Selassie I University in Addis Ababa. He received other administrative training during his 28 years in management of Ethiopian Airlines. A key leader in Ethiopia's Meserete Kristos Church in the 1970s, 1980s, and 1990s, he authored *I Will Build My Church*, the Amharic language history of the growth of the MKC. He then served as prayer minister and church relations consultant at Eastern Mennonite Missions from 2001 to 2011. He and his wife, Hiewet Tsegay, live in Columbia, Maryland, and attend the Ethiopian Evangelical Church Baltimore. They have three adult daughters.

Richard Showalter worked as a pastor and teacher in the United States and missionary in Kenya and the Middle East before serving as president of Rosedale Bible College (1989–1994) and as president of Eastern Mennonite Missions (1994–2011). Currently he serves as chair of the Mission Commission of Mennonite World Conference and coach for the International Missions Association, of which he is also president emeritus. Richard, who was born in Monticello, Wisconsin, completed undergraduate studies at Eastern Mennonite University and graduate studies at the University of Chicago Divinity School (MTh), Anabaptist Mennonite Biblical Seminary (MDiv), Fuller School of Intercultural Studies (courses), and Gordon Conwell Theological Seminary (DMin). He and his wife, Jewel, are members of West End Mennonite Fellowship in Lancaster, Pennsylvania, which is their home base while they serve in Asia. They have three adult children and ten grandchildren.